NOW WRITE!
SCREENWRITING

NOW WRITE!
SCREENWRITING

Exercises by Today's Best Writers and Teachers

SHERRY ELLIS
with LAURIE LAMSON

JEREMY P. TARCHER/PENGUIN
a member of Penguin Group (USA) Inc.
New York

JEREMY P. TARCHER/PENGUIN
Published by the Penguin Group
Penguin Group (USA) Inc., 375 Hudson Street, New York, New York 10014,
USA • Penguin Group (Canada), 90 Eglinton Avenue East, Suite 700, Toronto,
Ontario M4P 2Y3, Canada (a division of Pearson Penguin Canada Inc.) • Penguin Books Ltd,
80 Strand, London WC2R 0RL, England • Penguin Ireland, 25 St Stephen's Green,
Dublin 2, Ireland (a division of Penguin Books Ltd) • Penguin Group (Australia),
250 Camberwell Road, Camberwell, Victoria 3124, Australia (a division of Pearson
Australia Group Pty Ltd) • Penguin Books India Pvt Ltd, 11 Community Centre,
Panchsheel Park, New Delhi–110 017, India • Penguin Group (NZ),
67 Apollo Drive, Rosedale, North Shore 0632, New Zealand (a division of Pearson
New Zealand Ltd) • Penguin Books (South Africa) (Pty) Ltd, 24 Sturdee Avenue,
Rosebank, Johannesburg 2196, South Africa

Penguin Books Ltd, Registered Offices: 80 Strand, London WC2R 0RL, England

Most Tarcher/Penguin books are available at special quantity discounts for
bulk purchase for sales promotions, premiums, fund-raising, and educational needs.
Special books or book excerpts also can be created to fit specific needs.
For details, write Penguin Group (USA) Inc. Special Markets,
375 Hudson Street, New York, NY 10014.

Library of Congress Cataloging-in-Publication Data

Ellis, Sherry, date.
Now write! screenwriting : exercises by today's best writers and teachers /
Sherry Ellis with Laurie Lamson.
p.   cm.
ISBN 978-1-58542-851-9
1. Motion picture authorship.   2. Motion picture authorship—Handbooks, manuals, etc.
I. Lamson, Laurie.   II. Title.
PN1996.E445   2010   2010029424
808.2'3—dc22

Printed in the United States of America
1   3   5   7   9   10   8   6   4   2

BOOK DESIGN BY GRETCHEN ACHILLES

Now Write! Screenwriting
is dedicated to the splendiferous memory of
Maeve Moses,
a very compassionate and loving young woman,
a brave and positive soul who loved the arts and everything creative,
a very best friend and "soul sister,"
a woman who breathed life and joy into those she met
and who died way before her time.

CONTENTS

CONTENTS

CONTENTS

CONTENTS

VERBAL AND NONVERBAL COMMUNICATION

A NOTE FROM SHERRY ELLIS
AND LAURIE LAMSON

In the summer of 2008, my aunt Sherry and I started talking about developing a book of screenwriting exercises. I had been impressed and inspired by watching her put together *Now Write!* (Fiction) and *Now Write! Nonfiction,* and suggested a third book for her series: *Now Write! Screenwriting.*

Sherry loved the idea and invited me to collaborate with her on the book. Working together as aunt and niece was an exciting adventure. Teaming up gave us the chance to share our love of screenwriting and to learn from each other in the process.

Our intention with *Now Write! Screenwriting* is to help budding and developing screenwriters hone and expand their skills. Thanks to the wealth of knowledge provided by our contributors, the exercises in the book are useful at almost any stage in a screenwriter's career. We hope that readers will find it a valuable resource and that it will help them bring their craft to the next level.

To all the screenwriters, teachers and consultants who contributed exercises to this book, we thank you very much for sharing your expertise.

CHOOSING YOUR STORY

MARDIK MARTIN

Start with a Conflict

MARDIK MARTIN is a highly esteemed screenwriter, who penned MEAN STREETS, RAGING BULL, NEW YORK, NEW YORK, VALENTINO, and other screenplays. He has also served as an uncredited script doctor for numerous other feature films. His documentaries include ITALIAN-AMERICAN, AMERICAN BOY and THE LAST WALTZ. He's also the subject of the acclaimed 2009 documentary MARDIK: BAGHDAD TO HOL-LYWOOD. He's currently a senior lecturer at USC and has previously taught at New York University. In 2006, the American Film Institute named RAGING BULL the fourth best movie of all time, and the Writers Guild of America rated RAGING BULL as one of the top 101 screenplays of all time. In 2008, Martin was honored with a lifetime achievement award from AFFMA (Arpa Foundation for Film, Music and Art).

The biggest trap in writing a screenplay is the starting point. Remember, you're going to spend possibly a year of your life on a feature film script. So don't make the common mistake of using a theme, premise or message to start your story. It's easier and more effective to build with a conflict.

Let's assume a friend of yours sees a movie and tells you, "I loved it. I completely identified with the main character."

That's bull, in my opinion. Your friend did not identify with the main character. She or he identified with the protagonist's *conflict*. Your moviegoer friend can never be that person in the movie, but she could have experienced the character's conflict, problem, or situation. That's why she loved the movie. It was the conflict not the character that involved her in the story.

So, when you create a story, keep the character's conflict at the forefront of your screenplay's starting point. In other words, don't obsess over a point you want to make or a theme, as Lajos Egri states in his popular book *The Art of Dramatic Writing*. He insists that the writer should start with a premise, such as "Love Conquers All" or "Foolishness Leads to Poverty." The problem with the premise as a starting point is that you will inevitably create *contrived* situations and characters to make your theme become a story. But it usually ends up being phony or heavy handed. You're hitting your audience with a premise that's obviously not based on reality but on a point you want to make.

A much better place to start is observing (or stealing) from real life. Collect anecdotes. You will want to observe real people around you and, more important, their problems, their situations, their conflicts.

Pay close attention to the people who cause those problems. In movies, we call these problem-givers the antagonists. You should study both the antagonists and the protagonists like a scientist. You don't make judgments. You don't want them to be tools of your theme. So become like an objective scientist and research the human behavior of your characters so they can be as real as possible.

EXERCISE

A good place to start a story is to look around at the people you know and observe their problems, and at the people who cause the CONFLICT. Maybe your best friend has a problem living with his mother. Or your sister is getting married to a wealthy man she doesn't actually love.

Like an objective scientist, observe the conflict and imagine it as a scene. Take notes. Try not to interject your own opinions of the people. Stick to the facts of what you see and what happens.

The main thing to concentrate on at this point is the antagonist. Most beginning writers are comfortable creating a protagonist that substitutes for themselves, who they are. However, what actually creates drama is the antagonist, the conflict-giver. So when you observe life and take research notes, be sure to pinpoint the actions, motives, and desires of the ANTAGONIST. The protagonist, while important, may not be the key to your starting point.

And by the way, the antagonist does not mean "the bad guy." Your friend's mother could be an antagonist. She might be the sweetest, nicest person in the world, but she's a total pain in the ass to live with.

So watch a real-life mother create problems for her son. Or, better yet, combine several mothers, each of who compounds the conflict. Here's where a little imagination can help you. Remember, you can only steal so much from real life. The great writer uses ingenuity to combine characters and their situations.

As an easy and obvious example, think of James Bond movies. Bond is always the charming, dapper, ladies' man who does his thing. He would be extremely boring and repetitious were it not for the antagonist. Every antagonist in the Bond films is the character that creates hurdles for Bond to jump. The more interesting the hurdles the antagonist creates, the more ingenious Bond has to be to overcome them. So, in your exercise, it's the "Goldfingers" (or "Goldmembers") who are the key to your story.

The starting point of your story will be the antagonist creating problems for your protagonist. Now create scenes combining your observations with your imagination.

HAL ACKERMAN

The Cringe Exercise

HAL ACKERMAN has been on the faculty of the UCLA School of Theater, Film and Television for the past twenty-two years and is currently co-chair of the screenwriting program. He is the author of *Write Screenplays That Sell...The Ackerman Way*. His play *Testosterone: How Prostate Cancer Made a Man of Me*, which concluded its premiere theatrical run in Santa Monica, California, won the William Saroyan Centennial Award for drama.

I like to do this one the first day of a new class, though it can also be done alone. It is a great icebreaker. Beyond that, it addresses several fundamental issues that go to the DNA of story. New writers are so often cautioned, admonished, brainwashed that movies must have a likable protagonist. We sometimes paralyze ourselves and eviscerate characters by trying too hard to invest them with characteristics that will look good on their college resumes and by engaging them in acts of gratuitous nobility. Whereas many characters that leave indelible impressions upon us are those who perform acts that may seem or may *be* reprehensible.

Think for a moment about the fantastic documentary WINGED MIGRATION. We have spent two hours in the most amazingly intimate company of flocks of migrating birds, flown the thousands of miles with them, endured with them hardships beyond imagination—freezing and starving at the Pole while sheltering precious eggs in their fur, living weeks without food. Now, at last, a group of them returns to their home nesting grounds in the familiar warm pastureland of France. As they pass overhead, a farmer raises a shotgun, fires twice, and a bird, whose name we never knew but in whose struggles we were active participants, falls dead to earth. God! Our hearts break.

Now think of the Donner party, a group of settlers trekking from the Midwest in 1848 to a new home in California. After hardship and misery, deprivation and loss, at last they are on the verge of the Promised Land. Only one more mountain to cross. They reach the peak of the Sierra above Reno and, exhausted, decide to rest the night before moving on. A blizzard hits and they are stranded for months. All their supplies are depleted. They have eaten leather and are about to resort to the unthinkable, cannibalism. One last chance: A few of them trek out into six-foot drifts with a rifle. A game bird appears. They are so weak it takes three of them to lift the rifle. They fire. Do we want that bird to be killed? You bet we do. Same situation. Different emotion. Why?

Ackerman's Axiom #1: Intimacy trumps morality.

EXERCISE

1. Write ten things you have done in your life that literally make you cringe when you realize that you actually did them. (Just a brief one-line description.)

   For example: Fed lighter fluid to my sister's fish because I wanted to make it an electric eel. Got drunk in junior high school and frayed the climbing rope in gym. On way to visit fiancé's parents met man on plane and joined Mile High Club. Be honest.

   If in a group: All the people read theirs aloud. The thing to notice is that listeners are fascinated, not turned off. This is also true in the case of characters! Audiences, too, will be fascinated.

2. Choose one of these events and write a two- to three-page prose story around it. Remember, your reader has never met any of these people, so use all your storytelling skills. All of your five senses. Put your audience in the world. Construct a real emotional truth around the event and character.

3. Adapt that story to a screen story. Screen stories are different. Would you start in the same place? Since movie audiences only know what they see and hear, as a screenwriter how do you make the inner life of your character, narrated vividly in your prose story, accessible to an audience?

ALAN WATT

Trusting Yourself

ALAN WATT works in Los Angeles as a screenwriter, playwright and novelist. He is the author of the award-winning *Los Angeles Times*–bestselling novel *Diamond Dogs*, which he recently adapted for the big screen. He is the founder and creative director of LA Writers Lab and teaches the twice-yearly workshops 90-Day Screenplay and 90-Day Novel.

Story structure is not a formula, though it is frequently taught as such. In my workshops I describe structure as an *immutable paradigm through which to explore our hero's transformation*. What I mean is that every hero has a journey, but there is nothing predictable about it. The desire to write is connected to the desire to evolve or resolve something in our lives that we don't yet fully understand. We are naturally drawn to ideas and images that allow us to explore these unresolved questions for ourselves. Operating from this premise, we begin to recognize that we are necessarily *uniquely qualified to tell our story*.

Sometimes we approach our story from a distance, out of fear. The following exercise is the first one I give to my writers. It is a potent means by which to shed our "idea" of our story, for the true story. Our fears, those hobgoblins we believe we must exorcise before getting down to work, are in fact our guides! What if we simply gave ourselves permission to write from this raw, vulnerable place? What if we explored the "nature" of our fears and allowed ourselves to write, without judgment, whatever arose? We don't have to become something more or something better in order to write our screenplay. What we need to know already lies within.

So, here we go.

EXERCISE

Take a couple of minutes and list all of your fears around writing your screenplay. List them on a piece of paper, from the trivial to the forbidden. Perhaps you are afraid that your family will know something about you, that you will be "discovered" for being the strange, twisted creature you really are. Perhaps you are afraid that you will fail, that you will have wasted your life on a pointless quest, that you are not really a writer. Or maybe you are afraid that you will succeed, and that you will have to become responsible, some better and more noble version of yourself.

Maybe you're afraid that this is your only decent premise and that you ought not "waste" it while you're still learning. And on and on . . . "People will hate me," "My relationships will end," "It won't be commercial," and so on.

List all of your fears.

OK? Excellent!

Now, why do we do this exercise? The first reason is obvious: We want to be conscious of our fears so they don't rule us. But that isn't the big reason. The big reason arises from the idea that "the desire to write is connected to the desire to evolve." What I mean is that our fears around writing our story are *identical* in nature to the fears that our hero has in the story.

There is often some initial resistance to this idea. You may look at your fears and say there is no connection between my fears and the fears of my hero. Continue to investigate, sit with it for a moment, and be curious if you don't start to see some connections. This is not to say that the situations around the fears are the same, but rather the "nature" of our fears is connected to those of our hero. For example:

1. "I'm afraid to write this script because it will be a waste of time and it will never sell."

    Ask yourself: Where in the story does my hero believe he might be making a terrible mistake? And also, is it possible that my hero is refusing to face or even acknowledge his fear of making a terrible mistake?

2. "I'm afraid people will know my darkest secrets."

    Ask yourself: Where in the story does my hero believe he will be abandoned for being different? And even, what is the secret that my hero may be in denial of?

3. "I'm afraid I'll discover I'm not really a writer."

    Ask yourself: Where in the story does my hero fear failure? What is the dream that my hero fears he may never realize?

Though our fears are real to us, they are also just regular garden-variety fears. Everybody has them. When we can shed our "idea" of our story and shift our focus to the *nature* of our characters, fears and all, we begin to realize that there is nothing to "figure out," that we are actually channels for the screenplay that wants to be told through us. It is from this place that the true structure of our story begins to emerge.

BRAD RIDDELL

Note Card R&D

BRAD RIDDELL has written feature scripts for MTV, Paramount and Universal, in addition to working with several independent producers. He cofounded The Kentucky Film Lab and teaches screenwriting at the University of Southern California and Spalding University.

It is critically important that aspiring screenwriters learn to fight on multiple fronts. Most professionals rarely work on just one project at a time, instead keeping several stories moving forward simultaneously in various stages of development. Think of screenwriting as your start-up business, and then consider that there aren't many new companies that succeed without continuous research and development. A screenwriter's R&D involves carving out time each week to keep the assembly line moving, to provide a quick transition to the next project and to arm himself or herself with answers to the question that even the most successful scribes always hear in meetings: "So what else ya got?"

To better kick-start our students' conveyor belts and fill their idea armories with blockbuster ammo, I teach a class at USC called Breaking the Story. One exercise I developed for that class was at first only intended to simulate the task of writing a studio assignment, but it has since grown into a useful tool for generating new ideas when R&D slows and the cache runs dry.

For many writers, working on spec from a totally blank, anything-is-possible, wide-open canvas proves to be a difficult challenge that can quickly cripple inspiration and momentum under the weight of too many options and too much indecision. But if you add a few immutable parameters to the project (as they exist in a studio assignment), suddenly you have a starting point. Several of my students have turned projects derived from the following exercise into feature scripts, and recently one earned Distinction on his USC thesis, which he first developed using "Note Card R&D."

EXERCISE

1. Gather fifteen blank note cards.

2. Separate them into three stacks of five.

3. On each card in the first stack, write the name of a prominent actor.

4. On each card in the second stack, write the name of a genre.

5. On each card in the third stack, write the name of an interesting location.

6. Flip each stack over to hide your writing.

7. Keeping them separate, shuffle each stack vigorously.

8. Select one card from the top of each stack.

9. Drumroll your desk before turning over each of the three cards.

10. Now use these cards as building blocks to develop a movie treatment.

It is important that you *not* allow yourself to reshuffle and redraw. What you get is what you get. The challenge (as well as the fun) is born from working within rigid parameters. These random variables are what give your creativity a starting point and free you from preciousness and indecision. Holding fast to your hand of cards will push you to work on ideas outside your typical comfort zone, and sometimes the best stories come from the most unlikely pairings.

For instance, I once had a student draw Denzel Washington, Period Piece, Japan, and turn it into a gripping World War II treatment. Another student wrote an excellent feature-length script from

Natalie Portman, Action, Las Vegas, even though she hated all three elements at first. Kate Hudson, New York, Sci-Fi once generated a hilarious romantic comedy, and Shia LeBeouf, Drama, Africa was the foundation for the aforementioned thesis script that earned Distinction at USC.

The stories you derive from your note cards may not always be home runs or lead to finished feature scripts, but they will inevitably help you to explore new characters, worlds and scenarios that may become useful to you in other projects down the road. Most important, they will serve to keep your R&D factory humming at full speed and brimming with potential.

CHANDUS JACKSON

Concept Is King

CHANDUS JACKSON is an award-winning screenwriter, having recently won the Walt Disney/ABC Writing Fellowship for his political thriller screenplay RENDERED. While at Disney he also developed and wrote the sci-fi/family THE COMPLETION. He has won several screenwriting awards to include top finishes in the Page International Screenwriting Awards and Austin Heart of Film Screenplay Competition. Chandus presently has feature and TV scripts in development.

One lesson I've learned in Hollywood is that right out of the gate a screenplay will be judged solely on its concept or premise. You may say that this isn't fair and that once a creative executive or agent reads your latest opus he'll realize it's the next blockbuster or Oscar contender. You may be right. But for most writers the first step is to get someone to just read their script. In order to create this desire for a read, the premise or concept must be locked tight.

So what's this premise or concept? It's the "big idea," or rather, the "high concept," as many in the industry are fond of saying. I call it the sticking point. It's that one-liner about a story that leaves the reader wanting more. It essentially signals to the reader whether a script will be going to the top of the pile for the weekend read or the bottom of the stack. As an audience member we make similar selections about what we read or watch in our daily lives. We can all relate to flipping past channel after channel with the TV remote because what we're reading on the screen doesn't pique our interest.

Such is the case with the concept of a screenplay. The truth of the matter is that solid structure, great dialogue and superb characters cannot substitute for a faulty premise or an ill-conceived story idea.

What this usually signals is that a script may be better suited for another medium such as a novel, teleplay or short story. As storytellers we must know what medium works best as we find the perfect vehicle to share our stories with the world.

How can we be so sure that what we've found is worth the investment of the next four months or several years? The short answer is: Test the marketplace. I test the market every time by pitching my premise to a group of trusted friends. If these friends seem confused or even lukewarm, then it's back to the drawing board. The primary goal is to determine whether this concept is market-ready before investing time and resources in writing. Many scripts in Hollywood don't do this and, as such, are "Dead on Arrival." You say, "I'll get some feedback," but hold on. There's more. As writers it's our job to understand the entire family tree of the concept we're writing. Whether it's a comedy, thriller or action script, we must know what films are similar to our own, with an understanding of why our script is different and what sets it apart. We must also understand the current marketplace. There's no worse feeling than spending months or years on a script only to discover that another writer's similar script has been green-lit for production. I say, cut your losses and start writing something else, because life is just too short. As a screenwriter you must learn to develop several concepts if you're going to make it as a Hollywood working writer.

EXERCISE

There are two simple exercises that can be beneficial during the development process.

Part A. Write out the family tree of recent concepts you are working on. How is your concept similar to what has already been made? What's different or unique about your project? What's fresh? Most of this information about past films and future projects can easily be found on IMDb.com.

Part B. This next exercise involves watching films that are similar to your concept along with reading the script. This is an excellent way to see how similar projects are executed. Still, this exercise isn't just for projects you are working on. Every time you come across a script that interests you and that has recently been sold, look up its family tree. Research the story and see how it's different from other scripts in the marketplace. This will only strengthen a writer's story-development muscle. This, of course, is critical to the success of a Hollywood screenwriter. Remember, concept is king.

BARRI EVINS

When Sally Met Harry

BARRI EVINS is a both a screenwriting teacher and a film producer. She has taught at the UCLA Graduate Producer Program, AFI, CineStory, Great American PitchFest and the L.A. Screenwriting Expo. As a producer, Barri has set up numerous pitches and specs at Warner Bros., Universal, Disney, Nickelodeon, New Line and HBO. Her current passion is a project with actor-producer Tobey Maguire and Academy Award–nominated writers Mark Fergus and Hawk Otsby.

In the delicious scene between Harry and Sally in Katz's Deli, Meg Ryan's character claims men can't tell when women are faking an orgasm. Billy Crystal, supremely confident of his own prowess, *insists* he can. Meg launches into an utterly convincing demo, right there amid the corned beef and knishes. Here in Hollywood, we'll always side with Billy. We can tell when you're faking it. Probably by Page Two.

When frustrated screenwriters say to themselves, "To hell with Hollywood; everything they make is crap. If that's what they want, that's what I'm gonna give 'em. I'm gonna write one of those pieces of crap and sell it for Big Money," *They inevitably fail.*

They're faking it.

The material is flat. Dry. Forced.

Even if it's impeccably crafted, something's not quite right. Like saying "When Sally Met Harry"—it just doesn't flow. What didn't excite you can't possibly turn us on.

When writers fake it, they ignore the very keys to their success.

Remember when you were a kid and nervous about fitting in? Mom said, "Just be yourself." As usual, Mom was right.

The secret to being yourself as a writer is to know what you do best as well as what really matters to you. What you're good at and what you want to say. Your strengths and your passions.

Combine those two ingredients with what I call a "hooky idea," one that ignites our imagination, grabs us and won't let go, and *eureka*—career rocket fuel! You've discovered the Magic Triangle.

FADE IN: A struggling writer taking bit parts in movies attends a boxing match where the underdog miraculously goes the distance with the champ. Inspired, in three days he writes a screenplay he titles ROCKY. Sylvester Stallone was offered $250,000 for the script but turned it down. He sold it for $25,000 and the starring role. Sly used a powerful idea combined with his strengths and passions to get where he wanted to go.

The most important decision you will ever make as a writer is what to write next. Your Screenwriting Strengths are one invaluable tool for determining, *before* you begin to write, if your idea can catapult you to the next level in your career.

EXERCISE

1. Identifying your Screenwriting Strengths:

   —What do you enjoy most about screenwriting?

   —Your favorite genre to write in and a few words about why.

   —Your least favorite and why.

   —What aspect of screenwriting comes easiest to you?

   —If as a screenwriter I never again have to _____,
   I'd be thrilled.

   —I'm most happy when creating:

Action	Ideas	Outlines
Fantasy Elements	Description	Theme
Twists	Researching	Dialogue

Visuals	Character Arcs	Plot
Characters	Relationships	Tension and Suspense
Typing FADE OUT	Or _____	

2. When writing a scene, I:

—Just hear the characters talking

—Close my eyes and envision what's happening

—Think about how the characters feel

—Focus on advancing the plot

—Concentrate on what I want the audience to feel

—Figure out how to reveal something about my characters

—Write everything I can think of, then cut, cut, cut

—Have no idea

—Other: _____

3. What kind of dialogue is your forte? Your second greatest strength?

Snappy romantic banter	Authentic kids' voices
Contemporary teen chatter	Brisk, straightforward action
Period-appropriate phrasing	Inventing a new vocabulary
Witty wisecracks	Character-revealing speeches
Sophisticated adult conversation	Clever, clue-laden quips
Milieu-specific jargon	Distinctive voices for similar characters
I hate dialogue	Real-life dialogue just sticks in my head

Or _____

4. Without stopping to think twice, complete the sentences:

—My favorite line of movie dialogue:

—The scene without dialogue that blows me away:

—My favorite relationship between two characters:

—The comic moment that makes me laugh so hard that popcorn spurts out my nose:

—The twist that rocked me in my theater seat the first time I saw the movie:

—The movie visual burned into my brain:

—The film that speaks directly to what I think is important in life:

—The movie I can watch again and again and again:

Of the above, which answers sprang to mind instantly and with utter certainty?

5. If I had a magic wand and could create your perfect imaginary screenwriting partner— POOF!—what would be his or her greatest strength as a writer?

6. Unlike a *Cosmo* quiz, this one doesn't come with a handy decoder. But I think—deep down—you know the answers.

    —My Biggest Screenwriting Strength is: _____

    —My Second Greatest Strength is: _____

    —My area of Least "Strengthiness" (tip of the hat to Stephen Colbert) is: _____

Knowing your Screenwriting Strengths is an essential element of your own personal Magic Triangle. When it comes to What to Write Next, now you can choose ideas in genres that showcase what you're best at.

As for me, when it comes to reading a well-written fake or a great idea based on strengths and passions, unlike Rob Reiner's mom in Katz's, I'll have the real thing.

CHRISTINA M. KIM

The Comfort Zone

CHRISTINA M. KIM wrote for the television series *Lost* for three seasons. She received a Writers Guild Award for her work on the show as well as a nomination for one of the episodes she wrote. She has also written for the television series *Ghost Whisperer*, was a writer and producer for the medical drama *Miami Trauma*, and currently writes for *NCIS: Los Angeles*. She can be found outside her comfort zone, researching creative ways to keep Los Angeles safe.

There's an old adage (or maybe it's a cliché): "Write what you know." That was one of the first things I remember hearing when I was in film school. It's an encouraging piece of advice to a new writer . . . just think about stuff that's happened to you or people you know and start writing. Anyone can do that, right? Easy!

We all have great stories, like my nutty aunt who, weeping, drove five hours one way with her dead dog in the front seat to her son's college dorm so that he could say a proper goodbye to "Daisy." Or the insane high school party in the woods that ended with a full-on cop car chase through the suburbs. While these are interesting characters or scenes, only "writing what you know" can be limiting. Sometimes you have to leave the comfort zone of your life experiences and "write what you don't know." It's scary territory, but the material that's just waiting to be written about is worth it.

I recently had an idea for a script that took place in Hawaii among a group of competitive lifeguards. I was familiar with the setting of Hawaii, but I didn't know the first thing about lifeguarding beyond what I'd seen on *Baywatch*. So I went to Borders and bought a bunch of books on lifeguarding techniques, rented any movie that took place on the beach, and did all sorts of Wikipedia and Internet searches. I got a good foundation in lifeguard training and basics, but I didn't feel like I could write with any sort of authenticity.

Living in L.A., I had the advantage of miles of public beaches policed by lifeguards, just minutes away. I asked around my group of friends, and it turned out that a friend of a friend was a part-time lifeguard. Perfect! (And also a lesson that you never know until you ask— your acquaintances, people on Facebook, neighbors . . . everyone is a valuable resource.) My lifeguard buddy, Greg, was kind enough to let me shadow him during one of his shifts. I went out to Venice Beach and just absorbed everything I could . . . from the "conditions board" that he updated as soon as he arrived at work, to the way he scanned the water "reading the waves," to the lifeguards' shorthand interaction with each other. I also noticed that Greg never made eye contact with me because he was constantly watching the ocean for signs of trouble. While I didn't get to see a real-life rescue, I got to hear all sorts of stories from him and his friends about past saves.

I returned home with an entire notebook full of anecdotes and details, and, more important, the confidence to write with my newfound knowledge. So, in a sense, I'd sought out what I didn't know, gained some experience, and was now back to writing what I knew. No longer was I imagining what it would be like to sit in a lifeguard tower; now I knew what it looked liked, smelled like, every detail down to the old 1980s telephone that sat on the rotted-out wood plank that served as a desk.

For the purposes of this exercise, I encourage you to leave your comfort zone and write what you don't know. Ask yourself: What makes you uneasy? What have you always wanted to try? Who are you curious about? Don't limit yourself . . . most people, even strangers, are open-minded (and flattered) when you say you're writing a script and want to ask some questions or shadow them. Once you do, I guarantee you'll have something to write about. And at the end of the day, you can retreat to the comfort zone of your computer, armed with your new research, and start writing about something you know again.

EXERCISE

Find a topic or person that interests you. It can be anything from "What's it like to work at a police station?" to "I wonder what it's like to be the doorman at that trendy bar." Track down contacts, make phone calls and arrange for a day or even just an hour to watch someone in action. Interviews can be a good resource, but observing people in their element is where you'll pick up all sorts of juicy details.

Jot down every observation that you can: what they're wearing, any lingo they use, what they eat for lunch, mannerisms, smells, sounds, etc. . . .

Now sit down and come up with a scenario that takes place in that setting. Or take the person you observed and put him or her in a different setting. It doesn't matter what happens; the key to this exercise is to use the research you've done to add authenticity and depth to the scene and the characters. You'll be amazed at all the things you've absorbed, just by experiencing something new. And who knows, you may even come up with a killer idea for a script based on your research.

PAULA C. BRANCATO

Finding Your Story

PAULA BRANCATO, an award-winning screenwriter and producer, serves on the faculty at the University of Southern California. Brancato executive produced the feature film SOMEWHERE IN THE CITY, winner of the Karlovy Vary Film Festival. She wrote the screenplays SUBTERFUGE, ELLEN JERSEY and THE WANTING (sixteen screenwriting awards). Brancato's most recent directorial work, HER FATHER'S DAUGHTER, won the Houston International Worldfest and Women of Color Film Festival and was a Sundance finalist.

A screenplay begins with the creation of a story. Unfortunately, not all stories deserve to be told. You've heard it said a hundred ways: "We're looking for a premise that's unique and unusual, a 'high concept' story." "Something new that knocks our socks off." "A tale with remarkable insight, never told before." One of our greatest poets was asked why he turned out only six to eight new poems a year. He said, "Because I only have remarkable insights six to eight times a year." So, how do you get the remarkable insight that generates the unusual premise that creates the story that's a winner?

It's done through sheer unadulterated work. *Plus* paying attention to what stays in one's head and what doesn't, the flotsam and jetsam of one's brain. This is the realm of the poet, the observer who lets many good and bad ideas pass.

The truth? The average professional writer will run through about one hundred story ideas—dead cat meets maker and finds out he's a dog, London schoolteacher launches science fair undoing MI5, a cyber house turns on its inhabitants—to get ten that deserve to be put on paper or even discussed in short treatment form. Out of the

25

ten stories deemed suitable for a short treatment, the pro will find that maybe only three have the meat necessary to become a screenplay. That is after he or she has already written maybe fifty pages.

The pros are ruthless and relentless about casting less promising story ideas aside, because each rejected idea brings the writer closer to that remarkable concept. Perhaps the dog as cat theme is appealing but not something this particular writer can write well. The London schoolteacher idea might have run out of twists and turns and become a really bad, really sappy romance. And how many interesting ways can a cyber house kill people, after all, if that is all it's meant to do? This writer's cyber house might be a *Twilight Zone* episode, but it takes more to make a strong feature film, and so on and so on. The pro whittles away and funnels down.

Of the three stories that do survive, the professional further knows that only *one* is likely to have that remarkable insight that will not let go of the writer—that's one in one hundred—and that this is the story that must be told.

So, if your screenplays aren't shaking anyone up, consider your premise before you start. Is this story something you know about, can learn about and can write? Is it fun? Does it turn you on? Does it excite you down to your very bones? Is there enough meat to warrant two hours of an audience's time, or is this story a one-note Johnny? Are you certain you have no particular axe to grind? Screenplays aren't lessons, they are insights, things you didn't even know yourself! Finally, do you just keep finding this darned story knocking around in your head no matter how hard you try to get rid of it? Then write, by all means.

In order to help spur your "story muscles," you might try the following exercises. I have found them useful in breaking through writer's block and spurring the imagination so writers can get to the flotsam and jetsam in their heads.

EXERCISE

1. The Warm-Up

   You are alone, asleep in your bedroom, late at night. You wake up. There's a sound at the window. Someone's breaking in. Your heart is racing. The intruder is inches away from achieving his goal. You remember you have a gun, but you've hidden it because of the children. You can't remember where you hid the gun. And then . . .

   Jot down twenty possibilities of what might happen next. *Do not think.* Just jot. Take a few minutes, then reread the list. Are there any that make you laugh, cry, cringe or otherwise affect you? Good insights, yes?

2. Completing the Story

   A man lives alone in the mountains. He writes jingles for commercials, song ditties. One night in the lot near his house, he hears a car pull up and a woman scream. He thinks nothing of it. He is hard at work, writing a ditty. There's angry talk, then the car takes off, screeching away in the night. He is so involved in his writing that he hardly hears.

   The next day the police knock on his door. They want to know, what does he know about what went on in the lot next to him last night? He says he heard a car pull up and a woman scream, but at three a.m., he was working on a Pepsi commercial and didn't hear much else. The cops tell him a jogger found a body in the lot at five a.m. Don't leave town, they say, we may want to talk to you again.

   That night, having completed his work, the man goes out to his regular bar. It's very crowded, lots of people, eating, drinking, celebrating. From across the bar, he suddenly hears, quite distinctly, a man whistling a tune—the very same ditty he's been working on for days.

   Write a five-page scene that shows what happens next.

GET WRITING

KIM KRIZAN

Binding and Gagging the Internal Critic

KIM KRIZAN is an Academy Award–and Writers Guild of America Award–nominated writer best known for her work on the critically acclaimed films BEFORE SUNRISE and BEFORE SUNSET. She was a featured performer in the films SLACKER, DAZED AND CONFUSED, and WAKING LIFE, and recently wrote the 2061 comic series published in Zombie Tales. Krizan resides in Los Angeles and teaches writing courses at UCLA.

I'm a firm believer in the power of stream-of-conscious writing—that is, really messy, wild, unstructured and unpolished writing—with no fear that it will ever see the light of day. I'm doing that kind of stream-of-conscious brainstorming now as I write this, knowing it will end up in a book that potentially thousands upon thousands of people will read: serious students, learned professionals, the whole of intelligent civilization, perhaps the Magi and God Herself. I imagine them reading, and I imagine them criticizing. For that's what we fear when we write: the critic.

The critic, *real* critic, resides *within us*. It's the left-brained self that developed at some point in childhood and put the kibosh on our free, playful, creative self. It's the self that learned how to please others and to fit in, the self that lost the joy of doing things and making things for the sheer pleasure of it. This internal critic is focused on the final product: a final product that will be scrutinized and must pass muster.

As oppressive as this internal critic might sound, he or she is necessary, making certain we turn in assignments and pay our taxes and don't walk out into traffic or embarrass ourselves too badly at dinner parties. Unfortunately though, this critic is not very helpful when it comes to our writing. This is because the critic is, yes, *critical* and

31

perhaps certain that most of what we do is *absolute crap*. The internal critic believes that if your work isn't on the level of Shakespeare and Baudelaire and Kierkegaard combined, *immediately, right out of the gate*, then all is lost and you might as well quit and eat a cheesecake in its entirety.

I begin every project with a lot of messy stream-of-conscious brainstorming with no fear that it must be "right" or "good" or even that anyone will read it. This brainstorming plants the seeds, gets the ball rolling, and allows the project to take shape organically, without the dictatorial controls of the critical self.

I basically force my students to do the following exercise. It gets a good story out of them much faster than asking them to be Shakespeare or Baudelaire or someone they are not. It brings out a story that is much more elemental, much more original, much less tied to pleasing the supposed experts who determine what they "should" write. And, in the end, it makes writing a lot of fun.

EXERCISE

Get out a piece of paper and a pen or pencil. Put th_ pen or pencil down on the paper. Record your thoughts. Yes, your private thoughts. Do not judge these thoughts; just transcribe. Don't worry about handwriting, spelling, grammar, punctuation, and especially not content. You're free to say absolutely anything. Your hand won't be able to keep up with your thoughts, but do your best. Include plans for total global domination or detailed rants about people who annoy you or even how idiotic this exercise is—literally anything that crosses your mind. Go for at least twenty to thirty minutes.

This exercise will clear some of the tensions of the day and quiet the mental static that gets in the way of writing. It also helps you contact buried feelings and thoughts that will be very useful to your project. Most important, it helps to disengage the internal critic and engage the freer, more creative self.

If it's particularly difficult to get into this exercise or if you are very ambitious, switch to your nondominant hand. (My students who complain the most bitterly about this are the ones who go on to tell me that it brings on huge revelations.) It will be hard to write legibly, and you'll have to concentrate just to form the words, but this exercise will help you contact your creative brain.

Be sure to hide this writing in a safe place where no one can find it and read it, because this stuff is not for public consumption. Or, if you've written something really incendiary, throw it away. The point is to warm up, open channels, and get words flowing without the fear of being judged or critiqued.

Do this exercise regularly, perhaps every time you sit down to write. Just like a singer warms up the vocal chords before singing or a dancer warms up the muscles before dancing, this stream-of-conscious writing will prepare you for "real" writing. And it will make that "real" writing a lot easier and more fun.

WESLEY STRICK

The Talking Cure

WESLEY STRICK began his writing career as a rock journalist in the late seventies. Since the late eighties he has written, rewritten or cowritten a dozen Hollywood movies, including TRUE BELIEVER, ARACHNOPHOBIA, CAPE FEAR, WOLF, THE SAINT, RETURN TO PARADISE, DOOM and most recently the "reboot" of A NIGHTMARE ON ELM STREET, starring Jackie Earle Haley. Strick's first novel, *Out There in the Dark*, was published in 2006.

My screenwriting exercise is simple. That doesn't mean it's easy; it's not. In fact, it's something of an ordeal and an imposition, and puts your human dignity on the line. But life is full of embarrassment and pain. Don't let that stop you. In the end this exercise will save you much trouble (and writing) down the road. I didn't dare try it till later in my career—I was too self-conscious before. Looking back, I wish I'd had the courage to use a method so basic, so natural for whipping a movie idea into shape rather than relying on clever shortcuts, tricks, tips and jargon to feel good about my scripts. And there is a significant upside: This exercise doesn't involve any actual writing. Guaranteed: You won't type a word.

EXERCISE

By now you've pretty much got the movie organized in your head or in outline form or however it is that you work out your plot and characters. If you're like me, you've accumulated four or five disorganized pages full of story ideas, beats, a theme or two, some character notes, a line about style or a paragraph on what inspired all this. Now you're eager to start writing scenes, get a feel for how this material will live on the page.

But don't. Not yet. Instead, set aside a little time with someone in your life, someone you like and trust: boyfriend, girlfriend, best friend, sibling, spouse. We'll call this person your audience and refer to her using the female personal pronoun.

Next, find someplace quiet and cozy for the two of you to sit, face to face: the couch, the backyard, the bed, the bathtub. (No tub if it's a sibling.) Pour some coffee, or wine if you prefer. Let your audience know you're going to tell her a story.

If she insists on knowing more, admit that it's your new movie idea. No big deal. Maybe she'd already guessed. That's okay. But remember, you're not "pitching" your new movie idea. You're telling it. The way you'd tell a fascinating tale—an account of something that once happened to you or recently happened to you. Or to someone you know or someone you heard about.

Now set aside, for the duration of the exercise, the fact that it's an idea for a movie. Questions of commercial appeal are moot. Forget your brilliant concept. Forget genre. Forget about the inciting incident, rising action, midpoint pivot . . . none of these count for the moment. All that you're doing is telling a story, pure and simple.

(Or maybe not so simple, but we'll come to that.)

Remember, don't put undue pressure on yourself—you want to engross your audience, you don't need to hold her spellbound. You're not Orson Welles; you're just a screenwriter. Of course that doesn't mean you can't ham it up a bit. Embellish, embroider, do character voices if you're good at character voices. Make it amusing, make it interesting, make it entertaining. Anyway, start talking.

The process should take about a half hour to forty-five minutes tops. That gives you (applying the classic Syd Field "paradigm") ten minutes for the first act, twenty for the second, ten for the third, plus or minus. That's a long time to yak, sure, but stick with it to the end. Stay relaxed, stay fluid. Pause regularly for a hit of caffeine or alcohol. Answer any questions that arise briefly, without excessive backtracking or backpedaling, then get on with it. Those questions are important; they point to weakness and blurriness and possible contrivance in your plot. Watch your audience's facial expressions and body language for signs of boredom, confusion, incredulity.

Watch yourself, too—that is, stay aware of the areas where you stumble or find yourself caught in thickets of exposition, justification and/or rationalization. If you feel that you're fudging here or there, make a mental note of that. It speaks to a fundamental (though almost certainly fixable, nonfatal) flaw in your story's conception.

Pay attention to the ebbs and flows, the rhythms, of your tale. Does it feel natural or forced? Are *you* getting confused? Does this thing stay on the rails? Does it pick up speed as it moves along? Or can you feel it jumping the tracks—or worse, stalling?

Whew, you're finally done. Is your audience smiling, nodding? Or does she look perplexed? Does she want you to go back and "explain again about the part where . . . "?

Okay, take a breath. Thank your audience and go find a peaceful, private place to lick your wounds and recover some measure of dignity. Then start rethinking, focusing on those areas where things went iffy and dodgy and slipped from your grasp. Start shoring up and patching the weak spots.

Then find a fresh victim, and do it all over again. *Again? C'mon, really?*

Yes, because I say so. Force yourself—just once more.

And this time, now that you've got the essence of your story under control, feel free to open it up. Let in a little more air, a little more light. Explore the characters, their side roads and B stories. Unwind the narrative, treating it like some long, elaborate joke.

Because a joke is a very specific kind of story with a setup, an elaboration and a payoff, just like a movie. Your payoff doesn't have to be funny (unless you're doing comedy), but it should be surprising and—if you get lucky—powerful. So, this time, tell your story as it if were a long, leisurely (but not meandering) shaggy dog story.

Okay, was it any better this time? More vivid, more organic, more convincing? Having talked through the story once again, is there still some magic left, some spark of life, or did it feel like you were flogging a dead horse? In other words, do you still have that burning desire to write the script? Do you still love your movie idea?

Good. Now sleep on it. Tomorrow, hit your laptop. Time to type FADE IN.

BETH SERLIN

The Almighty Verb

BETH SERLIN cowrote the German film JENSEITS DER STILLE, which was nominated for the Best Foreign Language Academy Award in 1997, and has since written numerous scripts for the German market. An assistant professor of screenwriting at Loyola Marymount University, she usually breezes into the classroom, sometimes saunters, occasionally trudges, but never does she just enter.

Powerful cinema stories—we all want to write them. Our brains run amok with premises and plot twists, characters by the dozen, structural mayhem—it's enough to drive a poor writer batty. Lucky for us there's a single word that elevates storytelling and breathes life into our screenplays. It's one of the most effective fundamentals in a writer's toolbox but also the one most overlooked: I give you the almighty verb.

When we think of cinema stories we think of action. The verb takes center stage when writing action, which really means movement toward an objective or, more specifically, movement toward a character's objective. Why then do so many writers employ the dullest verbs in the book? A perfectly good scene can be hijacked by "He takes the gun from his pocket and goes into the 7-Eleven." Armed with proper verbs, you can transform the mundane into a memorable visual moment that reveals character: "He fumbles the gun from his pocket and trips into the 7-Eleven." Now we've got a sense of this guy's inexperience and reluctance, which creates automatic tension before anything even happens. What's more, we abide by screenwriting's one and only rule: Don't be boring. If someone would rather feather dust his bookshelf than read your screen direction, you've essentially lost the "screen" before the "play" even begins. After slugging through development of an original idea with unique characters and sizzling dialogue, why belittle all that effort with some version of the most hackneyed, dog-eared verb in the English language: *to be*? Remember, this verb didn't work out so well for Hamlet either.

So what can we do to suck in and rivet our readers? We want them spellbound, ignoring the phone, the doorbell, the urge to go to the bathroom, because they can't wait to see what happens next. The answer is deceptively simple: Find verbs that contain emotional connotation and can stand alone, without needing adjectives to qualify their existence. These almighty verbs evoke tone, atmosphere and feeling. They excel at externalizing the internal landscape of a character. Different images spring to mind when your hero *darts*, *struts* or *slithers* across a room versus when she or he *moves* across it. Specificity makes a verb potent and therefore more efficient. This is critical for the screenplay form that has as much white space as black marks on the page and thus requires that every word propel the story forward. I always remind my students (and myself): The picture that paints a thousand words is written with the fewest. Almighty verbs help make this happen, and you can too by creating a personal Writer's Thesaurus.

EXERCISE

Zeroing in on almighty verbs requires a simple, mindful practice: the creation of a personal Writer's Thesaurus. This essential reference will help transform boring verbs into brilliant ones. Start with the ten dullest verbs you can think of. My current favorites are: *to enter, to exit, to look, to walk, to sit, to hit, to move quickly, to get, to stand, to think.* For each of yours, find ten almighty verbs that mean the same but evoke specific emotion. Every time you come across an interesting verb, add it to your list. Consciously practice using these verbs, and before long the list will become second nature.

No matter what kind of story you weave, the journey to create a captivating screenplay may detour into the land of nod. With a personal Writer's Thesaurus in your first aid kit, you can easily "wake up" your writing and keep your reader turning the pages.

ALEXANDER WOO

Throw the Book Away

ALEXANDER WOO is a writer and co–executive producer on HBO's *True Blood*. Previously, he was a writer/co-producer on the Showtime series *Sleeper Cell*. Other television staff credits include *LAX* and *Wonderfalls*. His stage plays include *Forbidden City Blues*, *Debunked* and *In the Sherman Family Wax Museum*.

Personally, I have a deep mistrust of books on writing. Same goes for graduate writing programs. Naturally, I've contributed to both.

The danger is that the writer's mind ends up overburdened by systems and methodologies, like a camel dragging traveling trunks across the desert. Of course there's something to be said for craft (and money to be made teaching it) but not when it dilutes the spark that makes each writer unique. Like snowflakes and hoecakes, no two writers' processes are ever the same. There is no One Way to Do It. We're storytellers, not accountants.

Which leads me to the only suggestion I can safely recommend to anyone: Instead of seeking out what works in the minds of others, figure out *what works for you*. No one knows you like you. If your best work comes when you write without an outline, you don't have to use one. If keeping a journal exhausts you, it's okay to toss it aside. If you're torturing yourself by getting up at six a.m. every morning to write, you can give yourself a break. It's your process. And if your process requires you to stop and read a magazine for an hour so you can recharge, no one should tell you it's wrong.

This is harder than it sounds. Consciously or unconsciously, we've become encrusted with years of advice—which we've since adopted as gospel—on how to make something good. Honestly, there's nothing more crippling than the pressure to write something really, really good. Often we wind up imitating something we consider to be good, which may already be a pale imitation of something else. Like photocopies of photocopies of photocopies, the result is derivative, diffuse and, ultimately, someone else's original idea.

The playwright Mac Wellman has a wonderful exercise where the writer is asked to create the worst piece of crap imaginable. In addition, the scene has to include a rat sandwich, a character with an emerald-green hoof, and twenty-three occurrences—no more, no less—of a seven-syllable word of the writer's own choosing. It sounds ridiculous (and it is), but it's surprising how much easier it is to approach an exercise without the paralyzing objective of making it really, really good. And the rat sandwich, the hoof, and the seven-syllable word? They're all distractions, intended to stave away the subliminal voices of how-to books and workshop instructors haunting your fingertips. Ultimately, what ends up on the page is less important than the experience of the exercise itself. It's open, liberating and—rarest of all when it comes to writing—*fun*. That, of course, is the Holy Grail or, better yet, the White Whale: to write with ease and facility while enjoying yourself. And while we may never get there, Wellman's exercise gives us a peek at how much closer we can get if we throw away the rule book.

One last piece of advice about the hazards of advice: Too often, concern for the big picture ends up obliterating the small picture. To use a culinary analogy: If you asked ten different cooks to make a soufflé, you'd get ten different soufflés. If you supplied each person with the same amount of eggs, milk, butter, flour and sugar, you'd also get ten different soufflés. If you gave each of them the exact same step-by-step recipe . . . you would still get ten different soufflés. The point is, you can have the concept, the ingredients and the recipe, but what makes each result unique is the hand that does the cooking. Don't gloss over the detail work for the sake of the structure. The detail work is what makes your writing yours. Otherwise, you're just making McNuggets.

EXERCISE

Make a comprehensive inventory of all the practices and idiosyncrasies that define your writing process. The following is a very incomplete list of questions you may ask yourself:

- What time of day do you most like to work?

- Do you set deadlines for yourself?

- Do you write in long sittings or in short bursts?

- Do you work in total isolation or in public places?

- Do you initially write in longhand or on a computer?

- Do you work off an outline?

- If you do use an outline, how often do you diverge from it?

- Do you write with a partner?

- Do you frequently bounce ideas off of others?

- Do you always start at the beginning?

- Do you keep a journal?

- Is your writing frequently autobiographical?

- Do you only write scenes you've already thought through and outlined?

- Do you ever work on two projects at once?

- What do you do when you take a break?

- Do you work from source material?

- When you get stuck, do you plow through, skip ahead to something else or give up?

- Do you constantly edit and rewrite passages before moving on?

- How much time do you spend thinking about your project when you're not writing?

- Do you write when sober?

The resulting set of personality traits form the DNA signature of your process. The next step is a set of experiments to challenge each trait, one at a time, to determine whether it's a vital part of who you are as a writer or a rut you've dug yourself into along the way. If you never set deadlines for yourself, try spending an eight-hour day with a deadline at the end of each hour. If you always start writing on page one, try starting in the middle.

Many experiments will confirm that what you've always done is helpful to you. But you may also surprise yourself. The goal is to get closer to finding what works for you. It's an ongoing process with no real end point. We're all constantly evolving as writers, which means our processes evolve as well. But the better you know yourself, the more what makes you unique will end up on the page.

DANIEL CALVISI

Feeling the Music

DANIEL CALVISI is a former senior story analyst and freelance reader. His past employers include Miramax Films, Dimension Films and Twentieth Century–Fox. He has written screenplays on assignment, has worked as a private story consultant and is the president of The Writers' Building, a networking group and online community for screenwriters.

When I was a full-time script reader for movie companies, I found that the best screenplays were the ones that immediately evoked a strong tone that made me *feel the movie*. In those crucial first few pages, writers prove themselves with a clear, decisive voice in their description and dialogue. There was no mistaking the tone that the movie playing in my head as I read the script would create in future audience members.

One of the most powerful yet difficult feelings to evoke in the reader is fear. That eerie, unsettling feeling you get when you watch a truly creepy movie.

When was the last time you were truly *scared* by a horror movie or thriller? You couldn't sleep that night, convinced there were things going bump in the night? It is rare to get that reaction from contemporary horror movies.

A script that I read on the job that scared me was titled *The Curse*, written by Sam and Ivan Raimi. It was the story of a young woman who races to stop a gypsy's curse from dooming her to eternal torture in hell. The horribly withered gypsy woman in the script was a terrifying presence, seemingly unstoppable, even after death, and the events triggered by the curse put me on edge just as much as the protagonist. The interesting thing was that the script was also funny, which is a double whammy when it comes to an effective screenplay! There was just the right balance between scares and laughs, so that I immediately knew this was a piece of material that could make for a fantastic commercial film.

It took ten years for the movie to be made, and it was released with the title DRAG ME TO HELL. I enjoyed the movie, but I can't say that I was legitimately scared; I was definitely on edge because the movie employed a series of merciless shock cuts and gross-out moments, and I never knew when the next one might come. It was a fun thrill ride, but I'll never forget the chills I had when I read the original spec draft.

I think one of the reasons the movie was not as scary as the script was the musical score, which was functional but not memorable. The music didn't evoke that tone of a truly scary horror movie. Think of the music from THE SHINING, THE EXORCIST, HALLOWEEN or even THERE WILL BE BLOOD, which features one of the most ruthless villains ever put on film (Daniel Plainview, the protagonist and villain portrayed by Daniel Day Lewis) . . . it makes the hairs on the back of your neck stand on end.

As I wrote my own scripts, I realized that I got many of my ideas for scenes and moments while I listened to music, most often at great volume from my Klipsch stereo speakers (much to the chagrin of my neighbors below me in my cramped New York apartment) or using my headphones. I was already feeling the rush of emotion evoked by great music, whether it was contemporary or classical, so coming up with a dramatic situation for a movie that evoked the same emotion was a little bit easier than normal. And listening to my favorite movie soundtracks was an extra nudge to get in the right head and heart space to write an evocative screenplay.

I found a couple of gems in a used-record store: two CDs, one titled *Arnold Schwarzenegger: The Greatest Movie Themes!* and the other a compilation of John Williams's music from the movies of Steven Spielberg.

If you can't write an action sequence while blasting Basil

Poledouris's theme from CONAN THE BARBARIAN or John Williams's RAIDERS OF THE LOST ARK theme in your headphones, then I'm sorry to say it's time to hang up your laptop, good writer.

These days I have a separate iTunes mix for each script I write. For my supernatural thriller mix, I have moody pop songs from Nine Inch Nails and Dead Can Dance, along with soundtrack music from Phillip Glass and Hans Zimmer. I've even been known to drop some Korn and Dio into my mix to help me summon the proper intensity for a particularly teeth-grinding scene, but that's probably not for the faint of heart and definitely not for the "cute-meet" scene of a fluffy RomCom.

EXERCISE

Pick three movies that are similar to your screenplay in terms of qualities such as genre, story, pacing and tone. Purchase the soundtracks for these movies and listen to them, picking out the tracks that evoke in you the feeling that you want the Reader and Audience to feel as they experience your story. Arrange them in an iTunes playlist in an order that best mimics the tone and pacing of your narrative. (You may want to include only instrumental tracks, as lyrics can be distracting, but it's up to you.)

Listen to your mix on headphones so the music envelopes you and completely stirs your emotions as you write.

And set your iTunes player to "Repeat," as you will, I hope, experience that wonderful feeling of losing track of time as you fall deeper and deeper into the world of your movie. You may "wake up" from a writing session to realize that it's been hours since you began, and your mix has played over and over several times.

The more you listen to your mix, the more it will slip into the background as you write, to compliment and accentuate the characters and dialogue in your screenplay. Just like a great soundtrack in a great movie.

Good luck and happy writing!

GLENN M. BENEST

It's the Read—Writing Great Film Narrative

GLENN M. BENEST has written seven produced screenplays and teaches professional screenwriting workshops in Los Angeles. Five films have been launched from these groups.

The most common mistake I come across in reading the many scripts I analyze is that the film narrative (or descriptive passages) are tedious and lack energy. As a screenwriter gets more and more professional, he or she realizes that *the read is everything*. What do I mean by that?

The narrative is not written with style or energy, it's just pedantic, it's way too long or it's confusing. The writer seems to be over-describing every stage direction rather than honing it down to crystal clarity; so that we get the entire mood of the scene or what a place looks like or who a character is in one line.

So what gets in the way of a great read? Big blocks of narrative.

Make every paragraph reflect a different shot. So we read the paragraphs just as though we're going from shot to shot: Here's Bill, and he's sighting in on the target. Next paragraph is Mary, who's running for cover. Next paragraph is Mary's mother, who screams for her to get down.

Clumsy narrative lines: "A raging fire burns through the building and brightly lights the fire crew trying to tame it." That's okay, but a little awkward and not as visual as it could be. The writer rewrites this to read: "A raging fire burns through J.R.'s building. It has turned night to day and lights the sky." Narrative lines in a screenplay are not comparable to prose in a novel. We want short, pithy images. More like you're writing a poem.

Here's an example:

"Amusement park rides glisten against a bright blue sky, and the weather's just fine.

Come closer. Teens shrieking by on the roller coaster, bikini-clad bladers, wide-eyed tourists from the Midwest munching corn dogs—can't believe this is March.

Enter a balding *tourist* in a loud Hawaiian shirt. He's barely a blip on the radar screen as he wanders over to a telescope, deposits a quarter. We take a look, too . . ."

This is a description of the Santa Monica Pier on a spring day. It's got energy and pacing and great images.

The following exercise will help you get the hang of writing energetic film narrative.

EXERCISE

Take the opening description of your screenplay, where you describe the setting and the characters.

1. Take the action words—the verbs—and see if you can make them even stronger and more visual. Instead of "He falls on the floor," find a stronger way to say that. For example: "He gets splattered on the floor."

2. When you introduce your protagonist (the hero of your story) find a great and succinct line or two to really nail who he or she is. Instead of describing your hero in general terms, give us an indelible impression. This is an example from FACE/OFF: "Jo Archer . . . older . . . unshaven . . . fatigued . . . his EYES reveal a man in the grip of obsession."

    This is a description of Dexter's sister, from the TV show of the same name: "And we see DEBRA (twenties) dressed as a classic cheap whore, her shapely body shrink-wrapped tight in a pink neon tube top, miniskirt, fishnet stockings and high heels, talking into her cell phone."

3. Break up the action into shots. Stay away from big, thick paragraphs.

4. Give us interesting visual images to look at. Your job as a screenwriter is to write in visual images. Figure out what your scene is about visually and then find the central visual image that tells the story of that scene. If you do this correctly, the scene will write itself and the dialogue will come easily.

5. Find a rhythm to your narrative. If it's a hard-boiled detective story, find a short, tough way to describe the action. If it's an off-the-wall comedy, find a way to make the reader laugh or at least smile on page one.

6. Make it easy to read and follow. Don't throw more than a few characters at us in the first scene. Make sure we know who the protagonist is and what genre this is: Is it action? Is it a comedy? Is it a dark comedy? I want to know that just by reading the first page.

What's crucial in this exercise is that your attention is drawn away from the fact that you're writing for yourself and instead becomes focused on the fact you're writing to amuse, entertain and/or delight the reader. Every sentence, every word is there for a reason. If the first page vibrates with energy and skill, then the reader has a great first impression of your screenplay. Put all your writing ability into that first scene. If done correctly, it will pave the way for your success.

NICHOLAS KAZAN

Dream On

NICHOLAS KAZAN wrote the screenplays for AT CLOSE RANGE, REVERSAL OF FORTUNE (Academy Award nomination), FALLEN, BICENTENNIAL MAN, FRANCES (coauthor), MATILDA (with his wife, Robin Swicord) and for several other films. He likes people but in general prefers the company of dogs.

EXERCISE

Lie down. Close your eyes. Let your mind drift over the scene or sequence you're about to write. Don't censor. Don't guide. Invoke the muse in all her beauty and bounty. When an idea comes, dig deeper . . . or just drift over it. Stay there until you can't stand it anymore and have to rush back to your computer.

The worst thing you can do as a writer, but more particularly as a screenwriter, is bore the audience. The most obvious way to bore people is to give them what they expect . . . to follow, in movies for example, a formula or a paradigmatic three-act structure: reversal on p. 23, catastrophic crisis on p. 100, every character has to have an "arc," etc.

So while it's important to be aware of the so-called rules or paradigms (I don't believe there actually are any, but that's another essay), it's more important to *break* them . . . if only (think Haydn's Surprise Symphony) to keep the audience alert.

That's what I'm doing here. I was supposed to begin with an essay and then talk about my own work and conclude with an exercise. Instead, I began with the exercise.

My exercise is based on certain precepts:

—The best writing comes from the unconscious.

—The best screenwriting is visual, and images are easier to find (or unlock) with your eyes closed.

—The best dialogue is "heard." It arrives after only minimal prodding and should delight—or at least refuse to obey—the author.

—If you're having trouble writing a scene or figuring out what your character or movie should do next, there are really only two possibilities:

1. You're trying to write a scene (or sequence) the movie doesn't need.

OR

2. You have a good—logical or unconscious—reason for wanting the scene (or sequence) and you have yet to reveal the reason to yourself.

This technique (or "exercise") can be used as often as you like. You can try it for every single scene. You'll be surprised if you do, because the unconscious almost always finds a unique and unexpected solution to your problems. Your logical mind will put you at a funeral, but your unconscious will have the body fall out of the coffin and roll down the hill. Or if that doesn't work (and it may not . . . the unconscious is also a fountain of provocative but impossible notions), you might see the corpse sit up and speak. Or the widow breaks into hysterical laughter. Or a strange man might appear, causing the deceased's family to wonder how he dares show his face . . . in which case, of course, you'll have to discover, to your own delight and that of the reader/viewer, who this mystery man is, what the backstory is, why everyone reviles (or is scared of or adores) him, and so on.

Caution/caveat: As I just suggested, the unconscious, while an invaluable repository of arresting dramatic ideas and images, is also a garbage dump. Beware of the kitchen sink . . . and of the feeling the process generates: Scenes that emerge out of this exercise are likely to feel primal, sacrosanct. They're not. They're just what's in your mind. Use them with care, and they'll make your script more visual, more surprising and precise. Treat them as jewels, and you'll find you have been blinded by gems that may not be appropriate for the dance to which you have invited your reader and audience.

I came up with this technique during psychotherapy. My shrink kept pestering me to bring in my dreams, but I so rarely remember my dreams and I was disappointing him . . . and I don't like to disappoint people, so I blurted out: "I can have a dream right here and now if you want." He wanted. I closed my eyes and went through a rather elaborate and terrifying sequence of images.

And with that, I realized I could do the same thing any time I wanted. I encourage you to do the same. If you have a visual imagination, this will probably work for you. If you don't, you may have a very difficult time writing screenplays.

WILLIAM M. AKERS
Random Thoughts

WILLIAM M. AKERS is the author of *Your Screenplay Sucks! 100 Ways to Make It Great*, a lifetime member of the Writers Guild of America and has had three feature films produced from his screenplays. He teaches screenwriting and filmmaking at Vanderbilt University.

I write with a massive feeling of inadequacy hovering around my shoulders. The "It's not good enough" gremlin long ago burrowed into my soul and lives there, gnawing away at my innards. Sometimes I can hear him down there, smacking his lips and slobbering and grinding his rotting, unbrushed teeth. Perhaps I should try to drown him with alcohol. Perhaps not.

The fear that whatever I put down on paper will be more on the lousy side than on the decent side (I don't even think about the "genius" side . . . that's for parents of six-year-olds) drove me to come up with a way to force myself to make the work better, despite my own screamingly obvious lack of talent, skill, imagination or chutzpah.

I do all this worrying because I don't write for fun; I do it for money. I pay for cars for my kids to wreck by selling material to Hollywood, and what I write has to be something "they" will want to buy.

Writing scenes is fun. Outlining is backbreaking. I loathe outlining, and once I start writing script pages, I never want to work on the outline again. I just want to go go go! Even if the outline isn't . . . quite . . . ready. Oops.

To combat this cunning, baffling, powerful weakness in my soul, I do a Random Thoughts version of my story before I start writing actual pages. The freedom to feel free-to-create can get blown to atoms when facing a neat laser-printed outline that looks done.

EXERCISE

Write a subject heading at the top of a page: "Scene 42. Artie gets gun in men's room." You can do Random Thoughts for specific scenes, production design, characters, possibilities for conflicts—any aspect of your story.

I like to do it with music up loud. Music triggers ideas.

Now make stuff up that has to do with your topic. Any kind of stuff: stupid stuff, clever stuff, goofy stuff, stuff that will never fit in, silly things your buddy said in second grade . . . anything and everything that even semi-relates to the subject at hand. Generate random ideas from every direction about any aspect of "Scene 42. Artie gets gun in men's room." Wardrobe, dialogue, character, stuff that might tie in later, motivation, jokes, plot—anything you want to throw in. It's kitchen sink time.

It doesn't matter how much dreck you generate at this point— that's what highlighters are for. Have wonderful ideas about this scene until you've squeezed yourself dry. The beautiful thing is, a thought will trigger a thought and then five more, and *whoooosh!* you'll be off in a world you never dreamed of ten minutes earlier. Some of what you write will be, naturally, garbage . . . but some will be magnificent and new and thrilling . . . and useful.

You can do it with structure: Churn out ideas on zigzags in your story. If you randomly generate ideas for Act Breaks, think what new directions your tale might take.

You can do it with character: Why is Consuela the way she is? Change the music from The Singing Nun to Metallica and see what happens to your Random Thoughts!

You can do it with conflict: In Scene 42, my hero, Artie, a nebbishy hit man, goes to a public restroom to retrieve a hidden revolver, as in THE GODFATHER. Doing my Random Thoughts groove thing, I started thinking about various conflicts he might have . . . and out of nowhere, I had the idea for him to *struggle with the gun*. That suggested a bunch of different kinds of conflict between man and weapon, including fumbling around while trying to load it, and then

I thought of Artie dropping a bullet and failing to stop it before it rolls out of the stall toward the sinks . . . and then I wondered whose foot it might roll next to . . . a cop's! Suddenly the scene was ten times more interesting because I'd pounded the conflict far harder than if I had just gone with my initial "Artie gets gun in men's room" idea.

When you're completely done with Draft A of the Random Thoughts Outline, save it as Draft B, print it, whip out your highlighter and mark what you want to keep. Cut out the heaps of chaff, and lo and behold, a detailed, ultracreative outline you will use to write your screenplay!

This can take a long, *long* time.

Writing is a process. This is but a step in that process. Do not worry this will delay your story from reaching the world; it won't. Taking this "pressure-free" creative time at the front end will shorten your rewriting process, because you will have done a more thorough job of creating your outline in the first place.

Random Thoughts is an exhausting step to take, but you will come up with amazing material you would not have found otherwise. Always keep in mind: That is what "they" want to buy, work that's amazing.

SUSAN KOUGUELL

Analyzing Your Characters

SUSAN KOUGUELL, author of *The Savvy Screenwriter: How to Sell Your Screenplay (and Yourself) Without Selling Out!*, teaches screenwriting and film at Tufts University and conducts seminars nationwide. Chairperson of her motion picture consulting company, Su-City Pictures, Kouguell has worked with over one thousand clients worldwide, including major studios. An award-winning screenwriter and filmmaker, Kouguell has associate-produced two features, has written voice-overs for Miramax Films and rewritten assignments for more than a dozen production companies, and worked with director Louis Malle.

In my former Su-City Pictures New York City office, I had a small couch, along with chairs and other furnishings. But it was the couch toward which my clients instantly gravitated. To my astonishment, during a script consultation, several clients ended up lying down on the couch and then revealing their innermost thoughts, fears, secrets, and so on. I reminded them (repeatedly) that I was not their therapist, that in fact I was a screenplay doctor and that our focus should remain on their scripts, not their personal issues. And please sit up. Now!

From physicians and attorneys to movie stars and fishermen, after twenty years of consulting on screenplays and films with quite a cross section of international clients, a general theme persists—aside from the fact that I still know more than I wish to know about some of their personal lives—my main criticism of their work is not knowing and/or caring enough about their characters.

This opinion about lack of character development, plausibility, and empathy is shared by film executives across the independent and Hollywood aisles. As your script unfolds, readers must *care* about what will happen to your characters during their journeys as they overcome obstacles to reach their goals. If your screenplay does not contain characters with whom an audience can identify and/or for whom they can feel empathy, movie executives are going to reject your script. The film industry is a tough business and the competition is fierce just to get your script read, let alone considered for production. So, if your characters do not deliver, your screenplay will not end up on the silver screen.

Successful and memorable characters are multidimensional, with distinctive physical attributes, emotional traits, appearances, personalities, intelligence, vulnerabilities, emotions, attitudes, idiosyncrasies, a sense of humor or prevailing despair, secrets, wishes, and hopes and dreams. Characters must have depth: They can be passive, aggressive, and even passive-aggressive, and they can manipulate, avenge wrongs, outsmart, outwit, scheme, and/or be fraught with contradictions.

The choices and decisions your characters make are ultimately based on their respective backgrounds and motivations. When you, the screenwriter, do not know who your characters *really* are and why they take the actions they do, the film executive will also know—and he or she will know that you do not know how to craft a good screenplay.

Put yourself in film executives' shoes when writing your scripts and understand what they demand, including a solid three-act structure, an engaging plot, correct formatting, and well-developed characters. Now put yourself in your characters' shoes and, specifically, in their minds by writing character biographies.

Whether you are just beginning your script or working on your final polish, writing character bios for both your major and minor characters, at every major draft, is an enormous key to a successful screenplay. This extremely useful if not imperative tool will help you dig deeper into your characters. Once you complete your character bios, you will be able to return to your screenplay with fresh new insight into both your characters and plot.

EXERCISE

Envision each of your characters on a therapist's couch; perhaps this is the first time that he or she has gone into therapy or maybe your character has been in analysis his or her entire life. Choose a scenario that will enable you to delve into the mind of each character.

Write character biographies for all your major and minor characters and in *their* voices; this will enable you to get inside your characters' minds in a way that doing this exercise in the third person cannot. The first-person character bio will help you further uncover your characters' goals, motivations, actions, attitudes, and backstory—all the elements critical to understanding what makes your characters tick. It will also strengthen your characters' dialogue, which will become more distinctive, such as their speech patterns, rhythms, slang, and word choices.

Write whatever pops into your mind and don't edit yourself. Avoid thinking about specific scenes in your script or even reading your script when writing these bios; just concentrate on your characters and let them speak for themselves. Don't worry about sentence structure, run-on or incomplete sentences; just allow your characters to talk. Write at least one page per character, but use as many pages as you need for each character.

Set the scene for each character. What does the therapist's office look like? Is it dark and drab or colorfully decorated? Knowing how the office looks and feels will help to inform your character and how he or she relates to this specific environment. Does your character look at the decorations on the walls or objects on the therapist's desk or twiddle his or her thumbs? Is the therapist paying attention to your character or fighting sleep? Is the office quiet or is there loud honking from the street and fire trucks driving by the open window? Is your character reluctant to talk or anxious to spill the beans?

The therapist's office can be a safe environment where telephone landlines and cell phones are turned off. There can be a comfortable couch for the character to feel relaxed enough to reveal his or her thoughts and feelings. Or, if the therapist is not ethical, this can also present new situations for some of your characters, such as phone interruptions or someone barging in. These distractions might bring tension to your character and, in turn, will help you find a different way to get inside your character's mind.

Now picture the therapist and your character together and then envision your character's reaction to seeing this professional. Is this a comfortable or stressful session? For some characters, finally getting someone to listen to them might be a novel and exciting opportunity to spill their guts, whereas for others it might be intimidating or horrifying. Think about how your characters are going to respond to the therapist when they reveal the specific events in their lives that made them the person they are today, such as compassionate, hateful, bitter, vengeful, neurotic, or compulsive.

The following questions are designed to get you thinking about each of your characters. You can have your characters answer some or all of these questions, or you can invent some of your own.

Therapist's Questions

How do you feel being here? Are you comfortable? Have you been in therapy before? If so, how was your experience? Why did you feel the need to see a therapist? Is there a specific event that just happened, or was it something in your past that brought you here today?

Tell me about yourself. Where did you grow up? Describe the home where you grew up and compare it with where you live now. What do you like about your present home? Are you close with your family? Tell me about them. Is there one member of your family with whom you are particularly close? Why do you feel close to this family member? Are there any family members you despise, and if there are, why do you think that is? Who are the most important people in your life, and why are they important to you?

How would you describe your personality? Do you think your friends and family would describe you in the same way? What aspects about yourself do you like and not like?

Tell me what a typical day is like for you. What are your favorite things to do? Why do you like to do these things? Are you doing what you like to do in your life?

Have you ever been in love? Are you in love now? Why do you love this person? Do you think this person loves you?

What do you really want out of life? What are your hopes and dreams? Speaking of dreams, do you have recurring dreams? What do you think they really mean? Describe your scariest nightmare. Why are you keeping secrets? Who are you really scared of? What happened that made this person your adversary?

If you could be anyone in the world who would it be? If there were something that you could change about yourself what would it be? Why should I care about you? What do you think about the couch you are sitting on?

KEVIN CECIL

The Power of Negative Thinking

KEVIN CECIL is a BAFTA- and Emmy Award–winning scriptwriter. He has co-created several programs in the UK and the U.S. His work includes *Black Books, Hyperdrive, Slacker Cats, Little Britain* and *The Armando Iannucci Show*. He has also worked on films, including Tim Burton's THE CORPSE BRIDE, GNOMEO AND JULIET and PIRATES!

One of the great things about being a comedy writer is that you get to make use of all the things that annoy you. Irritation is ammunition.

When Andy, my writing partner, and I meet at our office, we'll often spend twenty minutes griping about things that have peeved us that morning. Perhaps something that one of us heard on the radio, or a particularly idiotic article in the newspaper. It could be a stupid advert or a social trend that we don't understand.

Or we have received some notes telling us to completely rewrite one of our scripts. That can be kind of annoying too. What's interesting is how often something that one of us says in our pre-working splutterings ends up as a joke or even a storyline in one of our scripts. It didn't feel like we were working, but in fact we were, and we were using the power of negative thinking to our advantage!

Yes, yes, all that stuff that everyone else has told you has a certain validity. Positivity is, in general, a pretty good thing. Hey, by the standards of comedy writers, I don't even consider us to be particularly dour people. But remember, negative energy can get you places as well. When you are next fulminating with indignity at the stupid, unjust, vapid and broken world we live in, stop for a moment and see if you can get some gags out of it. Comedy is about people's faults, about failings, and when it works it can provide a logical explanation for an illogical world.

George Costanza, the neurotic, vain, penny-pinching, dishonest creation of Larry David and Jerry Seinfeld is one of the greatest sitcom characters ever devised. He runs almost entirely on negativity and petty grievances. When we were writing scripts for Dylan Moran's sitcom *Black Books*, we could put any of our annoyances about living in London, whether it was dealing with the heat in a city or the soulless nature of the big bookshop chains, straight into the show. All our frustrations with computers and technology got extrapolated and then found their way into our science fiction sitcom *Hyperdrive*. If we come across someone in our career who drives us mad, we'll try not to let him know, but certain things he does and says will turn up on a screen one day. You're turning rubbish into something useful; surely that's just good recycling.

Of course we are not exempt. If one of us messes up, makes an idiot of himself, gets into needless trouble, we tell the other one, and there is often a scene in it. There's gold in them screwups.

So every now and again, let yourself have a moan, a kvetch or even a gripe. What gets your goat? It's quite likely that it will niggle other people too. We are lucky because we can use those things that would depress other people to make us laugh, and if we are really lucky we can make other people laugh too.

But, you say, I am too positive a person to whine. Nothing bad ever happens to me; each day I count my blessings and I run out of fingers *and* toes. Well the wider lesson is this: Anything that happens to you, everything you hear about, everything you notice in the world is something that you could potentially write about. Everything is research. Remember that, be a bit self-conscious about it for a day or two, then stop being self-conscious and get on with life. Then, when you get stuck, think of something that has happened to you, change it enough so that you don't get sued, and put it in your script.

EXERCISE

I would like you to start by making a list of all your faults. Be honest about it, and if you can't be, list "not honest" as one of your faults. If you are one of those people who do not have any faults, then pick one of your mortal friends and make a list of all of his or hers. Once you have your list, exaggerate them. If you are someone who occasionally gets a bit flustered when you're stressed, think about someone who is always stressed and in a permanent state of chaos because of it. If you suspect that you spend too much time thinking about food, create someone who finds it very difficult to think about anything else. Mix the failings together until you've got a person.

Now come up with someone with a different set of failings whom your first person would find really annoying. Don't think that the two people need to be opposites; there are a million and one ways in which two people are unable to get on. Choose a way that seems interesting and original to you. Write a scene in which they have to carry out a task together.

When you have finished, go and have fun. You've earned it. The next day, look at your piece and see what you dislike about it. What about it could have been funnier? What annoys you about it? Use your criticisms and insecurities to spur you on to rewrite it to make it funnier, slicker and better realized than ever. But once you are writing, put the negativity aside for a while. Just concentrate on getting it done.

Soon you will have something brilliant. Turn it into a show and send the script off. Then use your frustrations from being unable to sell the script, being able to sell the script but not for as much money as you would like, or being able to sell the script for so much money that friends are jealous of you as fuel for your next script. You now have a career in show business.

HESTER SCHELL

When Great Writing Meets a Great Actor: Writing for a Star

HESTER SCHELL, MFA, is an acting teacher, director, writer and film-maker. She has appeared in numerous shorts and festival features, and her original short films have played festivals. She is the CEO of Bay Area Casting News and the author of *Casting Revealed: A Guide for Independent Directors*.

We've seen it; we've felt it. When it happens it creates a sense of awe and wonder: when an actor completely morphs into a character. It moves us to a new level of seeing and believing. It's the magic we strive for at the intersection of character performance and transcendent writing. Daniel Day-Lewis in MY LEFT FOOT comes to mind. Meryl Streep in SOPHIE'S CHOICE, or more recently as Julia Child; Johnny Depp as Captain Jack Sparrow, Philip Seymour Hoffman as Truman Capote, Jamie Foxx in THE SOLOIST or as Ray Charles, Halle Berry in MONSTER'S BALL. These actors went deeper and created amazing screen moments of raw human condition and consciousness.

What these scripts have in common is they give actors things to do rather than describe what they feel. Good writing describes action, and the action speaks for itself. The action creates emotional response, first in the mind of the reader, as the words lift off the page and into imagination and visualization. The action stimulates the reaction. The movie stars want to perform extraordinary moments; it wins awards.

Read the scripts of the films mentioned above to study how the writers describe each of these screen moments. Consider the closing scene in MONSTER'S BALL on the back doorstep with Halle Berry and Billy Bob Thornton. We're not sure if the relationship is going to survive. He takes her hand, and everything changes. The collective sigh of relief: the torment on the character's face, while she waits for him to make a choice. It is the moment that won Halle Berry the Oscar. Next, take a look at Diane Lane on the train heading back to her home after stealing away to the city for her afternoon delight in UNFAITHFUL. Notice how it is written. Actors are looking for great moments like these when they read scripts. Begin and end your scenes with actions and activities, described with verbs. Verbs are what resonate with actors. Verbs are the action words of speech.

What about stars who shepherd a project to play a role, as Salma Hayek did with the Frida Kahlo biopic directed by Julie Taymor, or when an actor is brought on board after the script is finished? Obviously you would need to research this on a case-by-case basis, as there are many ways to get a film into production. Salma Hayek moved to Los Angeles from Mexico, working her connections for ten years, building her network, searching for funding and the right director, producer and designers to make her vision come to life.

Great moments are going to get known actors interested in your script. Submit only what is polished and perfect. Submit through your agent, and wait. And wait. Follow up. Submit again.

Clearly it's getting more difficult, more competitive to get a script launched; it's essential to have a good solid story with interesting characters in interesting situations doing interesting things. Beyond that looms this question: Should you write for a specific celebrity?

In a word, yes. Absolutely. Writing for a particular "A-list" actor can improve your chances of putting together a deal. Regardless of what happens to the big studio pictures, or that AVATAR made back its $200 million price tag in just a few weeks, movie stars are going to continue to develop new projects. It's your job to be the one that matches. The question is how to do it while in a recession. We read that the studios are cutting back on acquisitions, while more and more low-budget movies will be made with very low, if any, script fees up front. The good news is you have options.

Do-It-Yourself options include the following:

Create interest—Woo a known actor. Get him or her interested in your project. Get that actor attached and slowly draw together the necessary ingredients.

Network with producers—Someone who loves the film script as much as you do will draw in the investors, which will draw in the known actor.

Find a director.

Submit to actors' agents.

Get a literary agent, or an entertainment attorney who can make submissions to legitimate actor representatives.

Build a team.

Contact that actor's agent's assistant—Find out who represents your "A-list" person by calling the toll-free number at the Los Angeles Screen Actors Guild office: Who Represents Whom. Once you have the agent's name you can check for a website, where often you'll find submission guidelines or a phone number to call and ask for the submission guidelines. Whether you find the information on the website, always make the call. The person who answers the phone will put you through to the agent's assistant. (Don't leave a message. Call back until you get a person. No one picks up voicemail.) Be really authentic with this person. Authenticity is respected and appreciated in the back offices. Never waste anyone's time. Be direct: "I would like to submit a script to (your chosen lead here)." Be sure to follow the instructions for submissions exactly. The assistant will explain the submission procedure and hopefully answer your questions. You will need to know: *How far in advance is this actor accepting bookings?*

If the actor likes, no . . . *loves,* your script, you could hear from him or her fairly quickly. Everyone is looking for the next project. Everyone. Nothing tastes so sweet as having a next project lined up and on the books, funded, except having three or four, and seven or eight down the road, which is really what you're looking at when it comes to the really big "A-list" stars. It could be years, which is fine. In the meantime you can work on funding. You've got to start networking with producers; the best way to lock in an actor is funding.

It's standard to submit a script that is "pending funding," which means *take a look, nothing is sold here, no one is attached.* Or, *director is attached* and you include the director's bio. You will be invited to pitch your script and meet the actor, so get some coaching with your pitch presentation before you head in the door. You could also opt to hire a professional pitcher.

The other avenue is through your network of colleagues, who can put your script directly into an actor's hands—the six degrees of separation made manifest. Someone you know knows someone who knows someone who can get the script to that actor. Continue building your network to find someone who can get the script into the hands of the actor. Never give up. Once you have an actor on board and interested, then you lock in a deal and go hunting for a director, a producer and the rest of the cast. So, go for it: Write with an actor in mind who works in your story genre and style.

There are other ways, contests, Web postings of your log line. But generally speaking, most movies are made by direct connections among the key parties. A friend says, "You need to read this!" A script comes in the door perfect for an actor, and, bingo, that next project is born. It happens every day. And here's the cincher: You can't really make a submission to an agency that represents an actor without a signed release and a literary agent. So get started on finding an agent, or a better agent.

EXERCISE

Make a list of the top ten movies you wish you'd written—and probably could have if you'd been given half the chance. What do these films have in common? What is the best genre for you? Are you clear with your genre and the elements that hold that genre true to form?

Your task is to match actors to the style and genre you most like to write. Find the style and genre that suits what you do best. Write several treatments before expanding into the three-act short narrative. Tell the story. Work the story out with your writing groups. Get it right. Be sure you have your script proofed and covered before submitting it to the agents of these potential leading "A-list" actors whom you've had in mind as you poured all this time into writing. Include copies of professional coverage with your submission packet. And never give up.

BRAD SCHREIBER

Police Investigation

BRAD SCHREIBER is the author of five books, including *What Are You Laughing At? How to Write Funny Screenplays, Stories and More*. Schreiber was nominated for the King Arthur Screenwriters Award for his script *The Couch*. He is currently vice president of Storytech Literary Consulting, founded in 1999 by Christopher Vogler.

I once wrote a book called *What Are You Laughing At?* It includes exercises for humorous screenwriting as well as prose. Many of those exercises can be applied to dramatic writing as well. One of the most challenging but, I think, most rewarding assignments is something I call Police Investigation.

I have always been fascinated by how characters who lie, who are self-deceived, who are fearful or who are operating with limited information impact a story. Thus, films like Kurosawa's RASHOMON and Christopher Nolan's MEMENTO have held a particular interest for me as a writer and instructor. One day, I saw the following true story in a newspaper:

An out-of-work taxi driver in Belfort, France, suffered fractures of his skull and both legs and wrists in a spitting contest. Trying to prove his boast, "I can spit you all into the ground," he spit from the second-floor balcony of a friend's house by taking a running start from a bedroom inside. He was unable to stop at the balcony and fell to the street.

I thought to myself, If I was the spitting image of this taxi driver and I had to explain what happened to the police, I would want to lie rather than admit what an imbecile I was. And if I were a witness who knew the taxi driver and particularly liked or disliked him, that might color my statement to the cops.

By inventing a situation and giving three different explanations of what happened, the writer explores the nature of story, character, viewpoint, setting and dialogue simultaneously.

EXERCISE

Create any situation that involves three characters and requires that all three make statements to the police.

Write each statement in the first person, using the speech pattern and vocabulary of three different characters. Each statement can be as short as one or two paragraphs but each statement should give at least a slightly different—and possibly radically different—interpretation of what happened.

To get you started, consider using the French spitter who fell out of the window, his on-and-off girlfriend, Fifi, and Mrs. LePlunque, the judgmental neighbor on whom the spitter landed.

For added benefit write two versions of the same Police Investigation, one comedic and one dramatic.

Write Truthfully in Imaginary Circumstances:
The Mythology Inside You

MARK SEVI is a professional screenwriter with eighteen produced movies, including DEAD MEN CAN'T DANCE and ARACHNID. He also teaches screenwriting and writes articles about the business and art of screenwriting. He is currently joyfully participating in the sorrows of life in Hollywood, California.

As a science fiction fan and screenwriter, I often chuckle at the axiom "write what you know," as if Isaac Asimov, a rather robust Jewish man, knew what it was like to be a spinster scientist or a robot. How exactly did J. K. Rowling, a then thirty-year-old, unemployed, working-class mother, create a young male wizard who went to an exclusive magical school in a mythical land?

People write young, old, male, female, alien, king, peasant, and every variation imaginable. What's their secret? Good research? A keen observational eye? Channeling a secret muse? Yes, and perhaps. But let me share what is really meant by "write what you know." It means write your truth—write what you already know as a human being.

Are women and men really that different? Don't we all share the sting of rejection, the joy of love? Emotionally speaking, isn't life, in all its myriad variations, fundamentally the same for those in the bush and those in the Hamptons? Is the inevitability of a terminal disease today different from what it was one hundred years ago?

So how to bridge the gap between what we know and what we don't empirically understand?

Simply, write your truth. Write what you do understand from an emotional place, not necessarily a directly experiential one. That's the key.

I am a hero, a villain, a young girl, a serial killer. I am one of two kidnapped girls following a rabbit fence home. I stand on the bridge of the *Enterprise*, fight bravely in Thermopylae. I am a woman whose child is missing, a Spider-Man. A crack mother willing to abandon her child to buy drugs. As the writer said, "I am legion"—at least inside.

We can infuse all characters with believable life because to some extent we are all those characters. It's common, shared, human experience that we're channeling. But writing effectively, truthfully, requires courage. It forces you to go deep inside, reveal things about yourself that you'd perhaps rather not. People ask me, somewhat askance, how I can write such effective serial killers. I also do well with female leads. Do I want everyone to suspect that I have thoughts about what it's like to have the absolute power of life and death? Do I really want to make everyone aware that I occasionally wonder about being a mother—to birth a child, to have that life growing in me? Yes, yes, yes! Isn't childbearing a symbiotic experience—almost a parasitic one? Wouldn't that be a good basis for a horror film about someone who had something growing inside her whose birth wasn't going to be such a blessed event?

You must be fearless. You must never back away from a revelation, a horrible insight, a cancerous emotional growth that has suddenly sprung up, unbidden, out of your control. You need to go inside, find your truth, no matter how ugly or bizarre, and bring it to the page. Fear of revelation is the surest way to write tripe. Trust me; I've written plenty of it myself.

Why was the movie CLUELESS a hit? Couldn't we all relate to those young girls' struggles for validation? How about SLUMDOG MILLIONAIRE—didn't we relate to the pain and triumph that Jamal experienced? Or DOUBT—what a powerful, enduring message of self-examination and, well, internal and external doubt? Were these writers young debs, homeless Indians, child-molesting priests or ultra-authoritarian nuns?

So here's the challenge: Write your truth and put that truth into your work—without fear. Keep a secret writing diary if necessary. Write the things that make you cringe, that embarrass you—ideas and concepts that you've never fully admitted or never committed to paper before. Be stupid, ugly, disgusting, horrible, fanciful—any adjective you can imagine. Don't censor yourself. Erase it all afterward if you want to, but take that first step out of your fear and force yourself to admit that you're a woman, a man, a child, a murderer, a unicorn, an angel—a writer.

Write truthfully in imaginary circumstances. You'll find out that most of us can understand and relate to that truth because we all have it hidden away somewhere inside ourselves.

EXERCISE

Explore these characters and scenarios—truthfully. If you're male, make the characters female. If you're young, make them old. If you're an extrovert, make the character an introvert:

I am a contract killer for the mob. It's not personal. It's a job. Until one night . . .

I am a brilliant misanthropic doctor who is afraid to admit that I'm lonely. I'll use sarcasm to keep people from suspecting. Until she walks in and . . .

I am a young girl in love with an older man who I know will hurt me, but I don't care. I will be with him no matter what I have to do. Including . . .

I am desperate enough to rob a bank to pay for my drug habit, which has gotten out of control. But I never considered that this would happen . . .

I am a salesman with a secret: At night I dress as a woman and walk the streets. One night I saw something I shouldn't have. Now I have to . . .

SAM ZALUTSKY

Postcards from the Edge of Creativity

SAM ZALUTSKY'S first feature was YOU BELONG TO ME. He currently teaches screenwriting at the low-residency MFA in writing at Spalding University in Louisville, Kentucky. He received his MFA in film from NYU.

I am an inveterate postcard collector: museums, airports, art galleries, odd tourist sites. If there is an interesting postcard to be had, I will find it. This obsession started with my early studies in art and love of travel but has continued into my life as a filmmaker. After all, what is a film but millions of postcards strung together?

But dipping into my large postcard collection is more than a walk down memory lane. It leads me to new places in my own mind and helps me return to what is essential to every dramatic story: character, protagonist, antagonist, want, need, place. When I am stuck on a project . . . When I'm trying to generate new ideas . . . When I'm teaching a screenwriting class, I use this exercise to reinforce basic screenwriting concepts. It's a fantastic icebreaker that gets students to leave behind their inhibitions and let their imagination take them away. And if a student has too much imagination, this exercise can pull him or her back to reality, to a specific scene with specific characters. You can tailor this exercise to whatever problem you're working on.

For my first feature film, a psychological thriller titled YOU BELONG TO ME, I was initially inspired by a postcard of Balthus's *La Chambre*. The psychosexual danger of this image, of a young girl seemingly trapped in a room by an older woman, evoked the same sense of danger that I wanted to explore in my movie. I kept the card pinned above my desk for years as I struggled with the script. Any time I was stuck, I would just stare at that postcard and write.

Whatever came into my mind. Sometimes I would write scenes with the characters in the image. Other times I would transpose my main character, a late-twenty-something New York male architect who gets trapped by his landlady, into the scene in place of the girl. It didn't always make sense. Very little of what I wrote made it into the script, but it kept me inspired, focused and in the right frame of mind.

EXERCISE

Find a postcard with a compelling image. It really can be anything: a portrait, two people, a Cartier-Bresson "decisive moment," an adventure photo, a Renaissance fresco, an image famous or obscure. Ignore the caption or source. Study it. Think about it. Let your imagination run wild. How would you incorporate this image into a scene? What is the dramatic conflict at its core? Who is the protagonist? The antagonist? What does each want? What genre is it? What happens immediately before or after this image?

Here are some favorites that I have used in the past:

The title of Richard Gerstl's 1908 painting, *Self-Portrait Smiling*, intimates that he is happy. But to me his euphoric state looks almost dangerous. So ask yourself: Who is he? What does he want? Why so happy, Richard? Is it happiness spreading across his face like a fire or something else?

Martin Parr's *United Kingdom* (1992), lends itself to a potentially volatile domestic conflict: A mother kneels by her Mohawk-haired daughter, staring into her eyes, while the daughter stares off into the distance. A rifle hangs above the fireplace, hovering behind them. In this scene, whom would you choose as the protagonist? The antagonist? Why do you think the daughter won't look at her mother? Why does the mother look so imploringly at her daughter? Would either of them use the rifle to get what she wants? What would that look like? Start your scene.

Compare this image with Carrie Mae Weems's *Untitled (Makeup with Daughter)* from her 1990 *Kitchen Table Series*. In this image, a woman sits at the long end of a kitchen table, putting on makeup in front of a small round mirror, while to her left her daughter does the same. Who is the protagonist of this story? The antagonist? Whom would you choose? Could you write it as a romantic comedy? Thriller? Action movie?

Mary Ellen Mark's *South Bronx, New York 1987* shows a young couple, the man in a suede coat holding some sad flowers and the girl staring off into space, with an empty lot behind them. Is it a romantic comedy or a *Romeo and Juliet* story of star-crossed lovers? What happens immediately before this image? Immediately after? What does each want?

Or Larry Sultan's 1992 photo *Dad Practicing Golf Swing.* An elderly man practices his golf swing. But he does it indoors on a thick green shag carpet in his boxers and polo shirt, backlit by a diaphanous curtain. Next to him, the TV shows a woman talking, perhaps about stock prices. Give this man a name. An occupation. A family history. What does he want? Does he ever go outside? Would you make it a drama or a comedy?

What makes this exercise so fulfilling and so easy is that there is no right answer, only a "write" answer. Take fifteen minutes. Write down whatever comes to your mind. You decide who these people are. Where they live. What they want. Make it up. Change your mind. Have fun. Let your creative juices flow. If there are two people, imagine a conflicting want or need. How long have they known each other? Who wins in the scene? Who gets what he or she wants? Think crazy thoughts. Don't be hemmed in. Yes, what you see within the frame is important, but what about just beyond the frame?

When you have finished, perhaps you have a new idea for a script. Maybe you have a fresh perspective on an old character. Or maybe you avoided your real work for fifteen minutes. Whatever. No judgments. But this exercise can take the pressure off, whether you are a writer struggling to think of something "creative" to work on, or a teacher trying to inspire and challenge your students.

As a teacher, you can assign a particularly outrageous image to a student who refuses to take risks or give a restrained one to a student who resists focusing his or her story ideas. You can give your whole class the same image to brainstorm one story together, learning collaborative writing skills. Or they can imagine their own unique stories for the same image, revealing the infinite possibilities of a single image and each student's unique perspective. Students can bring in their own images to swap. Or treat yourself like an unresponsive or insecure student. Take an image that suggests a genre that's new for you, one that you're scared of. Choose a comedic image and write it as horror. The possibilities are endlessly surprising and surprisingly endless. Try it.

COLEMAN HOUGH

Found in Translation

COLEMAN HOUGH is a screenwriter and playwright. She wrote FULL FRONTAL and BUBBLE, both directed by Steven Soderbergh. She currently lives in Los Angeles and teaches screenwriting in the MPW program at USC.

If the dream is a translation of waking life, waking life is also a translation of the dream. —RENÉ MAGRITTE

You're still working out the problems in Act One—the inciting incident seems contrived—implausible—there needs to be more conflict—more character development—maybe a voice-over in the beginning. You start to panic. You give off the scent of fear. Every social occasion becomes an opportunity to pitch your story—get reactions, approval, advice, opinions. You pull a notebook out of your bag, and when you get home you can't read your writing.

Stop. You're letting form overwhelm your discovery of story—the spark. Let it make a fire at its own pace. Often the story is elusive because we don't trust the organic nature of our idea.

So what is your idea? What parts of it do you know? The less coherent, the more half-baked, the better. How does it resonate with running themes in your own life? Sit with it. Look for clues in what you have written. There's no need to pound nails in the story yet. See it as a dream that you are trying to remember. Details will emerge as they do.

Here's a workout that will get you out of your head and deeper into your story. Try it—and let go of any literal thinking. This is a chance to really depart from what you already know of your story and hear it in a variety of rhythms. I adapted this exercise from one

I learned from Irene Borger in a Los Angeles writing workshop. I use it in my class to shake free what needs to fall from the story tree.

EXERCISE

Write your story, or as much as you know of your story, in a few paragraphs. Read it—read it again and again until it appears to be written in another language. Detach yourself from the logic of your original story.

First, you are a translator who speaks the language of emotion. Write the story again in that language.

Next, you are a translator who speaks the language of the absurd. Write the story in *that* language.

Next, you are a translator who speaks the language of riddles . . . and on and on if you like.

Finally, write your story again in your native tongue. How has it changed? What did you find?

STRUCTURE

CHRIS SOTH

The Most Important Thing I Know and Teach

CHRIS SOTH is the screenwriter of FIRESTORM, his USC thesis, which was sold for $750,000 and the forthcoming OUTRAGE, as well as author of the Internet bestseller *Million-Dollar Screenwriting: The Mini-Movie Method* and the DVD *SOLD! How I Set Up Three Pitches in Hollywood.* He has taught at USC and UCLA.

Really, there are two important things that I or anyone else can or ever will teach you as far as screenwriting is concerned.

When I was young and would see a great movie, I'd always be baffled. What made it so good? Why did I like it so much? CASABLANCA, IT'S A WONDERFUL LIFE, as well as more modern greats such as DIE HARD, RAIDERS OF THE LOST ARK and THE USUAL SUSPECTS. When I hit college, I found the answer in Sigmund Freud's early work *The Pleasure Principle*, in which he states: "All pleasure comes from Tension Reduction."

The pleasure from eating reduces the tension of hunger; the pleasure of a good night's sleep reduces the tension of exhaustion and fatigue; the pleasure of sex comes from the buildup and release of sexual tension. Ever had a massage? What a pleasure! And all due to the release of tension—and aren't the best parts when your tensest muscles are focused on? More tension equals more tension reduction . . . equals . . . more pleasure.

And you must have heard this term thrown around: "Dramatic Tension."

So, if I liked those movies . . . they must have been building and releasing a tension in me. I must have taken all that pleasure from the buildup and release of dramatic tension. Every good movie builds up and releases tension. That's why we enjoy them.

Now, knowing that, can you go write a great screenplay?

Not yet. While you may have warmed to the idea that tension is the source of all the pleasure we take in movies, do you know what tension actually is and how to create it?

Not yet. I'm about to reveal the source of all pleasure in drama and tell you how to create it. Tension is two ingredients in dynamic conflict, fighting, pulling, pushing, one against another, suspending us between them in agony until the tension resolves toward one or the other. What are they?

Hope.

Fear.

In every movie, we hope for one outcome and fear another.

So, a quick and simple equation to help you remember how to create tension in every movie sequence and scene would be:

$$\text{TENSION} = \text{HOPE } versus \text{ FEAR}$$

Or:

$$T = H\, v.\, F$$

There it is. In every screenplay you write, hold on to that main tension and every sequence, scene and beat of action or line of dialogue moves us: From hope to fear or from fear to hope, from hope to fonder hope, from fear to greater fear . . . you'll never write a boring movie, scene or sequence ever, ever again. Every scene and movie you write will build and release tension and give your reader or viewer immense pleasure. In my telecourses, live seminars, e-book and DVDs, I teach *The Mini-Movie Method*, a structural outline that breaks the monolithic structure of three acts into six to eight "sequences," "reels" or, as I put it, "Mini-Movies"—why Mini-Movies? Because they're movies unto themselves. Why? Well, what's the defining aspect of a movie?

It's hope versus fear. It's a tension.

And Mini-Movies have a tension of their own, on which the main tension of the movie itself relies, like a chapter in a novel. And the Mini-Movies' tension relies on the outcome of the tension of each scene or beat within them. So structure is a series of dependent tensions. Seem simple? It can be.

EXERCISE

Decide what the main tension (hope and fear!) of your movie is. Break the story into six to eight Mini-Movies, each with its own tension to support the main tension. As you get to each Mini-Movie, brainstorm a scene and beat list of events and interactions with their own hope and fear to support the tension of the Mini-Movie.

DAVID TROTTIER

The Character/Action Grid

DAVID TROTTIER has sold or optioned ten screenplays, including HER-
CULES RECYCLED and THE PENNY PROMISE. He has helped hundreds
of writers break into the writing business. He is a script consultant and
author of *The Screenwriter's Bible*. As "Dr. Format," he writes a column
for *Script Magazine*.

I was stuck. Five drafts and I had lost the big picture. I wasn't sure
where my story was going or even if it existed anymore. And I
was tired of the age-old practice of pinning three-by-five cards to
my pockmarked wall, one card for each scene of my screenplay. So
I threw my three-by-five cards in the air and stared at them on the
floor. It was there that the idea of a new writing tool was born.

I sat down at my desk and developed my first Character/Action
Grid. It helped me see what was working and not working in the
structure and character development of my story. I wanted my story
to flow like a river, and now—at a single glance—I could see the
flow, the logjams, and the channel breaks.

Soon, I finished my screenplay, but I didn't sell it. However, it
found me work and a meeting with Walt Disney Pictures. Ten sales
later, I am still using The Grid, as are many of my students and clients. In fact, this tool has been used to craft many produced screenplays and published novels. I use it to outline my screenplays, and
then I return to it when I revise. Naturally, I end up revising The Grid
before revising my script; it keeps me focused.

So what is this Character/Action Grid? As you can see from the
worksheets, The Grid has two sections: (1) Character and Story, and
(2) Actions.

EXERCISE

1. Character and Story

    The Character and Story worksheet allows you to develop four main characters on one page. Not every cell in The Grid needs to be filled. In fact, you should make this tool *your* tool and create your own categories. Better yet, create your own grid.

    At the bottom of The Grid you have room to think through your main turning points in terms of each character. Obviously not every character will be involved with each turning point. I'll briefly explain each of the turning points.

    The *Catalyst* is the inciting incident. It's the event that takes place around page 10 that upsets the equilibrium of the story and gets things moving. The *Big Event*, however, is the event in your central character's life that really changes his life; it's often where he loses control of his life. This is the event that ends the first act in the traditional three-act structure.

    The *Crisis* is the low point or event that forces the key decision by the central character. It leads to the *Showdown* or climax of the movie. The *Realization* is the moment in the third act where the character, the audience, or both realize how the character has changed or understand the point of the drama. The *Denouement* is the tying up of loose ends (subplots).

    Feel free to use your own terminology in creating your own Character/Action Grid. Perhaps, you'll want to add the Midpoint, which is the central character's point of no return or the event where the character becomes fully motivated.

    Have fun adapting The Grid to your specific purposes. For example, one of my clients created a Character/Character Grid. In this grid, "Every character tells what he thinks about the other characters, and, of course, what he thinks about himself."

2. Actions

    You will not be able to plot your entire screenplay on just one sheet of paper. You may need two or three worksheets. In the top row of the chart, write the names of your five main characters. Then in the remaining rows and columns simply list each action a character takes. Dialogue can be considered action when it constitutes or creates movement.

The Grid allows you to see the entire story on just a few sheets of paper. It helps you notice if a character is static or uninvolved in the action or if a character's actions are repetitive rather than building. In other words, you can more readily see if you have a rising conflict or a stagnant story.

The Grid helps with pacing and spacing. Is there a major twist every so often? Are the subplots supporting the main plot? Are character actions crisscrossing throughout the story? Are all of your other major characters fully involved in the story? Does a character disappear for half the story? (That can be good or bad, depending on the story.)

I recommend use of The Grid after the first draft or when you are stuck. But you are the captain of your ship. Use The Grid when you wish or not at all.

Character/Action Grid example:

I designed the following story idea as a small example of how to use The Grid. I created only three characters. I won't take you through the entire grid with them, nor will I outline the entire story. I just want to give you a feel for The Grid's use. You will want to list every important action of your main characters from the beginning to the end of the story.

CHARACTER/ACTION GRID—*Character and Story*

CHAR:	JIM	SALLY	MAX
ROLE:	Central character/hero	Love interest, 2nd opposition	Main opposition
OCC:	Investigative journalist	Animal rights advocate	Circus owner

CHAR:	JIM	SALLY	MAX
GOAL:	Exploit Blimpo the Elephant for a story	Save Blimpo the Elephant from exploitation	Become #1 Circus Act in U.S.
MOTIVE:	Salvage career	Blimpo saves her life (later)	Prove he's not a loser
NEED:	Be more caring	Trust and love Jim	Respect animals
FLAW:	Anything for a story	Only trusts animals	Inhumane

CHARACTER/ACTION GRID—*Actions*

JIM	SALLY	MAX
Fired but then gets last chance	Only trusts animals	
Dumped by Sally	Dumps Jim; can't trust him	Whips Blimpo
	Kidnaps Blimpo; is chased	Chases Sally
	Hides Blimpo in Jim's yard	
Next morning: Finds Blimpo		

From David Trottier, *The Screenwriter's Bible*, David Trottier (Silman-James Press, 2005), p. 106.

Continue outlining your characters' actions to the end. When The Grid is completed, you will be able to see your entire story on just a few pages. The structure, pacing, motivation, and plot lines will be easier to work with. Good luck and keep writing.

JIM HERZFELD

Writing in the Dark

JIM HERZFELD began his career cowriting the comedic cult film IAPE-HEADS before working on sitcoms such as *It's Garry Shandling's Show* and *Married ... with Children*. Following his first solo feature credit on Disney's MEET THE DEEDLES, Jim was hired to write MEET THE PARENTS and its sequel MEET THE FOCKERS and continues to work developing TV sitcoms and feature films.

Quick confession: I've never read a screenwriting manual. This is not unusual; I know a number of fellow screenwriters who take pride in this admission of omission, convinced that reading any of the more popular "how-to" books will invariably result in formulaic and predictable storytelling. They might be right . . . I don't really know. In my case, I never read any such books because: (a) there weren't any such books when I started out and (b) I started out at UCLA Film School, where motion pictures were our books. We didn't have required reading; we had required *viewing*. And because I was a Bruin in the early '80s—before home video, DVDs, Netflix, the Internet, and the ability to watch a movie on your phone—viewing a film meant sitting in the film school's theater to watch film after film after film in the dark.

If you weren't serious about your studies, having a dark movie theater instead of a classroom was a great excuse to kick back and enjoy the show (which a lot of nonmajor frat boys taking film classes certainly did). But whenever I sat down to watch a film—be it Buster Keaton's THE GENERAL or a Hitchcock thriller or Truffaut's THE 400 BLOWS—I had a felt Flair pen in my hand and a blank yellow legal pad sprawled across my lap. And then, from the film's opening credits to the final fade-out, like a poor man's stenographer, I would jot down, as quickly and legibly as possible, virtually everything that happened up there on that screen.

I say "everything that happened" as opposed to "what I saw or heard" because my focus was less on describing the scene and more on *what happened* in the scene. Which is not to say I didn't write down *any* visuals or dialogue. If an image or a spoken exchange described or summed up the scene (consider the single line "Plastics" in THE GRADUATE) then I wrote it down. Remember, as a student, I did this because I *had* to. I was in a crowded theater, with zero ability to stop the film, back it up, and watch it again. So if I needed to remember or "study" the film after viewing (typically to write a paper or study for a test), I had only my notes to rely on.

Two hours later, the house lights would come up and illuminate the results of my speed-writing marathon: eighteen to twenty single-spaced pages of sloppy, crooked, chicken scratch seemingly penned by a drunk eight-year-old on the deck of a pitching ship. It mattered not; I could almost always read my own writing, and it would suffice for studying purposes. But what I didn't realize at the time was this: The learning "process" became more valuable than the lesson itself. Because by repeating this write-it-while-u-watch-it ritual several days a week over the course of years, and by being selective and economical about what I chose to write down, and by focusing only on what mattered in each scene, *I essentially created an "outline" for every movie I watched, from beginning to end.*

It's been said that people learn things by writing them down. Veteran screenwriter and director Nora Ephron once said she learned to be a screenwriter by retyping one of William Goldman's screenplays. Well, by reverse engineering or re-creating the outlines or "beat sheets" of dozens of brilliant, classic films over the course of my film school years, I believe I taught myself something invaluable to a writer: the nuts and bolts of film structure.

EXERCISE

The next time you sit down to watch a film (or a TV show, if that's your focus), get out a pen and pad and start writing, scene by scene, what happens. It can be a film you've seen before or one entirely new . . . it doesn't matter. If you decide to do this in a theater, see if you can find a pen with a built-in light. While writing, feel free to use a hybrid of script and prose, specifically using things like slug lines (INT. HOSPITAL) and transitions (CUT TO:) but avoid over-quoting dialogue (unless, as mentioned earlier, it's vital to describing the scene). Remember, try to write down only what's important to the narrative.

Also, if you're viewing the film on a DVD or the like, I would suggest you not stop or pause a scene so you can "catch up" and write everything that's going on. If you are truly selective and focused on the "what" and "why" of each scene (aka the plot lines), then you shouldn't have to write that much. Try to be "active" while viewing: Think about what's going on and whether it's worth writing down or not.

EXAMPLE: If you're watching THE WIZARD OF OZ, you could write the scene following Dorothy's arrival in Oz like this:

EXT. A COLORFUL PLACE—Dorothy and Toto exit house. Small people hiding in bushes. Glowing bubble arrives. It's Glinda—a good witch. Glinda tells Dorothy her house fell on and killed the witch. Munchkins come out and celebrate, sing. CHAOS as ANOTHER WITCH arrives. It's Wicked Witch of the West. Dead witch was sister. WWW wants slippers. Glinda puts slippers on Dorothy's feet. WWW threatens Dorothy. Dorothy wants to go home. Glinda suggests The Wizard. Suggests Dorothy follow the Yellow Brick Road to Oz.

EXT. YELLOW BRICK ROAD—Dorothy/Toto reach a fork. A SCARECROW offers to help. (And so on.)

When the film's over—once Dorothy's back home in Kansas and vows to never leave again—your outline is complete. If you typed it while watching, clean it up (eliminating minutiae) and print it out. If you penned it by hand, you might benefit from retyping it (à la Nora Ephron) and being concise. Then take some time to analyze your outline and ask yourself some of the following helpful questions:

Where are the three act breaks? How many scenes are in each act? What scenes are setups for other scenes to pay off? What is the narrative or causal linkage (where one thing begets another) between scenes? What was a reversal or a surprise? What conflict or character need is driving each scene, or, in some cases, each act? (Example, Act Three is driven by the Wizard's desire for Dorothy to get the witch's broom). In each scene, what choice does each character make that then drives the plot to the next scene?

Breaking down a successful film into a "tight" outline (with act breaks and clearly defined sequences) will prepare you well to create smart, lean outlines for your own original screenplays. And if you create enough of these outlines (as I was "forced" to do in the dark of film school), you'll also start to develop an instinctual and valuable understanding of narrative, structure, and the symbiosis between story and character. And who knows? You could soon be on your way to penning your own classic film that will someday be studied by future would-be filmmakers. (Hey, frat boys, next time, pay attention . . . !)

LINDA SEGER

The Newspaper Exercise

LINDA SEGER began her script consulting business in 1981, based on her doctoral dissertation on what makes a script work. She has consulted on over two thousand scripts, has taught screenwriting in thirty-one countries on six continents, and is the author of eight books on screenwriting. The third edition of *Making a Good Script Great* was published in 2010.

Writing is both an art and a craft. Many screenwriters learn to write by writing one script, then another, then another. But since there are many elements that make up the art and craft of screenwriting, a writer can practice the elements separately and then later combine these learned skills by integrating them into a script.

A writer can learn and practice the skill of structuring stories and dimensionalizing characters by simply reading the newspaper and filling in the blanks.

For instance, writers need to understand how to structure their stories so the story can be told in around two hours. Writers need to understand the three-act structure and be able to tell stories where there are clear beginnings (Act One), middles (the development of the story in Act Two) and ends (the pay-off of the story in Act Three.)

EXERCISE

To practice structuring stories, read a story in the newspaper and first identify whether it is about a beginning, middle or end. If the story is about "man murdered in park, no leads to killer" the murder is probably the catalyst for a story in the beginning. If you then made up the rest of the story, the story might include looking for clues and an investigation (Act Two), and then finding the killer (Act Three). If the story said "man arrested," it's the end of the story, and you can reconstruct Act One and Act Two.

You can further develop this exercise by researching the crime, and then figuring out how to put it into dramatic form. Look at what needs to be included and what can be left out. Where might you take dramatic liberties to make the story more cinematic and more dramatic?

Even a story about a social problem—such as "child sues parents"—can imply a story as well as a theme. The suing might be the action of Act Two, but there are ideas and issues to explore in a story such as this. You can practice by figuring out what the story of Act One and Act Three might be. You can also practice how to integrate ideas into a visual form, so you don't have to create long speeches about children's rights but instead show the issues through images rather than just talk about them.

The newspaper can be used to practice the development of character. You can read the longer obituaries, which are filled with fascinating character information. Many times an obituary not only tells what the person has done but also adds fascinating details that round out the character. For instance, an obituary might read: "Madeline, age sixty-seven, taught Spanish for thirty years at Austin Bluffs Middle School. She was also an avid hot-air balloonist." Unexpected details about the character are being revealed. However, in most cases, you don't want to just pile one interesting quality and another interesting quality to create a character. You want these qualities to be "paid off" and integrated into the story. So, you might try a creative exercise of figuring out what kind of story could connect teaching Spanish with being a hot-air balloonist. Might this character go to Spain or South America and have a hot-air balloon adventure? Or might she have to escape in a hot-air balloon from a South American dictator? Or perhaps fly across the ocean from Cuba to Miami?

Or . . . ??? The idea here is to practice combining two different qualities that ordinarily would not go together and integrate them in a story so the avocation as well as the vocation pay off.

Once you come up with an idea about a story or a character from the newspaper, you can then try to think of movies that use this technique and watch and rewatch the film to study how it's done. For instance, in MY COUSIN VINNY, the girlfriend (Marisa Tomei) saves the day when she appears on the witness stand and (unexpectedly) knows all about cars and tires because everyone in her family is a mechanic. Or if you were playing around with the "child sues parents" story, you might watch various social-issue films, like NORMA RAE or ERIN BROKOVICH, to see how social issues are explored in film.

By practicing the techniques needed to become a good screenwriter, writers can shorten the learning process as well as exercise the imagination and further develop their creative process.

NEIL LANDAU

21 Questions to Keep You on Track

NEIL LANDAU is a screenwriter whose TV and film credits include DON'T TELL MOM THE BABYSITTER'S DEAD, *Melrose Place, Doogie Howser, M.D., The Magnificent Seven* and *Twice in a Lifetime*. He currently teaches in the MFA screenwriting and producing programs at UCLA's School of Film, Television, and Digital Media, and in the MFA writing program at Goddard College. He is the coauthor of *101 Things I Learned™ in Film School*. Neil lives in Los Angeles.

My "big break" arrived about a year out of film school. I was young, brash and my dream of making a living as a screenwriter was coming true—despite my tenuous grasp on story structure, my secret shame. At that time, everything came from instinct. Even when I would go through the motions of outlining each scene, I would finish the latest draft of a screenplay with a vague sense that *something* was missing. But what?

Years later, I began to investigate in earnest what really makes a great movie tick from the inside out. I obsessively read every screenwriting craft book I could get my hands on—an informative, enlightening, and ultimately overwhelming endeavor. Each author had his or her own "take" on what makes a classic screenplay. But I always had trouble applying their sage advice to my own writing (and to my students' work as well).

I wanted more than a template and a set of "rules"; I wanted a list of structural questions that would synthesize the bulk of information into one accessible planning document. It would help me help my students face the blank page armed with a blueprint and scaffolding.

EXERCISE

These twenty-one questions are designed to expose these flaws so that you can renovate (or tear down) a shaky foundation and rebuild a solid one in its place.

A few words of advice before you begin:

- These questions are intended as a diagnostic exercise to help you get started on creating a structural blueprint for your screenplay or to address problems in a completed draft.

- Although these questions are numbered 1–21, this is *not* necessarily a chronological exercise. You may find it preferable to answer them out of order. Start at the end and work backward, or jump around to what you know first.

- There is an infinite number of answers to each question. Challenge yourself to find the freshest, boldest, most resonant approach. Transcend the obvious.

- If you experience exasperation as you endeavor to answer these questions, do not despair; this is an extremely challenging task. Remember, you are creating a world. Be patient. Take your time; this isn't a race.

- These questions are suggested guidelines for building and refining your screenplay and are *not* intended to be an absolute formula.

1. What's the "catch"? That is, what is the "hook" or central conflict of your premise? *This will be the "but" at the center of your premise.*

    Examples: ERIN BROCKOVICH: A single mom takes on a giant utilities conglomerate, but she's uneducated and broke. LITTLE MISS SUNSHINE: A family of losers pins its hopes on a children's beauty pageant, but the road to victory is paved with misfortune and their finalist daughter is hopelessly gawky. THE BOURNE IDENTITY: An assassin is being hunted but has no memory of his past. KNOCKED UP: A slacker must prepare for fatherhood, but he's still an immature child himself. AMERICAN BEAUTY: A lost man falls in lust, but with his teenage daughter's best friend. *Notice the central conflict in each idea.*

It's essential to clarify your "hook" before you begin writing your screenplay! The "but" will provide you with the foundation and narrative drive for the second act.

2. (a) What genre and tone are you establishing? (b) What is the main setting of the story? *Hint:* Think of setting as another charac-ter in your script. (c) What is the primary time period of the story? Present day? Period piece? The future? Be specific. (d) What is the time frame of the story, i.e., over how many days, weeks, months, years (or hours) does the entire story take place? *Hint:* It's "easier" to sustain suspense over the shortest amount of time possible.

3. (a) Who is your protagonist? (b) How old is he/she for the bulk of the movie? (c) What is most relevant about his/her backstory? (d) In what way is he/she desperate in act one? (e) Why does his/her story start today?

4. What is the most valuable aspect of his/her "Ordinary World"? Hint: This should ideally be something of value that your protag-onist stands to lose if he/she fails to act in the face of the crisis at the end of act one. This will establish the stakes (both emotional and tangible) in the second and third acts.

5. What is your protagonist's main character flaw? *Hint:* This will be something that limits him/her in the "Ordinary World," and that he/she will have the opportunity to overcome in the course of the story.

6. What is the "inciting incident" or threshold of the crisis? *Hint:* This will occur in the middle of act one (around page ten) and will facilitate your protagonist's taking some form of risk.

7. Who/What is the antagonist? *Hint:* This person or force will directly impede your protagonist from attaining his/her main goal. On an existential level, your protagonist will always also be his/her own antagonist, but you will also need an *external* one.

If your plot is lacking dramatic tension/conflict, you'll need to make your antagonist stronger. Ideally, in acts one and two your antagonist will appear to be more powerful than your protagonist, and your protagonist will need to get stronger and bolder by act three in order to overcome this threatening force.

8. (a) What is the specific incident that occurs at plot point I (the end of act one)? *Hint:* Think of plot point I as your first act climax. This specific incident will create a crisis in your protagonist's life. (b) What is this crisis?

9. (a) What action must he/she take in the face of this crisis? *Hint:* Think of this active goal as plan A. Ideally, your protagonist will have both a positive and negative goal; this +/– polarity will generate dramatic tension (or "heat") to keep the story engine running. (b) What will happen if this goal is not achieved, i.e., what's at stake?

10. What is the central mystery in the plot? What hidden or obscured truth comes to light by the end of the movie?

11. (a) What is the midpoint of the plot? (b) What unforeseen obstacle is now in the way? (c) *How does this unexpected event place your main character in an "existential dilemma"?*

12. What is plot point II—the second-act climax that occurs at the end of act two? *Hint:* This will be another specific incident that causes your protagonist to abandon or dramatically alter his/her original plan (the plan A set up at the end of act one) in favor of a new plan B. Which specific incident sparks this shift in goals?

13. (a) What epiphany does your protagonist have about his/her life that creates new choices about his/her future? This will put your character at a crossroads. (b) What are the two roads/choices? How do the stakes intensify as a result of this epiphany?

14. Your protagonist's decision about which road to take will spark a new goal at the start of act three. (a) What is this new goal (plan B)? (b) How is plan B substantively different from plan A?

15. What is the "ticking clock," or deadline, in which this new goal must be accomplished?

16. (a) What is the *big climax* of the movie? (b) What is the content of the showdown between protagonist and antagonist? (c) How has the above-mentioned character flaw been overcome? What truth emerges in your protagonist's life?

17. How does the central mystery resolve?

18. What is "The End" place of your movie? How much gets wrapped up?

19. What is the theme of the piece? That is, what does the entire screenplay stand for?

20. (a) Why is this story emotionally gripping? (b) Why are you compelled to write this? (c) What would you like the audience to come away with? (d) What will compel the audience to care about your characters?

21. What is your working title—and why?

Key Things to Know About Your Script
Before You Write

BARBARA SCHIFFMAN is a member of the Story Analysts Union who reads scripts and books for major Hollywood feature producers, cable networks and agencies. She also provides writers, producers and directors with "first look" feedback and pitch coaching.

The scariest moment is always just before you start," wrote Stephen King. "After that, things can only get better."

After reading more than ten thousand scripts as a story analyst for major Hollywood feature and cable producers, I'm always amazed when writers leave basic elements out of their scripts. Usually these elements are in their minds but don't wind up on the page. This makes readers—agents, producers, directors and stars, plus story analysts who write script coverage—work hard to figure out when, where or who the story is about. As you can imagine, this usually weakens our interest in the script as well as in the writer.

To be sure the key story elements readers want to know are on your script's pages, it's helpful to learn what these elements are. Answering these story questions before you begin writing also lets you focus on other important aspects of storytelling—theme, plot and structure, humor and/or suspense, dialogue and characterization— as you craft and revise your script until it's ready to send out.

EXERCISE

Here are some of the most basic things writers often leave out of their scripts or fail to make clear to readers:

1. *Who are your main characters?* When you introduce your protagonists or antagonists and other key characters for the first time, always include their full names, age or age range, gender if unclear, ethnicity if not Caucasian, plus a few words about unique physical or personality traits.

2. *Where and when does your story take place?* Make both specific if possible to help readers "see" the story in their minds. If your script is set in rainy Seattle, it will look and feel different from how it would if it occurs in sunny Miami. The world felt and looked different in 1776 from how it did in 1976 or 2006. We experience the story's time and place by what your characters do and wear, what they talk about and how they talk, and what's happening in the world around them.

3. *What genre is your script?* This sets the tone and pace of your story from page one. Is it a dark or broad comedy, a thriller, intrigue or film noir, a horror, sci-fi or fantasy? Each type has a distinctive tone on the page. If readers can't figure out whether your script's a comedy or drama, they won't laugh or cry about what your characters are experiencing.

4. *What's your main character's motive or goal?* Also what's in the way of his/her goal and what happens if he/she doesn't succeed? If the script is an ensemble story, this is important to know for each key character.

5. *Who's your antagonist, and what's his/her/their goal?* It's better for antagonists to be a single person rather than a group or a concept like "society." If your antagonist is not human, it should be specific, like the tornado in TWISTER or the shark in JAWS. The

antagonist's goal is often at odds with that of the protagonist, which creates tension and obstacles.

6. *What's the story's message?* The audience should learn something from your main character's experiences or at least have fun watching the story unfold. What makes this story important to you and why do you want to write it? If you don't know your story's message or it doesn't touch your emotions in some way, it won't impact readers or audiences either.

7. *What's your story's catalyst and conclusion?* The initial setup should hint at where the story will go so we can sense when it's getting close to the end. This builds tension and suspense by escalating the stakes and consequences via the obstacles to your main character's goal.

8. *What influences how and when the story ends?* Whether your hero runs out of time or options affects pacing, tone, events, what we'll see onscreen and what we won't. For example, 48 HOURS had a ticking clock while MIDNIGHT RUN had limited options, i.e., the mob accountant feared flying, so the bounty hunter had to bring him in via buses, trains and cars, which made travel longer and more complicated.

9. *Who's your audience?* If you don't know who they are and why they'd buy tickets to see your film or stay tuned to their TV, the reader will find this hard to envision. Your audience often depends on who your main character is and/or the story's message.

10. *Is your film's best marketplace movie theaters, TV or both?* If it can be a theatrical feature, does it have special effects requiring a big budget or is it character-driven and qualify as either an independent or studio project? If it's a telefilm, which networks might air it—Lifetime, Showtime or USA? If it's an epic saga, could it win awards as a limited or miniseries on a cable network like HBO?

Make sure the answers to these questions are clear on your script's pages through action, description and dialogue. Readers are then more likely to get your story the way you intend it and give your script its best shot. Especially in scriptwriting, first impressions always count.

MARILYN HOROWITZ

Four Magic Questions of Screenwriting

MARILYN HOROW Z, the creator of The Horowitz System, is an award-winning New York University professor, a producer, screenwriter, and New York–based writing coach. She's written five books on screenwriting, including her latest, *The Four Magic Questions of Screenwriting*.

When I sold my first novel and was asked to adapt it into a screenplay, it seemed impossible even though I was a film-school graduate who had sold a short film to cable. In desperation, I worked my way through the available information on screenplay writing. I read every book, tried all the different methods and took many classes. It all seemed like math to me, which was not my best subject. The night before the producers were going to give the adaptation to another writer, I had a sudden moment of mental clarity that gave me the techniques that became the basis of my writing method and helped me to successfully complete my own screenplay.

Aristotle's *Poetics* is considered the bible of dramatic structure. In it, he suggests that good drama should follow a paradigm called the three-act structure. He believed that every story should have a beginning (act I), a middle (act II) and an end (act III). Since the earliest days of film, this has been the model for screenplay structure. Writers always have struggled with the long middle, roughly sixty pages or minutes compared with roughly thirty minutes or pages for the first and third acts.

My life changed when I realized I could break the second act into two parts: act II, part 1 and act II, part 2. Suddenly, my writing became manageable and much more intuitive.

Because of my upbringing at the hands of my parents—a lawyer and a philosophy professor—asking a question was the obvious technique for finding any solution. By asking and answering a specific question for each section of the screenplay, I clearly understood my characters' motivations and, consequently, intuitively how to structure the right plot! This was the breakthrough that led to The Four Magic Questions of Screenwriting.

1. What is the main character's dream?

2. What is the main character's worst nightmare?

3. Who or what would the main character "die" for (literally or figuratively)?

4. What is the resolution of the dream or the beginning of a new dream?

Let's use the film THE GODFATHER, its hero, Michael Corleone, and its villain, Don Emilio Barzini, as an example of how to apply the 4MQS.

Here's a brief synopsis of THE GODFATHER:

Michael Corleone—a war hero and the youngest son of Don Vito Corleone, the powerful head of one of New York's five mob families—wants nothing to do with the family business. So when his father is shot, Michael is forced to save the Don's life by shooting the men who attempted to kill him. While hiding out in Sicily, Michael falls in love with Apollonia, but his father's enemies kill his new bride. Heartbroken and hardened, Michael returns to America and, in an orgy of violence, takes control of the business and prepares to lead the family into a new world.

1. Michael's dream is to live a life free from the Mafia.

2. Being dragged into the family business is Michael's nightmare.

3. Michael would have died for Apollonia, but didn't have the chance.

4. Michael forfeits his dream and becomes the new Godfather.

The answers to the 4MQS for Don Barzini are:

1. His dream is to take over the Corleone family.

2. His nightmare is that he won't be able to.

3. He would die to take over the family.

4. He fails to take over the family and is killed.

EXERCISE

(A) Answer the 4MQS for your main character:

1. What is your main character's dream?

2. What is your main character's nightmare?

3. Who or what would your main character literally or figuratively die for?

4. Will your character realize his/her dream or find a new dream?

(B) Answer the 4MQS for your villain or obstacle:

1. What is your villain's dream?

2. What is your villain's nightmare?

3. Who or what would your villain literally or figuratively die for?

4. Will your villain realize his/her dream or find a new dream?

(C) Write a brief synopsis of the story:

Take the answers and the basic story and write a summary of the screenplay plot following the example given above for THE GODFATHER.

(D) Create distance:

When the synopsis is written, it's best to put it aside for a little while and then reread it as if it were a film that is currently playing in a movie theater. If the writer would go see it based on the synopsis, then the script is ready to write. If not, the writer should go back and repeat the exercises until it clicks.

RICHARD STEFANIK

Creating Unpredictability Using Subgoals and Plot Twists

RICHARD MICHAELS STEFANIK is the author of the book *The Megahit Movies*, which analyzes the dramatic and comic elements found in commercially successful movies. He is also the author of the novels *Elixir* and *Entanglements*.

Stories must be entertaining for the audience. The worst thing that a writer can do is to create a piece that is predictable and boring! If the audience anticipates how things will turn out for the characters, then they will lose interest. That is why we must create stories that are unpredictable, that contain surprises and plot twists the audience does not expect. How can a writer do this? How can he or she design a story that will be filled with surprises? Writers can make their stories unpredictable by designing subgoals that will result in plot twists.

Subgoals (or subtasks) are minor objectives that a character must achieve in order to obtain his or her primary objective. Subgoals and plot twists are closely related. The audience is made aware of the relationship of subgoals to primary objectives when the characters discuss their plans and strategies. Plot twists occur when the accomplishment of a subgoal does not get the expected result of helping a character achieve his or her primary objective. This technique creates surprise and unpredictability and is found in many popular films.

RAIDERS OF THE LOST ARK uses this structure. Jones's primary objective is to find the Ark of the Covenant. To accomplish this, he has the subgoal of finding the Headpiece to the Staff of Ra. Once he finds it, he must use the headpiece to accomplish another subgoal, to locate the Well of Souls. Once that is found, he must next retrieve the Ark of the Covenant and get it to Cairo before the Nazis can gain possession of it. These are all connected to the unique primary objective: possession of the Ark of the Covenant.

In THE WIZARD OF OZ, Dorothy's primary objective is to find a place where she will never have problems. In order to achieve this, she attempts to accomplish several subgoals. Dorothy runs away from home in order to save Toto from Elmira Gulch. Dorothy returns home to help her "sick" Aunt Em, but a tornado takes her to Oz. This is a plot twist. Dorothy goes to Oz to get help from the Wizard to get her back to Kansas. This is her first major subgoal in the Land of Oz.

The Wizard will not help her until she gets the broomstick of the Wicked Witch. This unexpected result produces another plot twist. Dorothy gets the broomstick, but still the Wizard fails to help her get home. This plot twist is generated by an unexpected consequence of successfully accomplishing a subgoal. Dorothy's next subgoal is to fly back to Kansas in the balloon with the Wizard. But this fails because the balloon takes off without her—another plot twist. The final subgoal is to click the heels of the ruby slippers and wish to return home. She then finds herself back in bed on her Kansas farm. In SPIDER-MAN, Peter wants MJ. To win her, he plans to get a fancy car. This means that he must get some money. He decides to enter the wrestling contest to win $3,000. He wins the wrestling contest, but he is only paid $100, which is the plot twist.

A plan or strategy is a series of actions that a character intends to take in order to achieve his primary objective. He anticipates certain and possible obstacles, then devises tactics to overcome them. These plans are usually communicated to an audience in an exposition scene. The character discusses strategy and tactics with his supporters. This exposition of a plan creates expectations about future events for the audience.

A story becomes unpredictable when things do not occur as planned. This happens when new, unexpected obstacles occur or when the planned tactics fail to overcome an expected obstacle. Excitement is created when characters become endangered by these unexpected developments. It is only through the exposition of plans and strategies that expectations about the future can be generated in the mind of the audience.

In STAR WARS, the Rebel strategists plan to attack and destroy the Death Star, but things do not go as planned, and Luke finally destroys the Death Star by using the Force. In the LORD OF THE RINGS trilogy, the Fellowship plans to take the Ring to Mount Doom to be destroyed. Frodo plans to drop the Ring into the river of molten lava but cannot. In the final fight with Gollum, Gollum bites the Ring from Frodo's finger, and then falls into the lava river, which destroys him and the Ring.

Therefore, the most effective technique for writing stories that are unpredictable is including plans and subgoals that create plot twists. These stories will be filled with surprises and entertain the audience!

EXERCISE

Create three major subgoals that the protagonist must complete in order to achieve his primary objective. Describe the plans that he makes to achieve each of these subgoals. Then describe what goes wrong so that these subgoals are not achieved, a plot twist occurs, and the story becomes unpredictable.

MICHAEL AJAKWE, JR.

Your Outline Is Your Lifeline

MICHAEL AJAKWE, Jr., is a two-time NAACP Theater Award–winning playwright/producer who has written and directed nine plays and produced sixteen. He won an Emmy as one of the producers of E! Network's *Talk Soup*, starring Greg Kinnear, and has written and produced for sitcoms including *Martin, Sister Sister, The Parkers, The Brother Garcia* and *Eve* and the Showtime drama *Soul Food*. He just completed season one of his Web comedy series *Who*...

I have always believed that what distinguishes the wannabe scriptwriter from the pro is the ability to write a good usable draft when you're under the gun, not inspired or both. As we are often told by the production companies, studios and networks that employ us, "That's what the money's for." If you can't write well when you're under pressure or when you don't feel like it, you probably won't be getting paid to write for very long.

The best way to ensure you finish the script you started is to *always* outline prior to beginning. When you outline, you basically summarize each scene in your film in a few sentences or a paragraph, explaining what happens, which characters are present and their function in the scene. You can even go as far as including dialogue. Often when outlining, the more you delve into it, the more details you are likely to include. Some outlines are like reading the script in shorthand, which is really the whole point of outlining—to make it as easy as possible to write your script.

Some scriptwriters don't like outlining because it can feel like double work, like writing the script twice. Others find outlining confining, like they're being boxed in creatively. I'll admit outlining can be tedious. I have written scripts with and without an outline, and to me there is no question that the process is much smoother and more efficient with one. It's more work but well worth it. And it's only as confining as you allow it to be. You don't have to be married to your outline, and you can make adjustments at any time, so there is no need to feel that your outline is holding you hostage. You don't work for your outline; your outline works for you.

Here is a great metaphor for the outlining process. You are looking for something special but have to enter a forest to get it. You tie a rope from your car and take that rope with you as you venture into the brush. It doesn't matter how far you go or which way you go; as long as you have that rope, you can always find your way out of the wilderness. That is how an outline should work for you. It keeps you from getting lost as you write your screenplay by allowing you to track your story and make sure your structure is working. Remember, it is much easier to fix your story in a 15-to-20-page outline than a 110-to-120-page screenplay.

With an outline, you never have to worry about writer's block or getting stuck, because whenever you are in these places, you simply refer to your outline and you are right back in the game. Outlines are especially effective when you're trying to finish a script but are mentally fried or when you have a looming deadline. It is during these anxious moments when I am most grateful to have an outline to work from, when my outline becomes my lifeline to finishing my script.

EXERCISE

If you have an idea for a screenplay, take thirty minutes to write three sentences for every scene you see in your first act. Just write what you see in terms of the story moving forward. Repeat this process the next day, but take an hour to write a short paragraph for every scene you see in your second act. Do the same thing on the third day but give yourself thirty minutes to outline your third act.

Put the rough draft away for a week, pull it back out and clean it up. This time, take an hour to flesh out the scenes in your first act by expanding the sentences into paragraphs. The next day, spend two hours doing the same thing to your second act. On the third day, take an hour to do likewise to your third act.

In two weeks, you should have a usable outline, and you should be ready to attack the first draft of your screenplay. And it only took you the equivalent of one eight-hour day!

JAMES V. HART

The Tool Kit—Resuscitative Remedy for Writer's Block and Blank-Page Elimination

JAMES V. HART grew up on drive-in movies and Saturday matinees. His first feature film, SUMMER RUN, opened the USA Film Festival. His writing/producing credits include; HOOK, BRAM STOKER'S DRACULA, MUPPET TREASURE ISLAND, CONTACT, MARY SHELLEY'S FRANKENSTEIN, and LARA CROFT: TOMBRAIDER—THE CRADLE OF LIFE. J. V. is currently in production on his first animated spectacle, THE LEGEND OF THE LEAFMEN, which is based on ancient faerie legends. Hart's first novel, *Capt. Hook—Adventures of a Notorious Youth*, was named one of the Top Ten Young Adult Books in 2006 by the American Library Association. *"Go with gravity"* is Hart's primary mantra for the writing life. Never grow up! Never give up!

Dear Writers:

In order to survive as long as I have writing screenplays in this ever-changing business, I have had to develop survival strategies to demystify the challenge of writing in the highly restrictive screenplay format. A more mechanical approach to the task of writing the screenplay. The way a techie approaches fixing your computer or an auto mechanic does your car. A way of jump-starting the process to get me off my bummyhunk and write.

If you are waiting for inspiration before you write, get a day job. As Jack London said, "Inspiration? You don't wait for it. You find the biggest stick you can, chase it down and beat all hell out of it."

After participating in writing workshops at Sundance, eQuinoxe France and Germany, and serving as an adjunct professor at

Columbia and NYU, several of my students and colleagues asked that I put down in writing my basic set of strategies, exercises, and jump-start secrets that I use every day in my writing life.

My tool kit is less than ten pages long and requires no expensive seminar and/or mega book by nonworking writers to suffer through. This is my survival kit. These are tools that work for me. I use them every day. The ones you choose that are suited for you or that work for you are the ones you will use most often—and most successfully. Maybe this kit will work for you. It has served me well.

Please remember, the tools, techniques, and strategies presented here are not hard-and-fast rules. They are guidelines for implementing craft. You must have a command and access to the craft of screenwriting before you can break the rules.

A special hat tip to Francis Ford Coppola for literally giving me part one of the tool kit in a casual conversation about writing. And to all the directors and producers I have worked with, whose impossible and challenging tasks forced me to find a discipline that helps me make it through the writing day and night and, whoops, day again, thank you.

EXERCISE

THE TOOL KIT: NEVER FACE A BLANK PAGE—100% GUARANTEE THE THREE QUESTIONS:

The following are the Three Kings of storytelling, in my opinion. You must answer these three questions before you can even think of writing a screenplay. Francis Ford Coppola gave me this exercise a year after we had completed working together on his DRACULA. I have used it ever since. I use it every day in my writing. If you can answer these three questions, plus the bonus questions, then you are ready to proceed to the next step in preparing to write the screenplay. *Answer the following questions in writing:*

1. Who is the main character(s) and what does he/she want? (What he/she needs is different; see below.)

2. Who are the characters, and what are the obstacles the main character must encounter and overcome in order to get what he/she wants?

3. In the end, does the main character get what he/she wants or not? Was getting it or not getting it good or bad for him/her, i.e., did the character get what he/she needs?

4. Bonus question and most necessary: Why do we care? What is so damn compelling about your story that it would make me give up two hours of my life to read/see it?

5. Bonus question and very important: What does my main character need? How does this differ from what he/she wants when we meet him/her?

   WANT = MATERIAL THINGS, EGO-DRIVEN WANTS

   NEED = INNER DESIRES AND CONFLICTS, SPIRITUAL
            GROWTH

   Note: The Rolling Stones had it down: "You can't always get what you want. But if you try sometime, you just might find, you get what you need."

6. Bonus question: Why now? Why is this happening to my characters now? What event, what conditions exist today that enable this story to take place? Why not yesterday or next year?

Answering these questions will prepare you to write a character-driven screenplay. Do this exercise for all your main characters and see how they interact. The bonus questions demand a deeper understanding of your characters and your story.

THE WRITER IS THE COMPOSER!

THE DIRECTOR IS THE CONDUCTOR!

And remember this, scribes: Nobody in our vocational field—no director, costume designer, set designer, lighting designer, director of photography, production designer, sound man, boom man, stunt coordinator, SFX supervisor, painter, driver, PA, intern, and certainly no actor—has a job . . . until you type THE END.

So what are you waiting for?

- *Ne jamais grandir!*

- *Ne jamais abandonner!*

- Never grow up!

- Never give up!

BONNIE MACBIRD

The Genre Game

BONNIE MACBIRD is an Emmy- and Cine Golden Eagle–winning writer/ producer with thirty years experience in Hollywood. As a feature film development exec at Universal Studios for four years, MacBird read thousands of scripts and worked on all in-house projects, mentoring many writers. Bonnie was the original writer of the Disney motion picture TRON.

This is a fun, rather short game I play with students in my screenwriting class at UCLA Extension. It has three parts to it, and while it seems trivial, the students describe the results as surprising and profound.

It serves as a reminder of how our prioritizing brain can sometimes get in the way of writing, impeding the state of "flow" we need to do our work . . . and it also teaches us surprising lessons about what it is that we really love about movies. I personally play this game along with my students and am sometimes surprised at my own results, which show a shifting emphasis in my taste and help me choose the project I should focus on next.

Before we play the Genre Game, I introduce several techniques to students to connect them with their subconscious, to get them really writing "at speed," disarming the inner critic and writing nonstop without editing. One is a form of free writing I call Write-Outs, detailed in my upcoming book, which is a technique similar to Natalie Goldberg's Writing Practice and Julia Cameron's Morning Pages.

Over the weeks in class, students are coached to try to draft in this loose, free state of mind, allowing their editorial brains to kick in later. Students take to this with more or less gusto and concentration, but those who really learn to write freely without stopping, inevitably progress faster and have an easier time with first drafts.

Later on I introduce the concept of flow as defined by psychologist Mihaly Csikszentmihalyi. Flow is that wonderful state of mind where time recedes, and whatever the task at hand is becomes all encompassing, effortless and satisfying. It is the psychological state associated with successful creative activity and peak performance in a variety of endeavors from sports to the arts.

Flow, as it turns out, can be nurtured in a variety of ways. And it can be prevented too. If the task at hand is too simple for our well-developed skills, we are bored. And boredom means distraction. If the task is too hard for us, we get anxious, and anxiety is the enemy of concentration.

So, the key, says Csikszentmihalyi, is to match the task to the skill level, pushing ever upward in increments just small enough to prevent us from being overcome by our anxiety. Granted, there is a lot more to it than that, and several good books on the subject.

Translating this to screenwriting is another challenge altogether. Many new writers expect their first draft to be perfect . . . or "the one." Even when coached otherwise and confronted with the rainbow pages of a shooting script, they still place too much emphasis on getting it "right" the first time. This kind of expectation chokes productivity and lessens the chance for "flow."

So I invented the Genre Game to show them just how much this "I've got to get this right" idea can actually get in the way. The game works best in a group.

Let's try it now. You'll need a page of lined notepaper, a pencil with an eraser, a timer, a large stack of tiny stickies (I'm referring to those small sticky papers—Post-its or similar) and some larger ones if possible. Some fun and fast music you like. And a list of movie genres, appended below. If you have a group and the means, you can post these genres, one each, on the larger stickies, all around a room.

EXERCISE

Try this without reading ahead. If you cheat and read ahead, it won't work quite as well.

Part 1. Ten Favorite Movies in Order of Preference

First, take your page of lined paper and number lines one through ten. Set the timer for three minutes. Now, working silently and carefully, list your ten favorite movies in the *exact order* of your preference. You can erase. DING. Stop when the timer rings. Look at what you've got. How do you feel about this list? Is it accurate? In the correct order? Inclusive? Did you enjoy doing this?

Most people hate this exercise. And they are not sure they have the movies in order or even have remembered them all. It's antithetical to the way we think about something we love. (In fact, I usually stop this in class after about thirty seconds, as it's really no fun.) Then I tell my students to get up and stretch, sit down again and take out the little stickies. Do that now, please.

Part 2. Movies You Love

Next we set the timer for seven to ten minutes, and the next task is to just randomly write, one per stickie, the titles of movies you simply love, in any order, any kind, as fast as you can! The goal is to fill up as many stickies as possible, at least thirty, but more if you can: classics, recent hits, old favorites, childhood memories—anything and everything.

In class, I have students call out their favorites, and if someone hears one she loves, too, then she writes that down as well. Working together, students write scores of little stickies in these minutes, laughing and calling out titles to each other.

No judgment; the goal is lots of stickies. And enthusiasm!

If you're working alone, you can work with lists, Internet sites or books about movies (as long as they are not just one genre) to help jar your memory. Work as fast as you can, and when you have about thirty or so movies listed, go on to Part 3.

No one has any trouble doing this. I remind them that this is how the first draft is supposed to feel. I think, I see, I remember, I imagine . . . I write. Just write. Fast.

SAMPLE GENRES

Action	Dark Comedy	Historical Epic
Romantic Comedy	Action-Adventure	Drama
Horror	Satire	Animation
Documentary	Martial Arts	Science Fiction
Art Film	Family Appeal	Musical
Thriller	Comedy	Fantasy
Romance	War and Antiwar	Coming-of-Age
Film Noir	Mystery	Western

Part 3. The Surprising Genre Score

Next I put some fast-paced music on and urge students to work quickly, placing their movie title stickies under the genres posted around the room. And here's an interesting part: Students find they are often quite surprised to see more of their choices bunching in genres they didn't realize they preferred.

Working alone, line up your stickies on the wall or on your desk in genre categories. Where are you "favorite heavy"? Are you surprised? What genres did you repeatedly select?

Write what you love. When students are surprised by their preferences, I encourage them to consider a spec in that genre, even if it is not currently in vogue. Hit movies often come from "out-of-fashion" genres because, as the saying goes, "Everything old is new again."

It's a nonstop cycle. And, as any writing teacher will tell you, your best chance as a writer is to write the movie you want to see.

Notice what inspired you. Secondarily, we discuss how easy it was in Part 2 of this exercise to simply connect to "what we like" rather than trying, as in Part 1, to fit our list into a rigid format before we'd even thought about it. In an odd way, the profound difference in how the two tasks felt demonstrates exactly the difference between the internal tension we place upon ourselves when trying to be perfect while drafting and the way we should be feeling when writing that elusive first draft.

We've demonstrated "flow" in action while reconnecting to something we truly love about the movies. It's a real boost to the writing process. I hope you enjoy it as much as my students do.

THEME

DANNY RUBIN

How to Move a Pile of Dirt

DANNY RUBIN began writing screenplays after many years of writing for professional theater companies as well as scripting industrial films and children's television. His screen credits include HEAR NO EVIL, S.F.W., and GROUNDHOG DAY for which he received the British Academy Award for Best Screenplay and the Critics' Circle Award for Screenwriter of the Year as well as honors from the Writers Guild of America and the American Film Institute. Rubin has taught screenwriting in Chicago at the University of Illinois, Columbia College, and the National High School Institute; at the Sundance Institute in Utah; the PAL Screenwriting Lab in England; the Chautauqua Institution in New York; and in New Mexico at the College of Santa Fe. He is currently the Briggs-Copeland Lecturer on Screenwriting at Harvard University. Rubin holds an MFA in Radio-Television-Film from Northwestern University. He is married to architect and Web designer Louise Rubin, with whom he shares two children and two dogs.

Screenwriters are frequently encouraged to write "character" stories as opposed to pure "plot" stories. But since even plot stories involve characters, sometimes it's difficult to know what kind of story you are writing.

In a character story, there is something specific to the nature of the character that is challenged. Only that specific character would be challenged in that specific situation, and if you put a different character into the same situation there would be no tension. If, for example, a bartender offers a drink to a character that has just sworn off alcohol, there is immediately a tension that wouldn't be present had he offered the same drink to a nonalcoholic.

Writers who are struggling with a scene will often rack their brains to puzzle through a plot invention that will help create tension in the scene or will help get their hero out of the trap. Maybe you decide that the hero needs to receive a well-timed telephone call. Maybe she needs to have been carrying a hidden weapon. Maybe he needs to know a secret password. These are all plot inventions.

The better choice when you get into trouble is to look to character. Maybe your hero stutters when under pressure. Maybe he is indecisive and can't make a decision. Maybe she is afraid of the dark. By going deeper into your character rather than complicating the plot, you are better able to solve your story problem, to create a stronger scene, and to engage the audience emotionally as well as intellectually. You will also be giving your actor a better role with more to do.

This lesson has good real-world resonance as well: Whether you are a soldier, a politician, a businessperson, a parent, etc., I think you will find that it is often character that will save you. You can wait for an external event to change your situation, or you can reach into your own character and summon courage, sacrifice, calmness, humor, leadership or love. Character can be a powerful force, and in the best stories the writer has found something specific to a particular character that is challenged by the central conflict.

EXERCISE

Try this:

Imagine a pile of dirt. You have a character who must move this pile of dirt from its current position, and doing so is the most difficult thing this character has ever done.

1. What is the situation?

2. Who is the character?

3. Why is the dirt so difficult to move?

Create a situation where the dirt is difficult to move for plot reasons, and then create a situation where the dirt is difficult to move for character reasons.

Character reason: The scene is a funeral. A mother is burying her only son, an act that is breaking her heart. In fact, her inability to move the pile of dirt is specifically showing us the mother's degree of emotional pain. The dirt will be very heavy in the shovel.

Plot reason: There is an explosive buried beneath the pile of dirt. The Bomb Disposal Guy needs to remove the dirt without setting off the bomb, which will, by the way, wipe out the better part of a very popular vacation destination filled with children and endangered species.

As you can imagine, we feel the tension as each shovel of dirt is moved, regardless of who is doing the digging. That's one way to know that this is a plot idea. You can, of course, make this a character story as well: The Bomb Disposal Guy freaked out last time he did this, and a dozen people were killed. So for him every shovelful of dirt is a test of his skill and self-confidence, his return to completion.

Try a few of these yourself. Can you distinguish between a plot story and a character story?

KAREY KIRKPATRICK

The Emotionally Charged Icon

KAREY KIRKPATRICK wrote and co-directed OVER THE HEDGE, which has grossed over $330 million worldwide. His other screenplays include JAMES AND THE GIANT PEACH, FLAKES, THE LITTLE VAMPIRE, CHICKEN RUN (nominated for a Golden Globe in 2000), THE HITCHHIKER'S GUIDE TO THE GALAXY adaptation, CHARLOTTE'S WEB, and the SPIDERWICK CHRONICLES, which he also produced. He contributed as a writer or story consultant to THE ROAD TO EL DORADO, SPIRIT: STALLION OF THE CIMARRON and MADAGASCAR. Karey directed IMAGINE THAT and is set to produce, direct and cowrite *The Best a Man Can Get* for Nickelodeon/MTV.

One of the questions I am always asking when I'm writing is: "How can I show it rather than say it?" Characters are best defined through action, and in screenwriting in particular it is very important to find visual ways to convey character because, with the exception of using voice-over, it is very difficult to get inside a character's head and know what he or she is thinking.

This is why I often introduce one of the favorite devices I learned in film school: *the emotionally charged icon*. This is very much what the phrase would imply: an object that has been charged with some emotional resonance because of what it represents. An obvious example would be a locket that contains a photo of a deceased loved one. If the owner of the locket suddenly got a blank look on her face and started fiddling with the locket, we would know that she is thinking of her long lost loved one. It is a fantastic way to shorthand a glimpse into a character's psyche.

Two of my favorite examples of the emotionally charged icon

are the wristwatch in PULP FICTION and the harmonica in THE SHAWSHANK REDEMPTION.

First, the wristwatch. Bruce Willis's character thwarts his own getaway and endures serious hardships (including a sadistic "medieval" torture chamber) to get his watch back. Because of its monetary value? No. Because of the emotion with which this icon has been charged. Tarantino even gives us a whole scene and monologue (delivered beautifully and memorably by Christopher Walken) that charge the watch with its emotional value. It was his grandfather's watch, which was passed down to his father, who carried it in a rather uncomfortable place for years in a Hanoi prison so that he could pass it on to his son, Bruce Willis. The watch, then, becomes a symbol of honoring his father's memory. To not have the watch is to lose all connection with his past and to shame all that his father did for him while in captivity.

In THE SHAWSHANK REDEMPTION, the theme is all about hope and how to keep hope alive in the soul-destroying, hopeless confines of prison. When Tim Robbins's character, Andy, expresses hope for his freedom, Morgan Freeman's character, Red, tells him, "Hope is a dangerous thing in this place." When Andy learns that Red once played the harmonica before he came to prison (i.e., when he was a free man), Andy gives him a harmonica as a gift. The harmonica becomes a symbol of hope. Red is angry when he receives the gift and promptly puts it away. Later, when Andy's persistence gets the prison a library and gets Red a job in the library—which is much better than his previous job—he takes the harmonica out of the box and gives it one small test blow. He plays one note and one note only. And now we know, since this icon has been charged and represents hope, that Red is giving hope a try. After Andy's escape, when Red is released on parole, one of the few possessions he takes with him is the harmonica, which he is now playing on a more regular basis. He has it with him when he reconnects with Andy in Mexico, and, indeed, the last line of dialogue in the film is Red's statement, "I hope, I hope."

I use this device often. In CHICKEN RUN, the cantankerous,

militant former RAF chicken, Fowler, suspects that the American rooster, Rocky (voiced by Mel Gibson), is a con artist and is not to be trusted—which is true. But later, Fowler softens and gives Rocky one of his old war medals for bravery. The icon becomes charged because it now means that Rocky's biggest doubter believes in him. When Rocky decides to desert the chickens rather than tell them the truth, he leaves the medal on Fowler's pillow, and now we know what he is thinking: that he isn't brave, that he doesn't deserve this accolade. The icon allowed us to use this visual shorthand. The entire sequence plays with no dialogue whatsoever.

Some authors use emotionally charged icons as their title: THE RED VIOLIN, THE GLASS MENAGERIE, THE PELICAN BRIEF, THE MALTESE FALCON . . . to name a few.

EXERCISE

Take fifteen minutes and go through your house or that drawer where every little piece of junk gets stored. Set a trash can beside you and start throwing stuff away. Whatever you can't let go of is emotionally charged. Write down why you can't get rid of it, what it means to you, who gave it to you, etc. Then think of characters in whatever story you are currently working on and think of icons you can give them that will add emotional clarity and depth.

MICHAEL HAUGE

True Love

MICHAEL HAUGE is a Hollywood story and script consultant who works with screenwriters, novelists and filmmakers on their screenplays, manuscripts, film projects and development skills. He has coached writers, producers, stars and directors on projects for Will Smith, Julia Roberts, Jennifer Lopez, Kirsten Dunst, Charlize Theron and Morgan Freeman as well as for every major studio and network. He is the author of *Writing Screenplays That Sell* and *Selling Your Story in 60 Seconds: The Guaranteed Way to Get Your Screenplay or Novel Read*.

Whenever I work with clients whose screenplays or novels contain love stories, I always ask these questions: Why are these two people in love? Why, of all the people they have encountered in their lives, are they each other's destiny? Why are they attracted to each other, why do they belong together, and why, in spite of all the hurdles and obstacles you're going to throw in their path, will they end up together at the end of the story?

Okay. I guess that's more like five questions, but you get my point.

In movies and novels, as in real life, good looks, sexual chemistry and "magic" may spark an initial attraction, but real, enduring love comes from something much deeper. So to make your own love stories credible and emotionally satisfying, you must start by developing your hero's backstory.

Start by asking yourself: *What was my hero's wound? What event or situation in the past scarred my hero so deeply that she has suppressed her pain and buried her memory of it rather than face it and possibly heal it?*

Let me use a few classic love stories as examples:

In TITANIC, Rose was raised by her mother (presumably without a father present), who kept telling her that a woman was helpless on her own. In A BEAUTIFUL MIND, John Nash was told, "You have twice a brain and half a heart." In other words, he was convinced that he was incapable of love. And in SHREK, our hero tells Donkey that people see him coming and turn and run the other way. "They don't even give me a chance."

At the beginning of your story, your hero is emotionally terrified of ever again experiencing the pain of that wounding experience. Your hero would never admit or acknowledge this fear—it's unconscious—but it's still defining your hero's behavior. Because when we're vulnerable and afraid, we look for protection. We put on a suit of invisible armor to prevent us from ever suffering that pain again. We develop an *identity*—a false self, or *persona*—that we present to the world to protect us from our emotional fears.

So Rose lives as a kept woman in a relationship with a pompous, controlling and immoral jerk, just because he's a millionaire who can take care of her and her mother. John Nash creates an entire imaginary world to provide him with the friendship, love and significance he believes he'll never get from others. And Shrek lives in a swamp inside a barbed-wire fence that says "Keep Out" (a perfect image of being emotionally cut off and trapped in one's identity).

So what does all this have to do with writing love stories? Simply this: *Your hero's love interest is the one person in his life who will see beyond his protective identity and will love him for the person that he truly is.* As Dorothy says in that wonderful line in JERRY MAGUIRE, "I love him. I love him. I love him for the man he wants to be, and I love him for the man he almost is."

This true self—what I call a character's essence—is what your hero has the potential to become in the course of the movie. If your hero can find the courage to risk letting go of all that emotional armor, to risk rejection and abandonment to live her truth, then she will have earned the right to live happily ever after with her true love. And if he cannot find that courage, if he is ultimately unwilling to take that risk, he is a tragic hero who will end up alone.

When Rose meets Jack, she has found the right person for her: the man who sees the passionate, independent woman she longs to be. As she struggles through the tug-of-war between her attachment to Cal (who embodies her identity) and to Jack (who embodies her essence), she gradually sheds her protective identity and risks everything—physically and emotionally—to be with the right person.

When John Nash is desperately torn between the imaginary world of his mind and the real love he has for Alicia, she stays with him, supporting his essence. "Maybe the answer isn't here," she says, as she lifts his hand to her head. "Maybe it's here." And she puts his hand on her heart. They are connected at the level of their truth.

This brings up an important principle for employing this identity-to-essence transformation in your love stories: *Your lovers must always be in conflict at the level of identity and connect at the level of essence.* So when your hero and his true love fight, lie, misunderstand each other or break up, it is always because one or both of them have retreated into their protective identities. When they fall for each other, grow closer and honestly express their love, it's when both have shed their identities—at least temporarily—to reveal their essence.

This is why lovemaking scenes in movies often follow moments of real vulnerability, honesty and emotional intimacy: because the hero has risked shedding his armor and reveals his fear, or who he truly is. In other words, your hero has to get naked in order to get naked.

This transformation from identity to essence is what is meant by *character arc.* As you can see, understanding the connection between your hero's wound, belief, fear, identity and essence doesn't just strengthen your love story; it gives you a wonderful tool for developing character growth and for touching your audience at a much deeper emotional level.

When your hero's deepest desire is to win the love of the person of his dreams, the only way he can succeed—and the only path to real fulfillment—is to face his deepest fears, let go of his protective identity and become the person he truly is. That's why it's called true love.

EXERCISE

As you develop your characters and your love story, re-examine your hero with these questions:

1. What is my hero's wound?

2. Was this a single event or an ongoing situation?

3. How will I reveal that wound to the audience: In a prologue or opening scene? In a flashback? Through dialogue? With an object (a photograph, a headline, etc.)?

4. What unconscious belief was created by that wounding experience?

5. As a result of that belief, what is my hero's deepest emotional fear?

6. What identity does my hero present to the world to protect himself? What is my hero's essence? What truth lies underneath his identity? Who is he really, or who does he have the potential to become?

7. What actions will my hero take, as the story progresses, to show that he is abandoning that identity and moving into his essence?

8. What actions will my hero's love interest take to show that she sees beneath his identity and is connecting with him at the level of his essence?

9. What will occur at the climax of the film to show that my hero has abandoned his identity completely and has earned the love of the other person by living fully in his essence?

JEN GRISANTI

Finding Universal Themes

In January 2008, JEN GRISANTI launched Jen Grisanti Consultancy Inc., a consulting firm dedicated to helping talented screenwriters break into the industry. Jen guides writers to shape their material, hone their pitches and focus their careers.

What is a universal theme? It is an experience that appeals to the masses. It's how your audience connects to your story and your characters. I love a writer who has the maturity and the know-how to execute such themes well.

After I lost my job at CBS/Paramount in May 2007, I went through a period of tremendous grief. I also experienced complete euphoria. It was very strange. I loved the idea of total freedom. I hated the idea of no security. I loved the idea of not having to wake up at the crack of dawn. I hated the idea of not having a purpose that forced me to wake up at the crack of dawn. I had worked in the corporate world for seventeen years, ever since graduating from college. Since Spelling and CBS/Paramount were sister companies, I had essentially been with one company for over fifteen years. What was I going to do with my life?

I drove up to Esalen in Big Sur and took a course called Completions and Transitions. I had dealt with a divorce nine years earlier by essentially marrying my job, so losing this job was like going through a second divorce. I am telling you this story because of the exercise that I did in this course at Esalen. Mary Goldenson taught it. She is the author of the book *It's Time! No One's Coming to Save You*. One of the exercises Mary had us do was to chart our life from birth to the present. She asked us to graph and label every high and low that added to our life thus far. Then, she asked us to graph every high and low that we expected to experience from the present until the time we died. She also had us pick our age at death. Then, we each got up and told our story to the class.

It was a scary exercise, but a very valuable one. When I started Goldenson's class, I was in a room of fourteen strangers. At first, when I heard their stories, I felt I had nothing that could compare to the pain that some of them had gone or were going through. But as I continued to listen, I recognized that we are all so similar. We think our stories are embarrassing and that only we know this kind of pain, but I realized there is nothing to be embarrassed about, nor a need to qualify or compare our story. Our story is just that, our story. When we can detach from our story and utilize it to pass on the beauty of story to others through fiction, we can heal ourselves as well as touch others. This is how you find your universal themes.

EXERCISE

How do we find universal themes? I teach that we can find them in our own stories. Think back on your life. Think of all the firsts you went through: the first time you rode your bike, the first time you got through a day of school without missing your mother or father, the first time you played a sport and excelled in it, the first time you got a good grade, the first time you were punished, the first time you felt real isolation, the first time you kissed someone, the first time you fell in love, the first time you had your heart broken, the first time you heard about your parents' divorce, the first time you felt betrayed by a friend or lover, etc. The list is endless. Superficially, we have a lot of these experiences in common, if not all of them. Yet no one experiences joy and pain exactly like we do. It's this unique personal interpretation that informs what most of us want to find: our voice.

In screenplays, universal themes are what draw us in. STAR TREK beautifully explores the idea of logic versus emotion. VICKY CRISTINA BARCELONA examines the themes of chaos versus security when it comes to love and making choices. In FROST/ NIXON, the impending downfall of a powerful man is made manifest when Nixon calls Frost and tells him that they are both looking for a way back to the winner's podium, but there will only be one winner. THE LIVES OF OTHERS does a beautiful job of exploring loyalty. Hitting these moments is your goal.

STEPHEN RIVELE

Refining the Idea

STEPHEN RIVELE is the author of seven books and coauthor of numerous feature scripts, including Will Smith's ALI and the Oscar-nominated screenplay for Oliver Stone's NIXON. He cowrote COPYING BEETHOVEN and LIKE DANDELION DUST. Recent work includes screenplays about Miles Davis and Jacqueline Kennedy, and a new project for Steven Spielberg.

Until recently, I had never read a book on the writing of screenplays, though I had often heard them discussed. And so, last summer, I bought a book on screenwriting, and frankly, what I found there, I found appalling. Essentially, the author says this: The screenplay is a form of mechanism, and if you assemble the parts in the right order according to certain formulae, it will become a thing of beauty and a source of wealth.

To my mind this is nonsense. It violates everything I believe or think or intuit about writing. A screenplay is not a machine, its parts are not mechanical, and there are no formulae for assembling them into a whole. A screenplay, to my way of thinking, is an organic being—a living thing. Its creation cannot be approached mechanistically any more than can the raising of children. The fostering of living beings has more to do with imagination, thought, feeling, hope, despair, invention, inspiration, care, insight, truthfulness, and love than it does with what part goes where, or how to arrive at a plot point on page sixty.

To begin with, you must have an idea: something of such intense dramatic interest or of such ingenious comic invention that millions of strangers will be able to relate to it. Further, it must be something only you can say in your own peculiar language, something you believe passionately that an audience needs to hear. It must be important and universal. It must be a truth.

Film is not necessarily the appropriate medium for every idea, and you must decide whether what you have to say is best said in screenplay form. You must ask yourself whether your idea is cinematically idiomatic. If it is not, then write it in some other medium. Better to write one great poem, or an important novel, or a well-made play than a lifetime of failed scripts in the forlorn hope of having lunch with Renee Zellweger or Will Smith.

EXERCISE

Having examined your idea and decided that it can best be realized in screenplay form, your next task is to reduce it to its simplest statement. You must be able to answer the question "What is this script about?" in no more than two sentences. One sentence is preferable, and if you can reduce that sentence to one word, so much the better. If you cannot do this, your script will lack the integrity that only an underlying vision can give it. And when we talk about the central idea of the script—about the story's meaning—we mean the vision behind the work and how best we can convey it through the medium of film.

NIXON was a twisted love story; ALI was about a man seeking God's will; COPYING BEETHOVEN was about a young woman falling in love with a man who was becoming God; the Miles Davis script is about a man deciding whether to play music or die; and the Jacqueline Kennedy script is about an extraordinary woman trying to balance her private life and her public destiny.

At every turn, at every scene change, with the introduction of every new character, this single, simply stated idea will be your guide. It will determine who and what you will write, and what value they will have in the script, because your choice of scene or character must serve the expression of your core idea. I have always found this to be true. Whenever I was unsure of what to cut to, or where the story should go, or which character I should focus on,

I reverted to my single-sentence expression of the central idea and asked: Does this scene or character or dialogue serve to advance and elucidate the meaning I am trying to convey?

This is where many young screenwriters lose their way. If they have read the standard texts on writing the screenplay, they have been told that it must contain events and even that these events ought to occur at specific points in the text. And while, as I have said, I think this is utter nonsense, it is true that film scripts should be a framework of events—of things that happen and that can be seen—*but only to the extent that that framework is dictated by meaning*. Character does not dictate structure, nor does plot; meaning dictates structure, and truth dictates everything. For, as is the case with all art, screenplays exist to convey a truth from the author to the audience. And herein lies the essence of screenwriting from my point of view: Screenplays are not essentially about events; they are about truth.

Therefore, as a screenwriter, you must know the truth—the truth you are trying to convey to your audience—and that truth will free you to write and your work to come alive.

BARRY BRODSKY

The Thematic Line of Dialogue

BARRY BRODSKY is the director of the Screenwriting Certificate Program at Emerson College, where he's taught screenwriting since 1998. He also teaches screenwriting at Lesley University's low residency MFA Creative Writing program and at Boston University's film school. He has won recognition in several national screenwriting competitions, and two of his screenplays have been optioned.

In this highly competitive, dog-eat-dog-eat-dog world of writing and marketing spec scripts, it's universally assumed that if you can't hook the reader in the first ten pages, you're toast. Your script will be tossed on that mountainous pile of broken dreams and bent brads, never to be seen again. Ten pages to hook the reader—what baits that hook?

A compelling or quirky or engaging protagonist is de rigueur, of course. A strong visual setting helps. Crisp, convincing dialogue can't hurt either. Everyone goes for these characteristics in the opening pages of a script, and some writers achieve most of them. There is one other tool at your disposal in this first "howdy do" with the readers that can also grab their attention, giving them an unmistakable signpost pointing toward the heart of your story. It acts as a flashing neon sign announcing to your reader: This is what the movie's about! It's the *thematic line of dialogue*.

A *thematic line of dialogue* is a line delivered somewhere in the first ten pages that lets the reader know what the film is going to be about. In her book *How to Write a Movie in 21 Days*, Viki King says that a line of dialogue will be delivered (usually in the first three or four pages) that will "ask the central question" of the movie. As a writer, you should be focused not only on posing a question, but more directly showing the reader the script's theme.

Miserable Melvin Udall has just tossed Verdell, a cute little dog, down an apartment hallway's garbage chute. Verdell's owner, Simon, comes out of his apartment and into the hallway calling for his dog. He asks Melvin if he's seen the pooch. Melvin insults Simon, making homophobic comments about him and racist comments about Simon's friend Frank, who has joined them in the hallway. Frank would like to sock Melvin, but Simon pulls him back toward his apartment, and as they retreat inside, Melvin and Simon exchange the scene's final dialogue:

> MELVIN
> Hope you find him. I love that dog.

> SIMON
> You don't love anything, Mr. Udall.

Simon has just delivered a *thematic line of dialogue* in the movie AS GOOD AS IT GETS. We're at the top of page four in the script. The reader now knows that this story is about miserable Melvin Udall finding love. And given what we've seen of Melvin, the reader will be turning pages to find out exactly how this is going to happen.

Frank Galvin is introduced in the opening page as a drunken ambulance chaser. He pays off a funeral home director so he can slip his business card into the hand of a catatonic widow whose husband had apparently died in an accident. A few scenes later, Galvin tries the same ruse at another funeral home, only to be out-ed by the dead man's son. The son exposes the fact that Galvin didn't know his father and was just an unscrupulous lawyer trying to hustle business from bereaved people. As this funeral home director leads Galvin out, the son shouts his *thematic line of dialogue*: "Who the hell do you think you are?" We are at the bottom of page three in the script.

THE VERDICT is about who Frank Galvin thinks he is. Is he the idealistic lawyer of days gone by, who believed that the courtroom was a place where people could actually get justice? Or is he what we now see, a washed-up drunk who's just looking for an easy buck? A few pages later the reader gets another *thematic line of dialogue* from Frank's old law partner, Mickey. He finds Frank passed out on his office floor, brings him around, castigates him, and then says, "You're never going to change." By page six, the reader now knows that this is the story of a man who must change if he is to find out who he really is.

Single mom Sammy tells her eight-year-old son, Rudy, that Uncle Terry is coming to stay for a while. We are shown the backstory in the script's first pages: Sammy and Terry's parents were killed in an auto accident when they were very young. The scene with the two youngsters at their parents' funeral tugs at our heartstrings. Now we learn that they haven't seen each other in at least two years. We then see Terry bumming money from his girlfriend, Sheila, in order to make the trip to see his sister. After she gives him money, he asks for more. He wants her to ask her brother for more money, which she doesn't want to do ("It would mean I have to talk to him"). Terry is not a very together person. On page ten, he delivers the script's *thematic line of dialogue*: "I am not the kind of man that everyone says I am."

YOU CAN COUNT ON ME is the story of the difficult relationship between a hard-working single mom and her ne'er-do-well brother, who drops in on her life every few years to get money and cause her endless trouble. A reader sees the contrast between them in the first ten pages. The reader also picks up on Terry's line and now will expect the script to show whether in fact Terry is the loser "everyone" says he is.

Miles has picked up his soon-to-be-married friend, Jack, and they are off on a road trip to enjoy California's wine country. Back at Jack's house, Jack told his fiancée and her parents that Miles's novel was going to be published. Now, with the two men in the car, we learn that it's only being read by a small publisher. Miles scolds Jack for embellishing the story of his novel. They argue about whether Jack should have mentioned it. Then, on the top of page eight, Miles says, "I've stopped caring. That's it. I've stopped caring." And the reader knows that one theme the script SIDEWAYS will explore is whether Miles can start "caring" again.

In the following pages Miles stops at his mother's house and goes up to his room to get some money out of a secret hiding place. He looks at a wedding picture of himself with a woman. We've already seen that Miles lives alone and, to put it mildly, is a bit on the slothful side. By page ten, in what appears to be a very character-driven script, what or who is going to make Miles "care" should be the question that will keep a reader turning the pages.

EXERCISE

1. Look at your own scripts. Is there a *thematic line of dialogue* in the first ten pages? If not, come up with one. Then be ready to do some rewriting, if necessary, to make that line resonate throughout the script.

2. Watch the movies and/or read the scripts for CASABLANCA, THELMA AND LOUISE, CHINATOWN, DAVE, DEAD POETS SOCIETY, MR. HOLLAND'S OPUS, THE AFRICAN QUEEN, ALMOST FAMOUS, MAVERICK. See if you can find a *thematic line of dialogue* in the first ten minutes.

3. Watch ten movies you haven't seen before. See if you can identify a *thematic line of dialogue* in the first ten minutes. If not, pretend you've been hired to insert one, and write one to place in the first ten pages.

KARL IGLESIAS

The Emotional Outline

KARL IGLESIAS is a screenwriter, script doctor and consultant who specializes in the reader's emotional response to the written page. He is the author of *Writing for Emotional Impact: Advanced Dramatic Techniques to Attract, Engage and Fascinate the Reader from Beginning to End* and *The 101 Habits of Highly Successful Screenwriters*. He teaches at the UCLA Extension's Writer's Program and online at Writers University, and has presented workshops at the Screenwriting Expo, The Great American Pitchfest, Sherwood Oaks Experimental College and the Santa Fe Screenwriting Conference. Karl is also a regular columnist on the craft of screenwriting for *Creative Screenwriting Magazine*.

The following is an outlining exercise I give my UCLA students in my Writing for Emotional Impact class, which focuses on one of the unshakable truths of storytelling: "It's not about what happens to people on a page; it's about what happens to a reader in his heart and mind." In other words, it's all about engaging the reader emotionally. That's what craft is all about. Your job is to seduce your readers, to make them have to turn the pages to see what happens next, to interest them so intensely that they are captivated, taken "out" of themselves into the world you've created. You want them to forget they're actually reading words on a page. In order to do that, you have to find the most exciting and emotionally involving way to tell your story.

If you've read the screenwriting how-to books, taken the seminars, and have mastered the rules and principles, you're only halfway there. Just because you may have a solid structure, or the plot points are where they belong, or your hero follows the hero's journey, doesn't mean you have a great script. I can't tell you how many well-structured scripts I've read that followed all the rules and yet bored me to tears. We've all been bored by writers and filmmakers who have told good stories badly.

Never forget that at the script level you're the only person responsible for the reader's emotional response. If it's not the *desired* response, if the reader is bored instead of captivated, that's it. Game over.

In my classes, I lead students to view their final product not as a 110-page blueprint but as the promise of an intense and satisfying emotional experience. Sure, it's easy to write 110 pages in proper format with slug lines, description, and dialogue. Keeping the reader interested and moving him or her emotionally is another story.

This is crucial because not only is the emotional experience the essence of storytelling, but also it is what Hollywood buys and sells. Hollywood is in the emotion-delivery business. The movie studios trade in human emotions, delivering emotional experiences carefully packaged in movies and television programs to the tune of ten billion dollars per year.

If you doubt this, look at the way the studios advertise their "emotional packages"—through movie trailers and newspaper ads. Next time you see a trailer, disconnect emotionally from it and put on your analytical cap. Notice how each split-second image or brief moment taken from a scene is there to evoke a particular emotion in an instant, the sum of all images promising the viewer a fantastic emotional experience worth paying ten dollars for.

It's the same with newspaper ads and the highlighted praises from film critics. Pay close attention to them, and you'll see words and sentences such as "will grab you from start to finish; energetically funny, gritty, intense, and unpredictable; a staggering, haunting, and intense movie-going experience; pulse-pounding, highly affecting, powerfully seductive, superbly gripping, an incredible ride; packs an emotional wallop, hugely satisfying." When was the last time you saw a movie ad that said "well-structured, great plot points, fresh dialogue?" No. What you see more often than not are emotional blurbs, which are promises of the emotional experience you'll have by watching the movie.

Can your script match these promises to a reader? You need to think of each of your scenes as having an intended emotional impact on the reader. And this is where this exercise comes in.

EXERCISE

Think about the emotions you, as a film viewer or story reader, like to experience when you view a favorite film or read a script. Here are a few of the most common ones: *amusement, anticipation, curiosity, romance, tension, suspense, wonder, relief, hope, worry, shock, fear*. And let's not forget *empathy for the heroes* and *enmity for the villains*.

Next, think about what you'd like readers to experience as they read your script and attach this desired emotional response at the end of every major plot event or beat in your outline.

The key to this exercise is to force you to look at your plot events in terms of emotional response. The perfect outline should have a wide variety of emotions as discussed above, not just unemotional events or events that repeat the same emotion ad nauseam, like a bad horror script (fear-fear-fear-fear, etc.)

Here's an example of how the first act of STAR WARS would look if I were planning an emotional outline for that story:

1. Princess Leia is chased by Darth Vader and captured (awe, empathy for Leia, enmity for Vader, tension).

2. But she manages to slip secret plans and a message to R2D2 and C-3PO, who manage to escape (surprise, tension, hope).

3. On the desert planet of Tatooine, we meet Luke, an orphaned farm boy who dreams of becoming a fighter pilot for the resistance (empathy).

4. Luke accidentally gets the message from R2D2, intended for Obi-Wan Kenobi (surprise, curiosity).

5. R2D2 takes off to find Obi-Wan, followed by Luke and C-3PO (surprise, tension).

6. They're ambushed by the Sand People (tension, fear, worry).

7. But they're rescued by Obi-Wan (surprise, relief, anticipation).

8. Obi-Wan introduces Luke to the Force and the truth about his father, a Jedi knight (insight, anticipation).

9. R2D2 plays Leia's message; Obi-Wan asks Luke to join the quest, but Luke refuses (tension, disappointment).

10. Luke returns home to discover the Imperial storm troopers have burned the farm and killed his aunt and uncle, forcing Luke to accept Obi-Wan's request and to travel to Alderaan (shock, anticipation).

PAUL CHITLIK

Writing from Experience,
or Grandma's Teeth Fell into the Soup Again

Screenwriter/producer/director **PAUL CHITLIK** has written for all the major networks and studios. He has received a Writers Guild of America award nomination for his work on *The Twilight Zone* and a GLAAD Media Award nomination, and won a Genesis Award. His book *Rewrite: A Step-by-Step Guide to Strengthen Structure, Characters, and Drama in Your Screenplay* was published by Michael Wiese Productions in 2008 and is in its second printing.

Teaching comedy writing can be a tricky business. While no one can teach a sense of humor, one of the most essential requisites for a comedy writer, you can teach certain techniques to make things funnier, ways to set up situations to pay off with laughter, and proven "rules" (there are no real rules in writing, but there are "ways") that will help you get to the funny parts faster.

Through my experience writing for television and teaching screenwriting at Loyola Marymount University and UCLA, I've learned that people have a bank of funny experiences they can draw on to use in their writing—from a situation to a single line—but that they often don't know where to start. The following exercises have two purposes. One is to access those memories that are really material; the other performs a completely different function: to loosen up the class, bring students together, and enable them to say anything—anything, I tell you!—in class.

Why do I want people to be able to say anything in class? Because the more uninhibited you are, the less internal censorship you maintain and the easier it is for the funny stuff to come to the surface.

Down the road, in the maelstrom that is a "room" full of comedy writers (as many as twenty or as few as two), it will be useful to come up with something funny in a matter of seconds. If you know how to access that place in your mind where funny associations are developed, then you will be way ahead of the game. If you can't, you'll be out before you can say, "But *k* words are funny."

So what are these secret recipes to group bonding and subconscious access?

EXERCISE

1. It is the easiest thing in the world, because all you have to do is remember the funniest experience in your life. Just one. Then write it as a scene of no more than five pages. I usually give this as homework and then have students read their scenes aloud in class. By the time we're done hearing twelve of these, we're laughing out loud at just about anything, and we know way more about each other. Think about it—the funniest life experiences of twelve people in less than an hour. Got to be funny, right? It is. It also brings the class together as a unit, generating trust and confidence and breaking down performance fear.

2. But there is a way to go deeper. And that's exercise two. It's often said, "If it happens to me, it's tragedy; if it happens to someone else, it's comedy," or some variation of that. So, the next week of class, I'll ask everyone to write the saddest moment of his or her life. The benefits are similar: We're brought closer as a class, students access their own lives for material, and we learn to find what's funny in tragedy.

   Okay, doesn't always work. I've had classes that have been dangerously close to tears. Classes where even I couldn't find anything funny in those moments (and I've heard everything, from the death of a goldfish to the death of a parent to a romantic breakup). But even through the tears, it's almost always possible to find something useful for the individual writer. If not, I remind them of *The Mary Tyler Moore Show* episode featuring the death of Chuckles the clown—a classic, hilarious episode.

So what I'm saying to you, the individual writer, is do these exercises and see if you and your readers don't laugh out loud. If you write enough of them, you'll have a full-length feature film that's funny and poignant, not to mention autobiographical. Hey, wait a minute; that's the film I'm planning to write.

MICHAEL RAY BROWN

Change Your Perspective

MICHAEL RAY BROWN is a Hollywood script doctor and the founder of Story Sense. A story analyst for seven major studios, he has contributed to the development of such films as LETHAL WEAPON, BRAVEHEART, RED CORNER, CONTACT and HART'S WAR. Michael is a working screenwriter and frequent lecturer on the topic of screenplay structure.

Everyone studied Shakespeare's *Hamlet* in school, and there have been more than sixty film adaptations. In the play, Rosencrantz and Guildenstern are two courtiers. They appear in only a few scenes and then disappear, never to be seen again. Another courtier eventually tells Hamlet, "Rosencrantz and Guildenstern are dead."

What if we told the story from the viewpoint of these two unlikely characters? That's what Tom Stoppard did in his play *Rosencrantz and Guildenstern Are Dead*, which became a movie starring Tim Roth and Gary Goldman in the title roles. In the play, Stoppard explores the same existential themes but in a style wildly different from that of Shakespeare. He even tosses in a Ping-Pong game. In so doing, he makes the story seem more relevant than ever. It's not just about something being rotten in thirteenth-century Denmark but about the helplessness we all feel as we cope with daily life.

Every story has a point of view. Its perspective on the human condition is what gives it meaning. Audiences (and producers) tend to favor stories that have a strong point of view. If the protagonist ventures into a strange world, physically or morally, he or she acts as our surrogate. We experience the story through that character's eyes. We identify with the character. That draws us into the story. If we shift to a different point of view, our identification gets split or diluted. Consequently, the story's emotional impact may be blunted.

In my work as a consultant, I've observed that many scripts tend to have the same problem: a lack of focus. I often ask my clients, "Whose story is it?" Sometimes scripts will introduce so many characters in the first few pages that none of them emerges as the one around whom the story revolves. Even after you identify the hero, you need to ask yourself, "Should I tell the story from that character's point of view?"

TAXI DRIVER would be a very different movie if it had been told from the perspective of Harvey Keitel's character or Jodi Foster's character. It's unusual for us to identify with the prototypical "lone crazed gunman," but we understand the disgust and frustration that drive Travis Bickle to such extreme acts. On the other hand, the shifting point of view in PULP FICTION is primarily what makes that film so fascinating.

There's a film by Robert Bresson, AU HASARD BALTHAZAR, that's about a girl who is mistreated by her sadistic lover, but it's told entirely from the viewpoint of a donkey. The Italian film I'M NOT SCARED has a simple plot, but it's very captivating, largely due to its strong point of view. There is hardly a scene in which the main character, a boy who stumbled upon a ransom plot, doesn't appear.

If we get information when the protagonist does, we identify with the protagonist. If we get it before the protagonist does, we find ourselves in the privileged position of knowing more than our hero. This can generate anticipation and put the audience on edge, especially if the lack of such information puts the protagonist in danger. The question then becomes: "If we shift our perspective, do we gain some insights, or do we just distance the audience?"

The main character (through whose eyes we see the story) does not have to be the protagonist (whose pursuit of an objective drives the plot). Who is the main character of the Sherlock Holmes stories? It's not Holmes; it's his assistant, Dr. Watson, who always tells the story. It is his point of view that makes the methods of Holmes seem even more mysterious and amazing.

Mysteries are often told from the viewpoint of the detective. The investigator asks the questions we would like to ask (if we were smart enough to ask the right questions). He also often sees things the audience doesn't. If we take the point of view of the perpetrator in a murder mystery, we may identify with the killer. We embrace that character's values (or lack thereof) because we are walking in his or her shoes. We can't help but root for the villain to get away with his or her crimes, as morally repugnant as that might be. That's one of the reasons why the film NATURAL BORN KILLERS generated so much controversy.

It's important to choose your perspective carefully, but don't be afraid to experiment. If the point of view in a murder mystery isn't that of a police detective but that of the victim's spouse, for example, that would lend a more personal texture to the story.

EXERCISE

Take a few scenes from a script you have written, pick one of the minor characters, and rewrite those scenes (or even the entire script) from that character's point of view. Strip away every scene in which this character does not appear, and see if you can still tell the story. If not, see if some other story presents itself.

We are all protagonists in our own lives. You may find that, in addition to making this minor character the main character, you can also make him or her the protagonist. That character's struggle might turn out to be more relevant to the concerns of your audience (and perhaps even more pertinent to your theme) than that of the original protagonist.

If your story is about a bitter divorce, for example, try telling it through the eyes of the couple's only child. You might even try telling your story through the eyes of a pet. But remember, this is a movie, not a book. You can't get inside the mind of your main character. In movies, unlike novels, we are limited to the physical senses of sight and sound. Imagine you're witnessing each scene through the viewfinder of a camera, and tell us only what you see and hear.

Even if you go back to telling the story from your original perspective, you now have more insight into your other characters. You've put yourself inside their skins. When you rewrite the script, you'll better understand their motives. You may find yourself changing a line or adding a reaction that brings to life a scene that had previously been flat. Free yourself to explore your story from all angles, and you may surprise yourself with the possibilities.

SCOTT ANDERSON

The Union of Opposites

SCOTT ANDERSON is the director of the Harvard Square Scriptwriters. He has been a professional screenwriter since the early 1990s and is currently teaching at Emerson College in Boston.

A common misconception about heroes and villains is that they are opposites. One is good and the other is bad. In the best screenplays this isn't the case. Even though they are fighting and the villain is more powerful (at least at the beginning of the story), the protagonist (hero) and opponent (villain) often have a great deal in common.

"Luke, I am your father" is a STAR WARS example of an opponent and protagonist with a lot in common, but there are many more. Consider THE WIZARD OF OZ. How are Elmira Gulch and Dorothy alike? The first question is: "Who is Elmira Gulch?" She's the mean old spinster who later appears as the Wicked Witch of the West. She wants to take Toto away from Dorothy because the dog dug up her garden and chased her cat. Dorothy turns to family and friends for help, but ultimately chooses to run away so that she can keep Toto with her.

Fast forward and Dorothy finds herself in Oz, where she meets the Scarecrow (wisdom disguised as foolishness), the Tin Man (compassion disguised as heartlessness) and the Cowardly Lion (courage disguised as cowardice). Through them she learns to recognize wisdom, compassion and courage and internalizes these traits. In the process she comes to see the Emerald City for what it is—a community—and the wizard for what he is—a regular person.

Dorothy demonstrates her transformation when she sacrifices her chance to fly home with the wizard/Professor Marvel in his balloon, instead choosing to stay in Oz with Toto, not for her own sake but for that of her dog. This change in attitude and behavior shows she is ready to return to the real world as a wise, compassionate and brave human being.

So how is Dorothy like Miss Gulch? If she didn't learn these lessons she would grow into a larger version of her bossy and selfish child self: In other words, she would grow up to be like Elmira Gulch. The opponent, then, isn't just whom the hero battles against; it is what the hero will become if he or she doesn't triumph by learning the lessons inherent in the story.

THE ROCK (1996) starring Sean Connery, Ed Harris and Nicolas Cage is an action/adventure example. The movie begins with General Hummel (Harris) leaving his military medals on his wife's tombstone. He's given up on the system and breaks the law to try and help the vets he once commanded. At the beginning of the movie, Dr. Goodspeed (Cage) tells his fiancée that he doesn't want to have children because, after a really bad day at work, he's ready to give up on the world too. Through the course of the movie (thanks to John Patrick Mason, a great ally character played by Connery), Dr. Goodspeed finds the courage, compassion and wisdom to have faith in the world once more.

But what happens in a love story? Pretty much the same thing. In most love stories the opponent is not a villain but instead the love interest, and the protagonist must adopt the values of the opponent in order to earn his or her love.

GROUNDHOG DAY is a wonderful example. Phil the weatherman (played by Bill Murray) must change from the selfish and self-aggrandizing but funny man he is at the beginning to the caring, generous and funny man he becomes by the end. Through the course of the story Andy McDowell's character, Rita, remains constant. She is both the opponent and the goal.

There are other love stories that have both principal characters changing, as in WHEN HARRY MET SALLY or THE SURE THING.

The key thing to remember is that no matter the genre, the protagonist's transformation is what conveys the story's values and themes and that those changes are conveyed by the choices he or she makes. Be they good or bad, these learning experiences or transformational moments create your protagonist's character arc.

EXERCISE

This exercise will help you develop a better understanding of your characters while making their character arc or transformation convey the values and themes of your story.

1. Write a conversation between your opponent and protagonist that could take place at the beginning of your story, in which your opponent explains to the protagonist how and why they are alike.

2. Write another conversation at the end of your story in which the protagonist explains to the opponent how they are now different. In all likelihood you won't use these conversations in your screenplay, but they will help you to understand your characters and how they have changed (or not!).

3. Now think about what your hero must learn and how he or she must change in order to be the opposite of your opponent by the end of the story. Make a list and pick three things that the two will learn. Create three scenes where your protagonist learns these lessons.

4. To make your story more interesting, have your protagonist make some choices that lead him or her toward becoming more like your opponent. This is the source of conflict both in your character and in the story. If the story is about revenge, the hero might act out in increasingly vengeful ways. Pick three choices that the protagonist makes that pull him away from his ultimate goal and hinder his transformation into the person he needs to be, and create a scene around each.

MICHAEL FEIT DOUGAN

From End to End: The Creative Compass

MICHAEL FEIT DOUGAN'S first feature screenwriting credit, PUBLIC
ACCESS, won Best Picture at the 1993 Sundance Film Festival. He works
as a freelance screenwriter, script doctor, story consultant and screenwriting instructor and is coauthor of the book *Developing Digital Short
Films.*

The pursuit of the perfect story ending is like the quest to sell
your screenplay without compromising either your creative
vision or your soul.

My first sale reinforced my belief that I belonged in the field of
screenwriting. However, my first failure, my first unfinished screenplay, left me doubting everything, feeling irretrievably lost. I'd have
sold my soul to find the perfect ending for my story. I needed a technique to help me discover and examine my storytelling options.
Hard work and painstaking research led me to design just such a
tool, which I rely on to this day: the Creative Compass.

The Creative Compass enables you to explore all your options
and decide how to steer your story to a satisfying conclusion based
on the protagonist's wants and needs. Wants are the protagonist's
external desires or goals, which are connected to the plot. Needs are
the character's innermost desires or fears, which come from within
and express the story's theme.

The Creative Compass points to four possible outcomes, depending on whether the character's need and/or goal are achieved. Triumphant and tragic endings match success with success, or failure
with failure; the character successfully achieves both the want and
the need or fails to achieve either.

However, mixing the successful achievement of one goal with the failure to achieve the other is a more nuanced approach that yields existential and transcendent story endings. In these endings, want is sacrificed for need, or need is sacrificed for want—like winning the battle but losing the war, or vice versa.

EXERCISE

Using the Creative Compass takes five steps:

1. Identify the protagonist—the central story character who will struggle, adapt, persevere or fail. In this example that character is a screenwriter.

2. Define the character's goals by writing down his or her want and need. These goals should read as a single simple phrase. For example, the protagonist wants to "sell my script" and needs to "maintain my vision"—the integrity of his or her story.

3. Draw two dials, one inside the other, to form an eight-point compass. The inner dial represents the character's want and need, and his or her attainment or loss. The outer dial points to four possible story endings.

4. Write the successful achievement of the want at the top left corner and the successful achievement of the need at the top right. Failure to obtain the want belongs on the bottom right, and failure to obtain the need goes on the bottom left.

    Then combine the nearest points of the compass to reveal the four different types of story endings. The "north point" represents a triumphant ending: in maintaining the writer's vision, the script is sold. The "south point" reveals the tragic ending: Even after compromising the story, the script remains unsold.

    This exercise's existential ending has the protagonist achieve the "want"—to sell the script—but does so by compromising the story's integrity for commercial concerns. In the transcendent ending, the protagonist keeps his (and his story's) soul intact, but does not sell it. With luck it might become an Oscar-winner in the hands of another producer who values the script and its author's vision.

5. Last, choose which ending works best according to your personal style and the desired story message or theme. Once the compass has revealed the story's ending, you are ready to outline the script by fleshing out how your protagonist's challenges, actions and decisions bring about the selected ending. In this way, the Creative Compass helps you find your ending, without costing your soul.

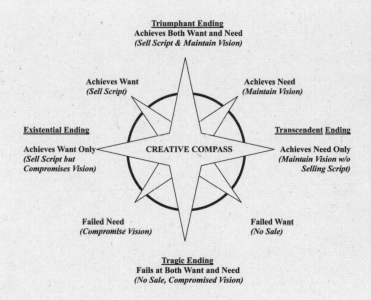

Triumphant Ending
Achieves Both Want and Need
(Sell Script & Maintain Vision)

Achieves Want
(Sell Script)

Achieves Need
(Maintain Vision)

Existential Ending
Achieves Want Only
(Sell Script but Compromises Vision)

CREATIVE COMPASS

Transcendent Ending
Achieves Need Only
(Maintain Vision w/o Selling Script)

Failed Need
(Compromise Vision)

Failed Want
(No Sale)

Tragic Ending
Fails at Both Want and Need
(No Sale, Compromised Vision)

CRAFTING SCENES

MICHAEL GENET

Rhythms, Levels and the Proper Respect

MICHAEL GENET won the 2008 Image Award for Outstanding Writing in a Motion Picture for Focus Features' TALK TO ME. He also cowrote SHE HATE ME for Spike Lee, the Olympic drama DREAM RACER for Daniel Rosenberg, and is now currently working on WITCHES BREW for Johnathan Dorfman and Gail Egan.

A few years ago, in the days before I became a writer, I was an actor at the Eugene O'Neill Playwrights Conference in Waterford, Connecticut, where I was blessed to be in the company of some of the finest writers and directors of our time. Directors like the late Lloyd Richards and writers like Academy Award winner John Patrick Shanley and Pulitzer Prize winner August Wilson.

August and I had struck up a friendship at the Yale Repertory Theatre on the second night of his new play *Fences,* starring the great James Earl Jones. He took me out for a drink afterward, and we talked for three hours, wherein he recited for me, word for word, line for line, the beginning, middle and end of what was to be his newest work, *Joe Turner's Come and Gone.* I remember the bar was so loud I could hear only half of what he said. But that didn't matter. Because August had a rhythm in the way he told a story that was to me better than Mozart, Bach or Brahms. When August "told" a story, it was like listening to the signature drumroll of a Motown classic, or the unbelievable riffs of an Ella Fitzgerald scat. Needless to say, he made an impression on me.

That summer we were both at the O'Neill conference, which was housed in the dorm of a local junior college. One night at about two a.m., we found ourselves headed down the hall to our respective rooms. Stopping midway, I asked August what the secret to being a great writer was. I knew it was a dumb question, but I was just looking for any way I could to get him to talk to me some more . . . about anything! To my surprise, August didn't think my question was dumb at all. In fact, he jumped all over it. Then, right there in the middle of a hallway in a junior college dorm, August Wilson said one of the most profound things I ever heard. He said, "Whenever you sit down to write, always approach it with the proper respect."

Those simple words cut through me like a knife. I was paralyzed. I couldn't move. I was so affected by what he said, that I didn't realize until I went to my room—at four a.m.—that we'd been standing in the hallway for two hours. Two hours in the middle of the night talking about writing. And the gift I was given was: "Whenever you sit down to write, always approach it with the proper respect."

So when I finally sat down at a keypad and decided to try my hand at writing, I remembered August's words and approached it very respectfully. Then I quickly went in search of what I believe is the second most important ingredient that any script must have: rhythm.

Rhythm is the spice. In essence, it's the writer's voice. Every script must have it. Every scene, character and line must pulsate with a writer's rhythm. A script without it is unreadable. A film without it is unwatchable.

However, finding your script's rhythm isn't as easy as it seems. For each story a writer tells, the rhythm is different from the one before. It can't be manipulated, duplicated or forced. Story dictates rhythm. Writers, if we are smart, realize that we are the facilitators. Because there comes a point in every script where the characters will invariably take over and start speaking for themselves. That is, of course, provided that the writer has approached his or her story with the proper respect.

EXERCISE

As an actor, I always give each scene I'm in a "level" rating of one to ten, meaning that each scene has ten levels I can reach to pull the best performance out of myself and embody my character to his or her fullest. Most "good" actors will regularly hit level six or seven. Truly great and dedicated actors will rarely settle for anything less than a level-nine performance. And if they're in a particular film, TV show or play long enough, they'll even reach level ten from time to time. When that happens, you usually hear someone say, "And the Oscar goes to . . ."

So our exercise here is to attempt to do the same thing as a writer. Once you've found your story, break each scene you write down into ten levels of richness, and see how many levels you can reach. To do this, finding the rhythm of your script/story is imperative. Patience and determination, or, as I like to say, a refusal to settle, are also keys to writing the best script you possibly can. I find that many writers, especially when writing for the screen, simply settle on a basic scene description or dialogue between characters. But if I were to tell you that if you started digging in a certain spot, half an inch down you'd find a shiny piece of gold, you'd start digging for it, wouldn't you? The question is, once you found that gold, would you be satisfied with it? Or would you then continue to dig until you found a bigger, better, shinier piece?

That's the essence of this exercise and, in truth, the essence of what it really means to approach your script with the proper respect and ultimately find its rhythm.

Write out a scene. It can be as short as three or four lines, or as long as five pages. Write it out, and then look at it. Read it over and over again. Hear it. Find it. Then feel its rhythm. Then, after you've done that, ask yourself, what level is your scene on? Did you find your gold on level one? If so, are you happy with that piece of gold? Or are you willing to dig several more levels down, possibly all the way to level ten to create the fullest, richest, most cinematically stimulating scene possible? That, to me, is what separates a so-so screenplay from a good one and a good screenplay from a brilliant one.

Writing is sometimes like scientific research: Historic men and women of science who discovered the great cures of the world were able to do so only after conducting hundreds and hundreds of physically and mentally exhausting experiments. At the top of the script for one of my screenplays, a romantic comedy called *Sunny Royal*, I posed one central question I knew I would have to answer at the end. The question was: "What is a woman?" That's a subjective question to be sure. There's no one right answer. But in posing it cinematically, I had to come up with an answer that was so deep and poetically profound that everyone who read the script or saw the film would in some way be satisfied that the answer rang true to the answer they themselves would have given. To that end, I remember I literally sat for eight hours trying to come up with the answer that was given in a speech by my main male character. I thought I was nuts for sitting so long on one speech, but in the end I needed those eight hours to get the speech and the scene to level ten, where it absolutely needed to be.

The charge is yours. Give respect to the task before you. Find the rhythm of your story, then start digging and see what level you reach in flushing out your characters and story arc.

This is simply one way of doing it. But the reward for such an approach to writing is often beyond measure!

COLLEEN McGUINNESS

Some Things Are Better Left Unsaid

COLLEEN McGUINNESS'S television credits include the NBC medical drama *Mercy*, *Miss Match*, *North Shore* and the Steven Spielberg–produced *On the Lot*. She has a number of studio films in development, including an adaptation of the Italian film L'UOMO PERFETTO (THE PERFECT MAN).

There's a Hall and Oates song with the above title. It's also a useful mantra to remember if you're a screenwriter. One of the jobs of a screenwriter is to provide texture and depth to each scene so that the audience can dig deep and discover what it is a character really wants as opposed to what he says he wants. What is a character trying to hide? What is the subtext? What is left unsaid?

When I completed my first screenplay, a trusted friend of mine read it and complimented me on its subtext. I thanked him but barely knew what he meant. Subtext? What was that? Did I really have it in my script? I hadn't purposefully added any subtext, but it was a character-driven piece, and naturally these characters were not always forthright about what they wanted. I decided my use of subtext here was just beginner's luck. While writing other projects, however, where mandatory plot and event were initially the focus, I was forced to become aware of subtext and how/where to include it. I had to make sure that each scene I wrote had more than one color to it. There is always the event of the scene, yes, but what lies beneath is often the most crucial aspect of the story.

There are lots of ways to work with subtext in a screenplay. Sometimes it's through dialogue: People say one thing and mean another. Or maybe it's through setting: The characters don't have to say much, but their surroundings say it all. Almost always, though, it comes down to behavior. What is the character doing that reveals what his or her true intention is?

It helps to look at a scene in three ways: (1) What is the event of the scene? (2) What is the subtext? (3) How is that subtext achieved and fleshed out?

Let's look at a very simple example from one of my favorite movies: PRETTY IN PINK. In a pivotal scene, Blayne (Andrew McCarthy) walks into the record store where Andie (Molly Ringwald) works. The event of the scene is that he buys a record from her. The subtext: He likes her and wants to ask her out. To take it further, you could note that he chooses to flirt with her on her turf, perhaps to make her more comfortable or maybe to learn more about her.

In the second part of the scene, Duckie (Jon Cryer) pulls Andie away from Blayne when he sets off the fire alarm (the event of the scene). As a result of this interruption, Blayne leaves before they finish their conversation. There is more subtext to mine from these events: Does Blayne's exit mean he is not yet fully committed or hasn't made up his mind about Andie? Do we intuit from this that he is torn between these two worlds? In contrast, for most of the scene, Andie, sure of who she is, sits firmly in her chair, rooted in her surroundings. Yet she is pulled away by something that appears urgent, that needs her immediate care. Does this represent the nature of the problems in her life and her role as someone who is metaphorically putting out fires for those close to her?

To work subtext into a screenplay, we must know how to find it in real life. As screenwriters, we must become keen observers of human behavior. If you stop to think about it, you'll realize that most people try to hide their true feelings. Someone gets the big promotion at work over you, and you're trained to say "Congratulations" instead of "I should've gotten that job! I'm so jealous." Someone who's drunk will try hard not to appear drunk. The person you've been dating for six months breaks up with you, and you try to hold back tears or say that your relationship "wasn't really working anyway" when the truth is, you really hoped it would, and you're about to cry your eyes out. In film/TV as in life, there is an event to a scene, and then there is the subtext—and it is the latter that is often the most interesting part.

EXERCISE

1. Take a specific period of time—an hour, a day, a week, what-ever—and look for ways in which people are saying or doing one thing when they really want something else. How do people cover up their behavior? What is the subtext of the interaction you are having with your mom, dad, sibling, boyfriend, girlfriend, coworker, neighbor, friend, person next to you in the grocery store? See if you can come up with ten interesting examples of real-life subtext.

2. Watch your favorite film and find both the event and the subtext in every scene. You can keep it simple to start, like my example above with PRETTY IN PINK. A movie like VERTIGO or AMA-DEUS might be more complex, which is fine, but start with a movie you know by heart and you'll be surprised at how clear the subtext is to you. Another great example of subtext comes with the film ORDINARY PEOPLE.

3. I believe in outlines, index cards, write-'n'-wipe boards—what-ever you can use to lay your story out in a concrete way. While outlining, make sure that you understand the multiple meanings of every scene you write. As you card each scene in your script, first make note of the event. Then make note of the subtext. Third, take note of how you have chosen to convey this subtext. Does everything (behavior, setting, wardrobe, tone, etc.) line up to support your intended subtext, your hidden event? Make sure you are saying something while leaving the bulk of it unsaid.

TOMMY SWERDLOW

Self-Knowledge Availed Us Plenty

TOMMY SWERDLOW wrote the screenplay COOL RUNNINGS with his partner Michael Goldberg. This led to credits on the family films LITTLE GIANTS, BUSHWHACKED and SNOW DOGS. Their television show *Brutally Normal* was on the WB in 2001. Tommy is also very proud of their being the original writers on SHREK. Though it was eight years later that the film was released, their creation of the Donkey character lives on. On his own, Tommy has written several pilots. He co-produced the film THE WARRIOR'S WAY and assisted with the writing.

One of the most powerful lines in the *Big Book* of Alcoholics Anonymous is: "Self-knowledge availed us nothing." Though that is true when it comes to battling an addiction, in screenwriting, self-knowledge can be indispensable!

I came to screenwriting (by *screenwriting* I mean movies and TV) as a poet and an actor, which is to say that I had a voice, an ear for dialogue and an understanding of how I liked words in my mouth as a performer. I had written a play that was a bopping rap of madness and sound—a real mash-up of esoteric and pop-culture references. Basically it was two guys talking about their girlfriends as they prepared to smoke a joint. The daily joint was their "ritual" as defined in their "scriptures." The actor with whom I performed the piece brought in a pal of his to direct. He made some comments about the script that startled me: "There's no conflict, no story . . . Don't get me wrong, I love it . . . But it could be better."

That day a partnership that endured for thirteen years (sadly, my partner Michael Goldberg became very ill in 2000) was born and produced some pretty good work, including all the movies that we "were known for," whatever that means. (Don't get me wrong; I am proud of my work, but the ego is the enemy of real creativity, and writers have massive egos.) When Michael asked for some dramatic conflict/stakes, my journey to becoming a playwright/screenwriter began. It's been twenty-one years, and I finally feel like I have some kind of understanding of story and structure (though understanding never replaces process, and by *process* I mean time in front of the computer, slogging away).

This knowledge can be both good and bad. The best screenplay I've ever written (in my opinion) was the first. It is called *Utopia Parkway* and has had a very rocky road to production, with a few close calls. (I am still hoping to make it and have worked on endless drafts and versions.) When I say "best" I mean it was the most personal. Unfortunately, the lead in this "personal" story is a very ill seventy-year-old man (based on my father, who had Parkinson's). This makes the film a very tough commercial sell, even in the independent world, and with every year that passes it seems to get even tougher.

Back in 1992, UTOPIA PARKWAY (a guileless first draft) got us signed by a great agent at a giant agency. Today, the climate in Hollywood has changed, and there is almost no chance that would happen, but I still believe that your first screenplay should be a very personal story. A story nobody else could tell (but if you have some big blockbuster just dying to get out, more power to you).

COOL RUNNINGS is something that I can mention, and people will know what I am talking about. Over the years, I have grown to love that script (and the movie), but it is a different animal from UTOPIA. There is nothing wrong with either. Every script has its own beauty and purpose. However, it is incredibly helpful to know what you are writing, for whom you are writing and what that person's expectations are. We'll call that knowledge of the project.

Still, those are professional concerns. Right now, let's stick with creative concerns and this issue of self-knowledge. *Know what kind of writer you are.* If you are a very structured, analytical and organized writer, it is probably best if you start out writing without an outline. If you are more of a "pure voice" (what I would consider myself to be, especially when I started), meaning a writer whose first impulse is to give his characters room to spew funny, powerful thoughts, then do as much outlining and organizing as you can.

Do not play to your strengths. Your strengths will take care of themselves. Be as honest with yourself as you can about your strengths and weaknesses, and always find someone you trust and respect to read your work. I can be clear with your script, but when it comes to my own work, there always comes a moment when I need a fresh pair of eyes. It is my firm belief that in *doing what is difficult, what does not come naturally*, we embrace the very nature of writing and process. For me, writing is often a painful, labor-intensive way to spend time, though a well-written line, scene or script is, for me, a profoundly satisfying experience.

EXERCISE

1. Outline a scene thoroughly (it can be something you're working on in your script or a scene created just for this exercise). Who's in it? What happens? Where does it turn (by *turn*, I mean, where does the key information or surprise happen)? Pick a specific page count you want to accomplish the scene in. If you're working on a scene from a script, ask how it fits into your overall screenplay? Are there any key plot elements or callbacks you can plant here? Were there any earlier you can reveal here? Now write the scene. (A *callback* is something planted in a script that pays off later. An obvious example would be having your lead character, who is adopted, break into a wildly loud sneezing fit in the middle of an early scene. Later, when talking to a man he doubts is his "real" father, this man breaks into an identical sneezing fit. That's a very basic example, but you can be as creative with callbacks as you like.)

2. Write a scene with absolutely no outlining or expectation. Just go. It can be about anything. Your characters can take on brand-new personalities. They can talk gibberish, speak in tongues, effect a sophisticated accent. You get the idea. Just blow, baby, blow.

3. Look at the two scenes you've written and make one scene out of them. This is an exercise; so don't go for results. You don't have to mix them evenly, but see what happens when you make a mash-up of these two seemingly contradictory ways of approaching a scene.

SARA CALDWELL

What Happens Next?

SARA CALDWELL is the author of *Splatter Flicks—How to Make Low-Budget Horror Films* and *Jumpstart Your Awesome Film Production Company* and a coauthor of *So You Want to Be a Screenwriter—How to Face the Fears and Take the Risks.* She has written hundreds of industry e-books, articles and reviews, and is a contributor to Constructing Horror.com, a site for horror writers. In addition, she teaches screenwriting and film production courses at College of the Canyons in Santa Clarita and is a frequent presenter at venues such as the Los Angeles Screenwriting Expo.

Good storytelling is about making a reader or audience want to know what happens next. In horror, it is also about surprising them with what happens next. That is the essence of suspense: combining the known and unknown with the unexpected.

In horror, we are creating unfamiliar worlds, places where our sense of reason can't easily be applied. A dark world where the very foundation of what we hold to be true is shattered, where there are such things as ghosts, alternate universes, mud creatures and other sources of ungodly evil—a place where characters lose control as unpredictable events escalate in terror and frequency.

Obviously we don't plod through our daily lives in a state of animated suspense punctuated by moments of pure terror. Our days are generally fairly structured and predictable. Even when we break the patterns with things like traveling, going to special events or trying new activities, we still have a sense of what to expect from previous experiences, research or listening to others. Sometimes the unexpected happens suddenly, from a dead car battery to getting fired from a job, but generally we've developed the coping skills to manage these situations, as painful as they may be.

But when something unexpectedly frightening happens, such as being on a plane that's in trouble or getting lost in a foreign city, sights and sounds become instantly heightened as all your senses go on high alert signaling danger. You want your characters to be in that same goose-pimple state of frightened alertness for the majority of your screenplay, and the more so, the better.

You've probably experienced such frightening moments. The two examples I gave are my own. I've been on a plane during liftoff when the flight crew suddenly shouted at everyone to run to the front (a weight imbalance was about to tip the plane tail down). I was also ten years old when I got lost in a foreign city and was running through the streets, crying, until a British couple saw my distress and helped me find my mother. Because of my high state of alertness in both situations, I remember them with absolute clarity. As bad as they were in the moment, these memories have become useful for creating that element of surprise in "what happens next."

In both situations, my expectations were shattered by the unexpected, which is frightening. What would happen next? Would the plane level off or crash? Would I find my mother or be kidnapped or harmed? While both situations turned out fine, I can (and did) imagine every other possible scenario. Remembering these moments and asking "What if?" is a useful technique for applying a similar thought process to your character's fearful situation and finding unexpected ways to surprise your audience.

EXERCISE

Write down what happened in one of the most frightening moments of your life. Include details, such as sights and sounds. Describe how you felt. Stop at the point that was the most frightening, where your heart was beating so hard you thought it would explode. Then consider all the worst ways in which things could have turned out.

Which is the most frightening, and why? Are there scenarios more frightening than death?

Now, what if the fear were to continue? What might follow this event to escalate things further? For example, a friendly old lady in the foreign city sees me crying and invites me into her home. I enter, and she locks the door before I see instruments of torture on her kitchen table. As you continue, push the envelope further and further, even if it seems ludicrous. Once you feel you've reached the edge, apply the same process to your character's situation, building from that first point of absolute terror and turning the knob to escalate it even further. Juxtaposing your own fears with your fictional ones is great for stimulating ideas that stretch far beyond formulaic clichés for those unexpected surprises.

CRAIG KELLEM

Scenes as Concepts

CRAIG KELLEM was an associate producer and talent consultant on the original *Saturday Night Live*. He produced THE RUTLES before becoming a development executive at Twentieth Century–Fox TV. Formerly a vice president in charge of comedy development at Universal, he also was a writer/producer. He then became executive vice president of Universal's Arthur Company, developing, selling and co-executive producing TV shows. In 1998, he founded Hollywoodscript.com, a company that helps writers develop their projects.

In the world of screenwriting, the word *concept* is usually associated with the overall idea of the movie. Once the concept is in place, scenes are then created to help tell the story. Ideally, the writer tries to come up with as many entertaining scenes as she or he can, designed not only to further the story but to intrinsically entertain us as well. But this tends to be the exception, not the rule. The predominant attitude appears to be one of getting by, plodding along by way of one supportive or "transitional" scene after another, preparing for that one humdinger just around the corner.

Not smart!

Professional writers understand that all scenes count. And there is no room for filler or bridges when true excellence across the board is the standard. Each scene should have its own magic, raison d'être, veracity and power.

An effective way of keeping yourself honest in this regard is to consider scenes concepts unto themselves. Adopting this attitude as the assembly-line prerequisite can prevent you from breezing through too many pages in order to get to the big moment. The scene in CITY SLICKERS where Billy Crystal and the boys are riding back to the ranch exemplifies this. What could have been just a "filler" scene of "the return" was elevated to an indelible cinematic sequence when the characters describe the best and worst days of their lives. Instead of simply being taken on another ride from A to B, we were given a memorable journey that will stay with us long after the credits have rolled.

Think of just about any film by the Coen brothers, who've made a living from delighting their audiences with "small stuff." Who can forget Jeffrey Lebowski, aka, "The Dude" (in THE BIG LEBOWSKI), buying milk at a supermarket. Not only does he come to the register with milk on his mustache, but he pays for the sixty-nine-cent carton with a check!

Getting to the final draft as quickly as possible may be endemic in our society and not conducive to the best creative attitude, so we encourage you to resist the impulse to rush and make it "good enough." Take the time to make those extra touches, small and large, because cumulatively, and sometimes quietly, they can make all the difference. Scenes are the bread and butter of your mood, your tone and the emotional currency of the story you are telling. So be sure to give every frame, every line a drop of inspiration imbued with integrity, imagination and soul.

EXERCISE

Make a list of ten possible scene ideas, big and small, which you might use in the project you are developing. As you ponder each scene, ask yourself, apart from the "functional" need of a given scene vis-à-vis the overall story (i.e., your hero must show up somewhere, somehow, meet someone by a certain page, etc.), is there a larger, subtextual aspect or characterization that can be unfolding in any given moment? How can the scene do more than functionally provide the "needed" beat?

If, for example, your hero gets lost and must stop at a gas station for directions, what added layer or layers can you massage into the exchange between your hero and the person he asks (even if only for a brief moment) that will reveal something new about your hero? Or suddenly add humor, depth or foreboding to the larger story? How can you make the very act of something, such as asking for directions, become more than simply "Hey, do you know how I can get to X?" How can you gently elevate the pit stop into a dramatic experience for your character?

It could be something as simple as our lonely protagonist hungrily stealing glances at a nice, young couple in another car as they play with their small child, waiting for their tires to be serviced. Or, maybe in addition to directions, he gets gas and sweats out the price mounting up on the gas pump in such a way that the attendant intuits his worry and they share a heartbreaking glance.

Take the extra time via this exercise to make every scene count just a little more. And then contemplate how doing this will further improve what's already probably really good, trusting that all those extra touches will hugely pay off for you in the end.

DAVID ATKINS

Crafting the Kick-Ass Scene

DAVID ATKINS has been a professional screenwriter since 1990 and has written projects for Paramount, Sony, Warner Brothers, Dreamworks, MTV, Lionsgate and MGM. These include ARIZONA DREAM, starring Johnny Depp and Jerry Lewis, which won the Silver Bear Award at the Berlin Film Festival, and NOVOCAINE, starring Steve Martin and Helena Bonham Carter, which he also directed. David has taught screenwriting and directing in the graduate film department at New York University's Tisch School of the Arts and in Columbia University's graduate film program.

I love a well-made scene. I love how a really finely crafted one functions, the way it enters a story with quiet efficiency and accomplishes a nice chunk of work in just a couple of minutes. When I first began working as a screenwriter, I was convinced that what made a great screenplay was dialogue. Pithy wordplay, short funny bursts, a punch line. Over time however, I've come to realize—not without a certain amount of chagrin—that the conversation between characters, while certainly essential, isn't the most important component. It's what's going on underneath the dialogue that really counts.

Don't get me wrong; I still love dialogue. The best kind of dialogue doesn't let you know what it's doing until it's already done it. It bounces back and forth, circling in on itself and riffing with little flashes of brilliance. Often it's interspersed with an obtuse moment or an errant thought because, wonderfully, this is precisely how real people speak. It's not until you reach the climax of the scene that you suddenly realize what has really gone on, and understand how deceptive the scene really was. Because while it seemed like all these characters were just fumbling for words and rambling in jumbled sentences, in fact what they were really doing was steadfastly pursuing their individual agendas.

That's what this exercise is all about: how to construct a scene in which the dialogue and action not only appear real, true to life, light, easy, breezy and effortless but also embody the tension and focus of a character passionately attempting to achieve a specific objective. This exercise focuses you on what you need to accomplish as a writer, while at the same time focusing your character on what he or she needs to accomplish as a character.

All right, let's get this out of the way: Writing is damn hard. I don't know about you, but I'm not out there belly-laughing my way through the day, knocking off twenty pages before breakfast. I actually need to trick myself into getting words on the pages. I find a blank page highly daunting. So if there's a device I can use to make that page *not* blank, I will put it in play every time.

Which is why I always have two items firmly in place before I begin a scene. First, I need the intention of the scene. If the scene doesn't have a specific job to do in the script, lose it immediately. Second, I have to know what each character is doing in the scene, what his or her dramatic action is. Like a scene without an intention, a character that doesn't have an essential action is extraneous. If he or she doesn't have something to accomplish in a scene, then get him or her out of there posthaste.

I like to think of a good scene like a kick-ass sword fight—all thrusts and parries. Each opponent has a mutually exclusive and well-defined objective, namely, to run the other guy through. I say mutually exclusive because only one character can achieve his goal. The other has to lose. If they both win, there's no tension. The more evenly matched the swordsmen, the better the fight. The more varied the technique, the more sophisticated the action. Similarly, characters in a scene must use whatever tools they are most proficient at in order to achieve their objective in the scene (and incidentally, the tools they employ will in turn define who they are as characters).

EXERCISE

Your first goal is to determine what the scene must accomplish to move the story forward. This should be articulated in one sentence. Let's say you determine the purpose of the scene is "to show that Fred is head over heels in love with Wilma." Now you have your scene's mission, its reason for being in the script.

Your next step is to determine the goal of each of your characters within the scene. Do this by articulating what each is actually doing dramatically. Begin by writing at the top of the page: "Fred wants to . . ." then free-associate a list of at least six different "to-dos" for your character. Pay careful attention to the verbs you use. Just as in acting, you want an action verb to drive your character's objective. A few examples:

- To trip up my adversary in a web of lies.

- To sweet-talk my boss into letting me leave early.

- To seduce a mark into believing I'm who I say I am.

Notice the choice of verbs: *to trip up, sweet-talk, seduce*. These are playable for an actor and therefore prime fodder for you as a writer. Imagine the myriad of methods your character can employ "to trip up." He can trick, confuse, corner, badger, win his opponent's confidence, lie, bedazzle, obfuscate or misdirect his opponent. Below are a few guidelines to consider when choosing the most appropriate objective for your character:

1. Make sure that your character's objective in the scene is in keeping with his or her overall desire in the screenplay.

    If Betty wants to win back Barney, don't give her a scene objective like "to pound home the fact that Barney is worthless." You make Barney feel worthless, and I don't care how much love you show him later on, he ain't coming back. Think about what your character wants in the overall story, then give the character a

CRAFTING THE KICK-ASS SCENE

specific objective for each scene, making sure the attainment of each of these objectives brings her one step closer to realistically achieving her overall goal.

2. Give the objective a cap.

   Open-ended objectives, such as "to save the world from evil," aren't effective, because there is no way to know when your character has achieved his or her goal. Make the objective finite and give it an end point. "Flattering an officious secretary into granting you an appointment," for example, clearly has a specific cap to the scene. Once the appointment has been scheduled, the scene is over. Now you know you can move on.

3. Make the objective fun or compelling to play.

   Your character is going to have to pursue this objective with all he's got, so it's important to give him something enjoyable to play. If a character is forced to carry out a banal errand such as "to convey a message," it's going to be an incredibly boring scene. "To drop a bombshell," for example, is a much more playful way to articulate this objective. Playful is good, by the way. Fun to write means fun to read, which means fun for an actor to act, which means fun to watch in the theater.

4. Make sure the objective has its test in the other person.

   In order for a scene to be dynamic, the characters must interact. This is the heart of a scene's tension: the interplay between characters, each of who is attempting to achieve his objective while preventing the other character from achieving his. If one character's agenda within a scene has nothing to do with that of the other character, then there is no interplay. Without interplay, you have no tension in your scene, and without that, you have no drama.

Okay, time to get it on the paper. Begin by jotting at the top of the page "My character wants to . . ." and then start free-associating possible objectives for your character. Don't think too hard. Just write as fast as you can, whatever you can possibly imagine your character trying to do in the scene. Get down as many different actions as you can think of. While you're at it, put some bad ones in there just for the hell of it—you never can tell. And don't forget your action verbs. Don't think. Just write.

When you're done, you'll have a minimum of six strong potential objectives from which to choose. Now cross out the ones that don't seem viable, enjoyable to write or in keeping with who your character is. Explore each of the remaining possibilities in your head. Which works best? Which would be most fun to see? Most important, which of the choices are you most dying to write? Because at the end of the day, the one that you most want to write will be the best choice almost every time.

When you've identified it, put a star next to it. That's your character's objective in the scene. Repeat this process for each character, no matter how small the role. Remember, every character has to be doing something in the scene, or he shouldn't be there. Once you have each of your character's objectives in place, you're ready to write. And that's how you write a kick-ass, razor-sharp, fun-to-play scene.

LARRY HAMA

Visual Storytelling

LARRY HAMA has written for TV animation and has worked in what used to be known as "Development Hell." He was cowriter of the film ALL AGES NIGHT with Gabrielle Kelly and is best known as a comic book writer for long runs on the Marvel Comics titles *GI Joe* and *Wolverine*.

I started out as a cartoonist and storyboard artist, so I approach every story I write from the visual side first. When I first started writing scripts (for comic books), I found that just working at a keyboard made me think in terms of dialogue, and as a result, my first efforts were way too talky and nonkinetic. When I reprioritized to work up the action first, everything seemed to fall into place.

I'm not just talking about choreographing action here. What I set out to do was envision the whole piece as a silent movie, so that character development, important plot points, character objectives, and so on, were all imbedded in the visual and not dependent on a character going into exposition mode. I could then concentrate on writing curt dialogue that wasn't burdened with explaining a plot point (a McGuffin) or covering up a logic flaw.

Although I have drawn storyboards for film and TV, I found that boarding commercials was the most instructive training for telling stories with pictures. The time is so limited that the information has to be brought across clearly and economically. Since the storyboard artist is the last guy in the chain and the deadline is always yesterday, you have to come up with solutions instantly.

A few years ago, I did a seminar on visual storytelling at a film school in Moscow. I asked the class to take a short scene from one of their own scripts and "board" it out. Being able to draw was not required. It could be stick figures or even a map showing character placement and movement, like a football play diagram. Even with the most rudimentary chartlike boards, new takes on character, motivation, and visual exposition were revealed.

It's hard to think of more meticulous writer/directors than Sergei Eisenstein and Akira Kurosawa, who both were known to sketch out their visions on paper, sometimes quite extensively. You would think that visionaries of that tier might be able to see the entirety in their heads, but they found it useful to work out their ideas in two dimensions before they set out to put them on their feet in front of cameras.

This is not to say that you should describe the shot. What I am suggesting is trying to see the scene from every possible angle, in order to make the visual narrative a cohesive chain of events. Even if you don't spell it out in the script, your knowing the underlying sequential logic will help to keep it all together. It might reveal an undetected violation of the fourth wall, or an omission that leads to onscreen deus ex machina. ("Oh, I guess you didn't see me pocket the poison pill when we were in the lab, huh?")

EXERCISE

Choose a scene that isn't an action piece—something in a restaurant, a living room, or on the street. Something with two or three characters and some interaction with the environment. Even if the scene is all conversation, don't think in terms of dialogue. Make the story come across in the pictures, but avoid silent-movie-style emoting. A long silence or a prolonged static reaction is sometimes better than verbalized exposition. If you can't even draw a smiley face, put down a circle and a notation: "She smiles awkwardly and turns away." If you do frames on index cards, you can rearrange and re-sort. You can even snap digital images of pose-able action figures. Just remember that you are not directing; you are putting the story on its visual feet so that you can understand it better.

ALLISON BURNETT

What Lies Beneath

ALLISON BURNETT is a screenwriter and novelist who wrote the scripts for AUTUMN IN NEW YORK, RED MEAT, FEAST OF LOVE, and the new FAME. His latest novel is *Undiscovered Gyrl*.

One of the striking differences between a mediocre film scene and a great one is subtext. Turn on your average soap opera or prime-time network TV drama, and you will soon discover that the characters know exactly what they think and feel at all times and are more than happy to state it as bluntly as possible, often with their fingers pointed in each other's faces. In real life and in the best works of art, this is never the case.

Beneath the level of our conscious mind lies a much larger and more interesting world of fears, resentments, wounds, hopes, memories, and yearnings. If you don't believe me, take a look at your dreams. It's pretty easy to see these secret forces at work in the speech and actions of others, but when it comes to our own words and actions, we are, for the most part, clueless. In other words, what we think we are doing and saying is rarely what we are actually doing and saying. The best dramatic artists understand this, and it is reflected in every page of their work.

Pick up a film script that you admire, then go to your favorite scenes and ask yourself two questions: "On the surface, what is this scene about?" and "What is this scene really about?" The answers will almost always be different. Now try it with a film script that you don't admire. The answers will almost always be the same.

Subtext is the third dimension of creative writing. It's what endows drama with resonance, soulfulness, reality, and poetic ambiguity. Without it, you have soap opera, sketch comedy, comic books, and cartoons. Subtext is like the patina of fine metalwork: It takes years to create but only a few seconds to obliterate. I have found that the last writer on a studio movie (the polisher!) is the one who usually wipes away all signs of subtext. I have also found that one of the pitfalls of actors who improvise their lines is a tendency not only to repeat themselves but, in the spur of the moment, to turn subtext into text.

EXERCISE

Think up a simple dramatic situation. For example, a high school boy walks a female classmate home from school. They linger outside her door for a minute or two. The boy asks her out for Saturday night. She says yes. They part.

First, write the scene knowing that the boy has been in love with the girl since grade school and that she has never given him the time of day. He is certain that he will be rejected when he asks her out. Because this is an exercise in subtext, he is not allowed to tell her how he feels, of course, but it should inform the scene. We should feel his love and fear pulsing beneath the action.

When you are finished, write it a second way. This time, the boy has never paid her any attention, but he has just learned through the grapevine that the girl has been in love with him since grade school. Flattered and noticing her beauty for the first time, he decides to ask her out. Again, nothing is stated, but how does it change his approach? How does it alter his behavior and the words he chooses? Try to keep this version as close to the first version as possible, changing the words only enough to reflect the new reality.

Finally, write the scene a third way. This time the boy and girl have been friends since they were kids, but only at school. They never hang out on weekends. Recently the boy has begun to feel romantic toward her. Asking her out on a Saturday night means changing the rules of their relationship. He is stepping into dangerous territory.

Now show your three scenes to a few trusted readers. When they are finished reading, ask them what they learned about the characters and their situation from each scene. Nothing is easier than communicating text; communicating subtext is much harder. See if you communicated your subtext. See if the buried lives of your characters reached the readers.

STEPHEN V. DUNCAN

Write Cinematic Scenes

STEPHEN V. DUNCAN is the author of *Genre Screenwriting: How to Write Popular Screenplays That Sell* and *A Guide to Screenwriting Success: How to Write for Film and Television*. He co-created the Emmy-winning CBS-TV series *Tour of Duty* and cowrote the Emmy-nominated TNT original film THE COURT-MARTIAL OF JACKIE ROBINSON. An associate professor, he's the chair of the Screenwriting Department at Loyola Marymount University's School of Film and Television in Los Angeles.

A film, by its very nature, is a visual art form. However, I've found that new screenwriters tend to forget that they've ever seen a film in their lives. Too often, inexperienced writers go right for wall-to-wall yakking when writing a scene or sequence for a movie. While verbal dialogue drives television scenes, you want to write dramatically effective cinematic scenes for a feature film.

An effective approach is to use *The Seven Elements of a Scene or Sequence*. Use them when you rough out scenes but especially during the rewriting process. I'm often surprised that some writers do not know the definition of a scene or a sequence. In screenwriting, this is important to know because, unlike novels or short stories, your scenes ultimately will appear on film, as translated by a director and a production crew. This process begins with the writer properly formatting the page with scene headings that describe whether it takes place interior or exterior, the specific location and the time of day. A scene takes place in a single location. A sequence is a *series of scenes* that tell a short story within the context of the larger story. Here are the seven elements and the questions you should ask and answer for yourself:

A protagonist. Who has the "most dramatic need" in the scene? In other words, what does this character want in the scene?

An antagonist. Who opposes the dramatic need in the scene? Ironically, this has the same meaning as the protagonist's: What does this character want in the scene? They should oppose in order to create conflict. If each wants the same thing, then they must disagree on how to get it. Otherwise, your scene will bore the reader (and, ultimately, the viewer).

Pivotal character(s). Who is for or against the protagonist and/ or the antagonist in a scene? These characters have two purposes in a scene: to keep the protagonist and antagonist engaged in conflict and/or to provide a different point of view about the problem in the scene.

Dialogue. How do the characters communicate with each other: through the spoken word, nonverbally (through actions, reactions or pure silence) or both? For example, a character can say "I love you," then turn her back and, by her expression, reveal to the audience that she's lying.

Intentions. Why is each character in the scene? Actors call it motivation. This is the driving force behind creating conflict in a scene.

Subtext. What emotions are bubbling underneath the scene? What is the scene really about? This element gets its cue from the theme of the screen story.

Context. How does the scene relate to what came before it and what comes after it? This element gives the writer the ability to give the same scene intense suspense or create comedic tone without even rewriting it.

While these seven elements may appear simplistic, the viability of a screenplay depends on writing entertaining scenes, and this approach can be an effective method for practicing and improving the style and content of your screenplay.

EXERCISE

Start with a single sentence idea. Here are some I've used to inspire scenes:

"A couple finds an old pair of wingtip shoes in an attic."

"A family pet gives his/her owner a piece of his/her mind."

"Infidelity in a marriage."

"Face to face with an alien being."

"A husband of twenty years is a serial killer."

"Love at first sight."

The goal is to improve your ability to write cinematic scenes and sequences. Pick one idea (or make up your own) and write it three different ways:

1. The first approach is using only spoken dialogue. Keep it short, around two to three pages.

2. Next, write the same scene using only actions and nonverbal dialogue. You need to translate the spoken words into recognizable visual actions and reactions.

3. Finally, rewrite the same scene focusing on improving the visuals, but this time write a single line of dialogue to capture the subtext (theme) of the scene.

You can take this exercise to an advanced level by writing a six- to eight-page sequence based on the same idea. Each scene as well as the overall sequence should use the seven elements. First, try this technique using only the spoken dialogue, then try it using a single theme-defining line of dialogue, and finally write a sequence combining spoken and nonspoken dialogue with visual action.

At the end of this process, your ability to combine both visual and auditory elements to create dramatically effective scenes should be significantly improved.

T. J. LYNCH

I Know What You're Thinking:
Dialogue, Context, Subtext

T. J. LYNCH was awarded a Nicholls Fellowship in Screenwriting by the Academy of Motion Picture Arts & Sciences for his screenplay *The Beginning of Wisdom*. He is the original screenwriter of the feature film A PLUMM SUMMER, which enjoyed a limited theatrical release in 2008 and was released on DVD in 2009. He is a citizen of both the United States and Canada, and lives in Los Angeles. When time permits, he does screenplay consultation for fledgling screenwriters.

D ialogue is a bit of a sticky wicket. It has to sound "natural." It also has to impart information. These two objectives often conflict. One of the ways to disguise exposition is through the use of *subtext*. A command of subtext is one of the most difficult screenwriting skills to master and one of the most elegant when executed properly.

Subtext is about what's not said. In real life, people often don't come out and say exactly what they think. They hedge. They deceive. They obfuscate. They save face. Subtext is what's underneath, the meaning behind what someone says. Whenever possible, it's good to have our characters saying something different from what they're actually thinking.

One may reasonably ask, "If they're saying something different from what they're thinking, how are we supposed to know what they're thinking?" The answer lies in *context*. What is the setting of the scene? What is the relationship between the characters? How are they staged relative to one another? More important, what are their respective behaviors?

What we do reveals as much about us as what we say. If we're tapping our fingers we're bored. If we're playing with our watchband we're concerned about time. If we smile when the situation isn't funny we're nervous (probably because we're lying). Behavior is the key to unlocking the subtext in a scene. If a character simply says something, we take it at face value. But if his or her behavior contradicts in some way what he or she is saying, now we have subtext. Suddenly there are two separate tracks for the audience to interpret—a much more interesting dynamic. The variance between word and deed allows the viewer to glean the meaning behind the words.

Here's an example of subtext from my screenplay *The Beginning of Wisdom*. The new housekeeper observes Harley, a recently widowed rancher, mooning over the loss of his wife. She says sympathetically, "You must've really loved her." Harley responds, "She was a fine cook." At first blush his response might seem a bit cold-hearted. But in the context of the scene as well as that of all the scenes that preceeded it, we recognize that what his response actually means is: "Of course I loved her; she took care of my every need. She was my life. But I'm too damaged by the loss to affirm my love for her out loud."

EXERCISE

Let's try an exercise. Pick out a scene from a screenplay you're working on. Not an action scene with lots going on, preferably a conversation between two characters. Is the dialogue spot-on? By that I mean, do they say pretty much what's exactly on their minds? Great! Now you have an opportunity to inject subtext into the scene.

Now rewrite the scene. First look at the staging of the characters in the room. How does the context change if one character has his back turned toward the other as they converse? Is he hiding something, afraid his expression will give it away? Or is he simply uninterested in what she has to say? What about her? Is she standing in the doorway as if she's afraid to enter or ready to storm out at any moment?

Next, give them each a behavior that in some way contradicts what they're saying. If he's assuring her that he's happy in their marriage, why is he fiddling with his wedding band as if it's uncomfortable on his finger? If she smiles and affirms she trusts him, why are her arms crossed? Why is she chewing her nails to the quick at the same time? Design the interchange between them so that we learn as much by what they're doing as by what they're saying.

Subtext is one of the screenwriter's best tools for parceling out exposition nonverbally. It engages the reader of your screenplay (and, perhaps, someday the audience of your film) more fully than dialogue alone. Moreover, it enhances your characters by giving them the option to lie and your audience the capacity to see through the lies. Words often deceive, whereas behavior often reveals an underlying truth.

VALERIE ALEXANDER
One-Page Character Introduction

VALERIE ALEXANDER has been a working writer, active Writers Guild of America West member, and dedicated mentor for the Young Story-tellers Foundation since 2003. Valerie developed the television series *Gangster, Inc.* for CubeVision. Her screen adaptations include the novel *Social Crimes* by Jane Hitchcock, and Michael Chepiga's stage play *Getting & Spending*.

There is a lot of great advice in these pages concerning what you need to know before you start writing. What I feel is most important is to know your characters.

If you know them, truly know them inside and out—likes and dislikes, personal styles, quirks, morals, ethics, inner spirit—that will go a long way toward avoiding two common mistakes of unseasoned writers:

1. having everyone speak with the same voice; and

2. developing a character that does something completely uncharacteristic.

One of the best ways to test how well you know your characters is to write the One-Page Intro.

EXERCISE

To start, write down everything you want your audience to know about your main character. What are the five most important traits I need my audience to know about my main character? (And please don't include things like hair color or height, unless that's highly relevant to the story.)

Now write a single scene where all of these traits are conveyed to the audience without using dialogue. In other words, no one says, "Gosh, Donna, you seem so lonely." Show us the raw palpability of her loneliness.

Once you've done this with your main character, pick two or three significant supporting characters and write a scene for each of them. None of these should be longer than a page.

For my main character, I like to make this the first scene in the movie. It can have nothing to do with the rest of the film, but it opens with a snapshot of who this person is and, ultimately, what the entire movie will be about.

As an example, consider the opening scene of my script *PR*, which follows.

FADE IN:

Through the back of a large fish tank are the water-distorted faces of ALEXANDRA, an attractive woman in her forties, who is crouched next to her two daughters, MELODY, 8, and TANYA, 5.

The three of them are happily giggling at the sight of the tank. The young girls excitedly point at different fish, proclaiming this one then that one to be the favorite.

While the girls stare at the fish, Alex stands and looks around for someone. She spots him.

ALEX
Todd.

TODD, Alex's husband, an imposing, handsome man, comes over. This is the picture of the perfect American family enjoying an outing together.

Alex nods her head to the side, and Todd nods in agreement.

> TODD
> Hey girls, let's go get dessert.

He takes the girls by their hands and leads them away from the fish tank.

Alex turns and motions to a MAN behind the counter.

> ALEX
> That one.

She points at a rainbow trout, and the man fishes it out with a net.
It turns out they're not in a pet shop or an aquarium. This is an upscale grocery store.

The counter clerk flips the unsuspecting fish onto a steel table and WHACK! He cuts off its head.

Now, there are a number of things you still don't know about Alex, like what she does for a living or her family background, but think about what you do know.

(*Note:* It's not an accident that there's no slug line. The scene loses all of its punch if it opens with INT. GROCERY STORE—DAY, so I chose not to include that, and it has never been a problem. If the writing is compelling enough, people ignore it when you break the rules.)

Now, back to what we know about Alex:

1. She's married.

   What do you know about her marriage? They're out together as a family, they have an unspoken understanding of what the other needs; they seem to be a good team. Overall, you can say this is a good marriage, and maybe go as far as to say it's a marriage of equals.

2. She's a mother.

   A good mother? She's giggling with her children, enjoying their company, but when it comes time to do something a bit shocking, she makes sure they are protected. She shields them from her own unpleasant behavior.

3. This family is not poor.

   In fact, they are doing quite well. They shop in the kind of grocery store where fish are swimming in tanks before you buy them.

4. She's ruthless.

   Did you see it coming, the beheading of the fish? That's important. I want the audience to be thinking about what Alex is capable of right from the start. They should also realize that things in this movie that seem to be one thing (a fun, public aquarium) can turn out to be something else entirely (the sudden, bloody demise of an innocent fish).

5. Between Alex and Todd, she's the one who does the dirty work.

   There's probably more that can be read into it, but those are the things I wanted to convey before I wrote the scene.

   This script has been optioned by three different producers, has had two directors attached plus an A-list actress, and continues to be my primary writing sample. Throughout countless development sessions, that scene—the first page of the script—has never changed. Not a word.

   That's how you know you've nailed it.

   So before you write your script, think about whose stories you are telling. Write a scene—especially an opening scene—that conveys it all on one page, without using your dialogue to tell us the details of your characters. If you can do that, you truly have mastered a key aspect of screenwriting.

HOWARD ALLEN

Better Than Irony

HOWARD ALLEN is a professional actor, playwright, director, screenwriter and literary manager/dramaturge who began as a journalist.
He was a featured speaker at the Sixth Annual Screenwriters Expo.
His production company is Coyote Moon Films. He is the writer and
director of SE HABLA ESPAÑOL.

While this should come as no surprise, screenwriting is closer
to writing narrative poetry and graphic novels than it is to
writing prose fiction. The final product is a blueprint for
other collaborators, especially actors and directors, to finish telling the
story. Working as both an actor and director has given me some fun
insight into this kind of storytelling.

Still, this form equips writers with at least one spectacular tool
for involving an audience (reader): *dramatic irony*. Better than plain
irony, dramatic irony creates wonderful anticipation and tension in
an audience—literally keeping them guessing and on the edge of
their seats.

Don't get me wrong; plain irony can be very entertaining: The
most superficial of women can become a successful Harvard Law
graduate if that's what it takes to follow her boyfriend (LEGALLY
BLONDE). Or a very honest and caring single mom can jump into a
dangerous criminal world by smuggling people in the trunk of her
car if that's what it takes for her to get the money to get a better
mobile home for her and her kids (the amazing FROZEN RIVER).

But I'm going to tell you right now that in those two movies, the
dramatic irony trumps the plain irony. Dramatic irony contains two
working parts in its little machine: (a) a secret the audience is in on

with at least one character and (b) the knowledge that at least one other character is not in on the secret.

Audiences love it when a confident screenwriter (or playwright or even a dang novelist) plays this game with them. Examples: It really works when we know that that same superficial woman is hiding her real qualifications and intellectual skills from everyone else at Harvard Law with very comic results (LEGALLY BLONDE). Or when we know the honest single mom has to hide her criminal activity from her kids, her ex, her family and even the friendly local sheriff who's taken an interest in her. The tension is palpable in the audience rooting for Melissa Leo in FROZEN RIVER.

There are whole movies built on dramatic irony. The two I love to use in my workshops are MRS. DOUBTFIRE and THE FUGITIVE.

What's the secret in MRS. DOUBTFIRE? Of course, we know and Robin Williams's character knows and his gay brother, whose partner is an expert in special makeup effects, know that the Scottish nanny is really Robin trying to get to be with his kids. His wife and kids and everyone else in San Francisco do not know. This situation creates tremendous comic tension through most of the movie.

What's the secret in THE FUGITIVE? Of course, we know and Harrison Ford's character and the one-armed guy know that Harrison's Dr. Kimble did not kill his wife. The federal marshal (Tommy Lee Jones), the police, the doctor's coworkers at the research hospital and everyone else in Chicago do not know he's an escaped good guy trying to prove his innocence rather than an escaped killer. Tremendous suspense comes from this device through most of the movie.

EXERCISE

So let's start the exercise right now:

Take out a story or screenplay of your own. Write down the name of your protagonist (impress your friends: call this person the POV, or point-of-view, character). Write what the character is trying to do in one scene or in the story as a whole. Is this goal a secret from anyone? If it is, or even if it isn't, write down another character that you can exclude from the secret of the goal. Now write a dialogue scene with that character and your POV character, who is still hiding the secret. See how much more tension this gives you?

Next, find or create a character to serve as your POV character's opponent. Write a scene with this opponent planning something really bad for the POV character. Now write a dialogue scene for the opponent—still hiding the secret—and your protagonist. The sparks you see flying in the audience or reader are from dramatic irony.

Do this exploration with any good movie you watch. You can thank me later—during your Oscar acceptance speech.

CHARACTER DEVELOPMENT

SYD FIELD

On Creating Character

SYD FIELD has authored eight books on screenwriting, including *Screenplay*, *The Screenwriter's Workbook* and *The Screenwriter's Problem Solver*. He is on the faculty of the Masters of Professional Writing program at the University of Southern California and teaches screenwriting and storytelling workshops. He has served as a screenplay consultant for Twentieth Century–Fox, Touchstone Pictures, TriStar Pictures and Universal Studios, and has also worked with many prominent filmmakers.

Creating character is a process that will be with you from the beginning to the end, from FADE IN to FADE OUT. It is an ongoing educational progression, an experience that continues expanding as you go deeper and deeper into your characters' lives.

There are many ways to approach writing character. Some writers mull over their characters for a long period of time and then, when they feel they "know" them, jump in and start writing. Others create an elaborate list of characterizations; some writers list the major elements of their character's life on three-by-five-inch cards; some write extensive outlines or draw diagrams of behavior. Some use pictures from magazines and newspapers to help them *see* what their characters look like. "That's my character," they say. They may tack the pictures above their work area so they can "be with" their characters during their work time. Some use well-known actors and actresses as models for characters.

Anything that makes it easier for you to create your character is a good tool. Choose your own way. You can use some, all or none of the tools mentioned here; it doesn't matter. What matters is whether it works. If it works, use it. If it doesn't, don't. Find your own way, your own style in creating character. The important thing is that it's got to work for you.

One of the most insightful character tools is a *character biography*. The character biography is a free-association, automatic-writing exercise that reveals your character's history from birth up until the time your story begins. It captures and defines the forces, physical and emotional, internal and external, that are working on your character during those formative years that fashions his or her behavior. It is a process that reveals character.

Start at the beginning. Is your character male or female? How old is she when the story begins? Where does she live? What city or country? Where was she born? Was she an only child, or did she have any brothers and sisters? What kind of relationship did she have with her brothers and sisters? Was it good, bad, confining, adventurous? What kind of childhood would you say your character had? Would you consider it happy? Or sad? Was it physically or medically challenging, with illness or physical problems? What about her relationship to her parents? Was it good or bad? Was she a mischievous child getting into a lot of trouble or was she quiet and withdrawn, preferring her own inner life instead of a social one? Was she stubborn and willful? Did she have a problem with authority? Do you think she was socially active, made friends easily and got along well with relatives and other children? What kind of a child would you say she was? Good or bad? Was she outgoing and extroverted or a shy and studious introvert? *Let your imagination guide you.*

EXERCISE

Write character biographies for two or three of your main characters in about seven to ten pages. More if you need to. Focus on their early years. Where was each character born? What did his or her father and mother do for a living? Describe each character's relationship with his or her parents. Does each character have brothers or sisters? What are their relationships like—friendly and supportive, or angry and combative?

Define the other relationships the character had in his or her second and third ten years, and see how these relationships formed his or her character. Remember Henry James's Theory of Illumination: Every character sheds light on your main character.

Before you begin writing your biography, think about your character(s) for a few days, then set aside a time when you can work two or three hours without interruption: no phone calls, no TV, no e-mail, video games or visits from friends. It may help to lower the lights or turn on some soft music. Then start "throwing down" thoughts, words and ideas about the character. Just let it come out. Don't worry about grammar, punctuation, spelling or bad writing. Just get your thoughts down on paper, and don't worry about anything else. You're not going to show these pages to anyone; it's only a tool for you to use while you discover your characters and "get to know them." If you want to include parts of your character biography in your screenplay, fine. But just get your character down on paper. Free-associate. Let your characters discover who they are.

Do the same with the professional, personal and private lives of your character. Write a page or two about what your character does for a living, his or her relationships and hobbies. You might even go into a "day in the life" of your character and write what his or her day looks like. What does she do from the moment she gets out of bed till she goes to sleep at night? Write it in a page or two. If you need to write more, write more. If you can do it in less, do it in less.

If you discover any areas in a character's life that you feel unsure or insecure about, write it in a page or two. Do some research, if necessary. Free-associate. The relationship between you and your characters is like the relationship between two best friends. You decide what you need, then define it.

If you don't know whether you should write something or not, write it! It's *your* script, *your* story, *your* characters, *your* dramatic choices. When you have completed your assignment, you will know your characters as if they were good friends.

BILL JOHNSON

Give Me a Dramatic Truth or Give Me Death!

BILL JOHNSON is the author of *A Story Is a Promise* and *Deep Characterization*, a writing workbook, and webmaster of a site that explores principles of storytelling through reviews of popular movies. He's taught storytelling at the Screenwriting Expo and at writing conferences around the United States.

To satisfy an audience a story must ring true. One way to create a story that rings true is for the storyteller to understand how to create characters and situations that embody what I call dramatic truths.

In THE WIZARD OF OZ, Dorothy wants to find her way home; the Tin Man, a heart; the Scarecrow, a brain; the Cowardly Lion, courage.

Rocky wants to be somebody.

The Velveteen Rabbit wants to be real.

Harry Potter wants to fit in.

Each character embodies a truth that defines that character. These truths are dramatic because they are in need of resolution. Will Dorothy find her way home, Rocky become somebody, Harry fit in, the Velveteen Rabbit become real?

Every story, every significant character in a story, even the environment of a story, can represent a dramatic truth. Conversely, a character, plot event or scene description that doesn't represent a dramatic truth can risk appearing to be literal and inconsequential.

That Dorothy is twelve and has black hair are literal truths. Literal truths describe; dramatic truths evoke who a character is and what he or she wants.

212

The point of getting across a character's dramatic truth with his or her introduction isn't to suggest that one has to "spill the beans" in the first scene of a screenplay. But to understand the dramatic truth of a story, of a character in a story or even the truth of the environment of a story (Kansas as well as Oz ring true) is to have a compass to what words to use to create visual images that convey purpose and meaning. This is vital in screenwriting because of the necessity of an economy of words.

Many writers, to avoid being overly descriptive, lean toward offering flat, literal descriptions that speak no dramatic truth. A woman is blonde, twenty-nine, athletic. A man is thirty-two, stocky, handsome.

I very often read scripts where characters have a role in a story's plot, have a presence in scenes, but where the characters and plot events represent no dramatic truth. Such stories can offer resolution, but they're like a bowl containing the ingredients of a cake instead of a finished cake. Such stories and characters are not fulfilling. I see this kind of presentation of literal truths about characters most often at the beginning of a story. It makes the beginning of a script the weakest part of the story.

I've found that many writers have been taught to never be obvious, but this leads many screenwriters to become obscure.

EXERCISE

To help writers create a dramatic truth, I use the diagram on the following page. I ask that writers start with an obvious statement about who a character is. I then ask the writer to create an obscure sentence that suggests nothing about what's "true" for a character, then a sentence that is dramatically suggestive of a character's truth.

Understanding the truth of a character can help guide a writer to making choices that are dramatic and suggestive.

Start a story with something that speaks clearly and directly to me as a reader, even if it's just a few words about a character or a story's environment. Make me want to know more. Make me want to share that character's journey in a story. Then you'll have larger-than-life characters that come off the page and embed themselves into the imagination of your script reader.

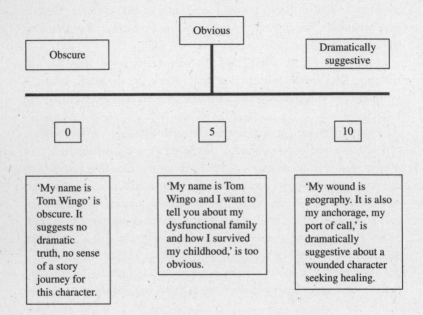

Obscure	Obvious	Dramatically suggestive
0	5	10
'My name is Tom Wingo' is obscure. It suggests no dramatic truth, no sense of a story journey for this character.	'My name is Tom Wingo and I want to tell you about my dysfunctional family and how I survived my childhood,' is too obvious.	'My wound is geography. It is also my anchorage, my port of call,' is dramatically suggestive about a wounded character seeking healing.

LINDA COWGILL

Creating Characters Who Work for You, Not Against You

LINDA COWGILL is an award-winning screenwriter, lecturer and author of the books *Writing Short Films*, *The Art of Plotting* and *Secrets of Screenplay Structure*. Currently, she heads the Screenwriting Department at the Los Angeles Film School, where she teaches. She lives with her family in Santa Monica.

One of the hardest concepts for new screenwriters to master is that of the active protagonist. Passive protagonists populate the pages of countless screenplays. As a screenwriting teacher and screenplay consultant, I see this all the time. But don't just take my word for it. According to a reader friend of mine who's read over a thousand scripts for Chris Columbus's production company, 1492, it's the single most common mistake among experienced screenwriters and novices alike. Even writers who are able to reach the highest echelons of the studio system are guilty of this.

A passive protagonist can hold a reader's interest for a while, but as the plot plods along with the protagonist moving from scene to scene with seemingly no real aim, a story loses tension and momentum, and the audience loses interest.

Beginning writers often confuse a strong protagonist with a complicated biography. Then they tell the audience about their characters in dialogue instead of showing them in action. Even when they pay heed to the old screenwriting adage "Show, don't tell," the true meaning is lost on them. They give information in flashbacks or in scenes where the writer "shows" the audience something about the character's backstory. Characters may have interesting histories, but this isn't what interests the audience. The audience doesn't want to *hear* the story; they want to *see* it. They want characters who act and make things happen. And they want to see characters with *character*. What this means is that the *strength* of a character's personality (that's Character with a capital C) is tested and demonstrated by the conflict of the story.

Drama needs action and conflict not only to create tension and momentum to hold the audience's attention but also to test the characters. Their actions under duress demonstrate who the characters really are, on the basis of their decisions and choices. This is what really interests the moviegoing public.

How do we create an active protagonist? The simple answer is that he must have something important he wants and will struggle for.

Time and again, new writers give their protagonists wants that are too abstract. "My character wants love," my students say. But you can't plot out a story if we don't know what "love" means to the protagonist. Romeo wants Juliet; she represents love. He acts on his desire in spite of the conflict between their families. Specific desires make the abstract real to the audience by illustrating why characters do what they do for their goals.

Some criticize this emphasis on the "want," saying that it flattens a plot. This can be true if it's all that's driving a character and story. To work, the *want/goal* then has to be dramatic and dangerous, and the action intense. Think RAIDERS OF THE LOST ARK or JURASSIC PARK.

But the *want* is only part of the equation. Great writers craft characters that are driven by *desires.* Plural. These desires are *wants* and *needs.* By focusing on them we reveal a character's different sides.

A want is a goal, a clear objective the character consciously wants. A need is an unconscious desire that motivates the character to act. If you were to interview your character and ask her what she wants, she could tell you what and why. Now, her "why" may not be the real motivating force for her actions, but this "why" would be how she understands her reasons.

A need prickles beneath the surface and influences a character's actions and behavior, often in surprising ways. April in REVOLUTIONARY ROAD needs to leave her unsatisfying marriage, but her goal is to convince Frank to quit his job and move the family to Paris. The conflict between her need and her want makes for a painful, tragic end to her story.

Sometimes the conflict among a character's stated goal, his want, and his unconscious need is what's most interesting in a story. Movies from CASABLANCA to THE READER use this incompatibility among goals, wants and needs to wrest powerful drama from their story situations.

If there isn't a full-on antagonist, the protagonist must still meet with a strong conflict. Whether it's THE DIVING BELL AND THE BUTTERFLY or TOUCHING THE VOID, characters must face a sustained dramatic conflict to create a compelling story.

EXERCISE

Once we know who the character is, four simple questions can help you craft answers that produce active characters instead of passive ones:

1. What does my character want?

    Make sure that the main characters' goals and objectives are specific, clear and difficult to achieve. There has to be enough energy in this goal to drive a plot for the duration of the movie. In SLUMDOG MILLIONAIRE, Jamal wants Latika and will stop at nothing to get her.

2. Why does he want it?

    The reasons for the characters' goals must be credible and authentic. Jamal wants Latika because he loves her.

3. Why can't he get it?

    When a specific protagonist/antagonist relationship anchors the script, the answers to these questions should be in direct opposition. In FROST/NIXON, David Frost wants the Nixon interview for the notoriety and prestige it will award him; Nixon wants it for the quick cash and believes he will squash the light-weight TV personality. Neither character really understands what he is up against.

4. What does he need?

A character's need can cause more conflict or be the solution to it. Either way, the need is *usually connected to the character's arc*. In both THE READER and REVOLUTIONARY ROAD, we see characters whose needs destroy them. In SLUMDOG MILLION-AIRE, Jamal's need sustains and fulfills him.

Keep handy the answers to these questions for all your important characters. They not only will help you understand who your char-acters are, but also will allow you to see what's driving them, so that they can drive your plot. It is a time-tested method to take a passive protagonist and turn her into an active one.

MADELINE DiMAGGIO

Approach Character Like an
Actor . . . from the Inside Out!

MADELINE DIMAGGIO, writer/producer/consultant, has over forty-five
hours of produced TV and film, including sitcoms, one-hour dramas, TV
pilots, soaps, animation, cable movies and feature films. She previously
has written under contract to Paramount Studios and is currently a
partner at Honest Engine Films. She is currently writing the television
movie-of-the-week *Panic* for Incendo Productions. She is the author of
How to Write for Television.

Screenwriters are often so busy with the hard work of writing that we stay on the outside of our characters, telling them
where to go instead of letting them talk to us. It's when we feel
them from the inside that great things happen.

I began my career as an actor and I have found acting techniques
to be very handy in helping writers with the "interior view."

ABOUT SCHMIDT opens on a private moment, with Schmidt
sitting in a cleaned-out, windowless office, looking up at the clock as
the seconds count down to his retirement. With each tick we sense
his life slipping away; we feel his dread. When the clock strikes, he
gets up, looks around one last time, then shuts the door. From this
moment on, Schmidt needs to find meaning in his life. We laugh at
him, we cry with him and we dread becoming like him. No matter
what our circumstances are in life, we identify with this character's
futility. Schmidt, played by Jack Nicholson, is so layered, so vacant,
so deprived of his own potential that you ache for him.

You might say it was the brilliance of Nicholson that made

Schmidt, but it was the character of Schmidt that brought the genius of Nicholson on board to play the part. Schmidt, created by novelist Louis Begley and superbly crafted by screenwriter Alexander Payne, was obviously felt from the inside out.

In LARS AND THE REAL GIRL, Nancy Oliver paints Lars as an emotionally wounded young man who lives in a garage apartment behind his brother's house. We first meet Lars dressed for church, looking out the window, obviously set apart from the world. His room is austere: There is one cup and one plate, and old furniture he's had since he was a kid. At church, we see he's a kind soul, always doing things for people. They like him, but he's painfully shy and awkward. Alone that night, in his garage apartment, Oliver has Lars sitting on his bed in the dark. He's still in his church clothes; it's four a.m. He hasn't moved. He's been awake all night. Later, when Lars goes to the mall, he wanders aimlessly and sees nothing but families and couples at the food court. "He feels his isolation," Oliver writes, "like a physical illness."

There is such a visceral truth in the character of Lars, we know Nancy Oliver somehow found that place of isolation somewhere within herself.

Great characters don't just happen; they are explored. As screenwriters, how can we do this? How can we find that emotional state, or memory, so that we can create from a place of truth instead of fiction?

EXERCISE

Sense memory is recalling a feeling. It is not enough to say your character hurts. What is hurt? How does hurt feel? How does hurt react? What is it like to feel truly alone or to feel envious? Find that place within yourself.

Try to use your five senses. Remembering the "why" or the circumstances of how you got this feeling is not important; what matters is the feeling. Think of where you were. Was it in a room? Were there objects you can recall? What were you looking at? Touching? Was there a sound, a view, a smell? Remembering your physical environment can be very helpful in taking you back to that place. Go there when you need to evoke a similar feeling in your character, or write a pivotal scene, or create a crucial tone in the story.

Sense memory takes you out of the peripheral "view" and out of your own way as a writer. You are drawing on your own truth to make characters live their truth. You are moving into their interior.

Subtext is the layer of action and dialogue where we all hide. It is where we camouflage our true intentions and feelings. Good actors are good observers. They study subtext and identify it in as many situations as possible. Like actors, witness the subtext in your own conversations and actions. Ask yourself, what am I really saying here? What am I really doing? What is happening beneath my words? What am I covering up? What do I really want? What am I afraid to hear? Go to this place with your characters. Go there when you're writing their dialogue.

It is the screenwriter's job to know the character's weak spots; how they are revealed separates the good writers from the great. Say the character's subtext out loud. Dialogue happens on two levels, the spoken and the unspoken. Think of writing subtext as playing a game of "hide-and-seek." Let the characters feel safe, allow them the cover-up, and then, in their most vulnerable moments, let their true motives and feelings start to peek through. These vulnerable moments are almost always a result of conflict. That's when we all let down our defenses. Like the actor, work with resisting obvious exposition. Example: If a character is weak, play him as covering up his weakness. Inner conflict and subtext always work.

Private moments are peeks into the character's soul. This is where the character is revealed in his or her most vulnerable and raw state. To reach this inner core, writers, like actors, should draw on themselves first. Who are you when no one is watching? Where is that most vulnerable, raw part of you? How do you hide it from the world? Is it ugly? Does it show fear or weakness? What is the best visual you could use to depict this character trait on film? Where are you? How could you reveal this secret? How can you show it without one word of dialogue? Now think of your character. Find that window into him or her.

You can find excellent examples of private moments in ABOUT SCHMIDT and LARS AND THE REAL GIRL (as described earlier).

BILLY MERNIT

The Character's Trailer Shot

BILLY MERNIT is the author of the screenwriting textbook *Writing the Romantic Comedy* and *Imagine Me and You: A Novel*. He has written for NBC's *Santa Barbara* and teaches screenwriting at UCLA Extension, while serving as both a private script consultant and a story analyst for Universal.

Supposedly the three most important aspects of screenwriting are *structure, structure* and *structure*. But as a script consultant and teacher, I find that the hardest thing for aspiring screenwriters (and a number of the pros) to get right is *character*. I read too many scripts where the plot points land on the right pages, but the screenwriters have neglected a crucial job: nailing down the essence of their story's protagonist.

All good characters have a clear purpose, are credible, and inspire empathy. And all great characters are complicated. We're fascinated by walking contradictions who seem to have complex inner lives. But developing complexity for a fictional creation can be a tricky pursuit. Sometimes so many elements go into the character mix concocted by a writer that what gets lost sight of is: What is *the* most important thing the audience needs to know about this person? What's the character's bottom line, the one aspect of his or her personality that truly defines who she or he is supposed to be?

Defining character in a clear, vivid cinematic shorthand is the purpose of an exercise I use in many of my classes. Though I generally have students do it early on in the development of their projects, it's equally helpful when they're approaching a rewrite. I ask them to imagine they're watching a trailer of the finished movie they're about to write or rewrite and to design the shot—one shot—that will tell the audience the *most important thing* they need to know about the film's protagonist.

You've seen such shots in trailers: the quick defining gag that tells you "Oh, he's *that* guy," or the brief intense dramatic moment that announces "She's like *this*." It might be a scruffy Al Pacino as a bank robber excitedly whipping up the crowd outside the bank, yelling "Attica!" or the outlandishly dressed, self-conscious, adorably all-over-the-place Diane Keaton as Annie Hall, muttering "La-dee-dah!" Take away the dialogue, and a strong defining character moment still resonates. What could be more iconic than that shot of John Cusack as Lloyd Dobler holding the blaster over his head in SAY ANYTHING, or Julie Andrews twirling around with arms outstretched amid those hills that are alive with THE SOUND OF MUSIC?

I once saw this moment in real life: On a busy corner in Los Angeles, a woman fumbling with her overstuffed bag nearly dropped it and thus nearly stepped off the curb into traffic before she righted herself. On that same corner, two men witnessed this: One instinctively moved toward her as if to offer help, and the other man just stood there, observing. I learned something about all three of these people's characters in that single "shot." You can learn even more by designing such a movie moment for your lead.

EXERCISE

1. The first step is sometimes the most difficult: identifying that single characteristic. Think about your protagonist in terms of "How would I describe this person to a friend in one brief phrase or even a single word?" This kind of meditation forces you to get down to essentials. If you were designing a single image for Indiana Jones, for example, would you go with his statement "I hate snakes"? No, because that's merely a personality tic. You'd more likely work with an image of, say, Indy snapping his bullwhip to swipe an apple from someone and then taking a bite out of it with a saucy grin. Is your character courageous? Indecisive? Quick

tempered? Shy? Determine the most basic aspect of who that character is and what personality trait he or she most strongly embodies.

2. Now think through your story and find a moment—written or as yet unwritten—where that primary characteristic is expressed. The trick is to think visually, to come up with *active imagery*. A handsome hunk smiles at a passing woman. Does she smile back, avert her eyes with a blush or ignore him? Say the woman smiles seductively and sniffs at the guy's aftershave as she walks by . . . then shows us she's lifted his watch. Ten seconds, and we know what that woman's about, so if you've resorted to dialogue in your shot, then try a rewrite that's nonverbal.

3. Describe your shot to someone who knows nothing about this character or your story. Did he get it? Or did he misinterpret your intention? Any reported confusion means you haven't been clear and inventive enough. This exercise is spinach for the imagination. And once you've created a trailer moment that works, you can use it as a touchstone for that character's essence throughout your draft.

CHRISTINE CONRADT

The Scene That Doesn't Exist

CHRISTINE CONRADT has written more than twenty-five made-for-TV movies that have aired on FOX, Lifetime, LMN, USA and other networks. Several of her screenplays have also been produced as independent feature films, such as SUMMER'S BLOOD, STRIPPED NAKED and HOTEL CALIFORNIA. She is a native of Lincoln, Nebraska, and currently lives in Los Angeles.

Writer's block is the nemesis of creative flow. There you are: Everything's going right. Punchy, clever dialogue rolls off your fingers. Your characters are dynamic, engaging, layered, sympathetic even! The acts are practically breaking themselves! Just as you embark on the scene they'll play as they announce your Oscar nomination, writer's block crashes your little creativity party and beats your muse into a pulpy, unrecognizable mess.

As a professional screenwriter whose mortgage depends on delivering a quality screenplay by a predetermined date, I don't have the luxury of taking time off from a project and hoping the muse will eventually reincarnate. Neither should you. Writer's block must be attacked head-on *immediately* and forced aside so that you may continue toward that resplendent FADE OUT. Early in my career, I learned a technique that's helped me time and again to overcome even the most crippling block: Remove your characters from the problematic scene and write a new scene that will never be in your movie.

Writer's block obviously comes from the pressure to write a scene we don't know how to write because we aren't sure what should come next. When this happens, we become fixated on plot and forget that there are actually two sources of conflict in a screenplay:

plot and character. In the blockbuster TITANIC, Rose's plot conflict is straightforward: She's on a ship that's sinking. Her character
conflicts come from her personal traits, strengths and deficiencies:
She's supposed to marry a man she doesn't like and she doesn't have
the guts to break off her relationship; her mother is relying on her
marriage for financial security; and she feels responsible for Jack's
bogus arrest. Focusing on these character attributes is a good way
to overcome your plot problems because the two are inherently connected. Shift your focus back to who these characters really are, what
drives them and what they really want by eliminating plot entirely—
at least for the moment.

EXERCISE

First, think hard about the two central characters in TITANIC: *Jack*
and *Rose*. On paper, write their names and numbers one to ten under
each. Then list ten attributes that define each of them.

JACK	ROSE
1. artistic/good at drawing	1. suicidal/feels trapped
2.	2.
3.	3.
4.	4.
5.	5.
6.	6.
7.	7.
8.	8.
9.	9.
10.	10.

What did you write for Jack? Did you remember that he was a
risk taker? That he won his ticket by gambling? Did you write that

he came from an impoverished background? That he was "socially unsophisticated"? How about Rose? Did you remember how comfortable she felt drinking beer and dancing with the third-class passengers? Did you write that her father had died? That the family money was running out? Did you remember she liked and collected expensive art?

Now write a scene between Jack and Rose that *would never have been in the movie*. Let's put them in a New York City pizzeria together. What would they order? Who would feel more at home? What if some drunkard were to spill beer on Rose? When the bill comes and they realize they don't have enough money, what does Jack suggest they do? How does Rose want to handle it? Focus on who these two are as characters by looking at their list of attributes and decide what would cause conflict between the two as a couple or for each individually.

Remember, the scene will never be in your script, so you can create anything you want. Maybe the pizza place is robbed while they're there. Maybe Jack sees someone from his past. Maybe Rose can speak a little Italian and realizes the owner knew her father in Europe. Anything can happen. Just write the scene without any pressure to make it "good."

This is the same exercise you should do with your own characters when you're blocked. Pluck them out of their situation and drop them into a scene completely unrelated to your story. Let them be stranded at sea, stuck in war-torn Bosnia, enjoying the state fair, lost in the woods, invited to the inaugural ball . . . Regardless of what you write, the process will produce character-related conflict or dialogue that you can then transfer to your screenplay to help you decide what should come next and hurdle right over that block.

JAMES BONNET

The Key to Charismatic Characters

JAMES BONNET was elected twice to the board of directors of the Writers Guild of America and has acted in or written more than forty television shows and features. He is the author of *Stealing Fire from the Gods: The Complete Guide to Story for Writers and Filmmakers.*

In the early 1990s, I was reading Homer's *Iliad* to fathom why that story had endured for three thousand years, when I suddenly realized that all of the major characters in the story were the ultimate best or worst examples of some important human quality, which is to say they were all personifications of some human quality that had been taken to the quintessential. Zeus is the most powerful god. Achilles is the greatest warrior. Helen of Troy is the most beautiful woman. Paris is the handsomest man, and so on.

I then looked at other great stories and discovered the same thing. King Arthur is the most chivalrous king. King Herod is the nastiest tyrant. Sampson is the strongest man. Great stories, myths and legends are, in fact, dominated by quintessential elements, and it is the real key to their immortality and success.

Taking a character to the quintessential means making that character the best or worst example of something. If you make something the most extraordinary example, you will make that idea more intriguing and more memorable. The quintessential can be applied to any element of your story, but is especially effective when applied to the professions and dominant character traits of your characters. If you take these dimensions to the quintessential, you can make your characters truly charismatic, and that will add significantly to the power of your work.

Harry Potter is a young wizard, but he is not just an ordinary young wizard; he is the most famous and powerful young wizard of all time. In GLADIATOR, Russell Crowe is the greatest gladiator. Sherlock Holmes is the world's greatest detective. Dracula is the quintessential vampire. Iago in *Othello* is the most treacherous servant. Jack the Ripper and Hannibal Lecter are quintessential serial killers. Superman is the greatest superhero. All of which adds considerably to our fascination with and interest in these stories.

Sherlock Holmes's dominant character trait is deductive reasoning. He is more skilled than all other detectives in that regard. Achilles' dominant trait is anger, and *The Iliad* is a revelation of that human attribute. Othello's is jealousy. Ebenezer Scrooge's is miserliness. Archie Bunker's is bigotry. Don Juan's is lust. Macbeth's is blind ambition. Hitler, as a story character, is the quintessential megalomaniac. Rick's dominant trait in CASABLANCA is disillusionment—he's a disillusioned patriot and lover. They are all quintessential personifications of their dominant character traits. That is the secret of their success, and that is the trick to making your characters truly memorable and even merchandisable. You take their dominant traits to the quintessential.

EXERCISE

1. As you are developing your central character (or any character for that matter), work with that character until you have defined his or her profession (doctor, lawyer, warrior, detective, spy, etc.) and have discovered his or her dominant character trait (prejudice, arrogance, conceit, courage, sincerity, generosity, loyalty, jealousy, lust, greed, etc.).

2. Learn as much as you can about those isolated dimensions by researching and by getting in touch with those dimensions in yourself through self-reflection.

3. Strive to create a definitive portrait of that character's professional function by making your central character not just an okay spy but a great spy, detective, warrior, lawyer or doctor,

who personifies the quintessence of his or her profession—into another Sherlock Holmes, Achilles, Clarence Darrow or Albert Schweitzer.

4. Then do the same with the character's dominant trait and develop this newly created character into the quintessence of that dominant quality. If you're creating a charismatic figure like Napoleon, take a quality like inflation or military genius and work with it until you develop that character into the quintessence of one of those qualities.

    If you're creating an immortal character like Dracula, take a dominant quality like blood lust and make that character the quintessence of that characteristic. But be sure to put that dominant quality in the context of a fully realized human being. If you just play the dominant trait and leave out the rest of the human being, you will create a stereotype or a cliché.

5. Monitor your feelings throughout this creative process, and identify the intuitive feelings that are helping you make creative decisions. The truth about anger and lust and greed, and all of the functions and skills of a great professional are inside you. When you use your intuition and a trial-and-error creative process to communicate with the unconscious source of your creativity, you are, in effect, teasing the truth about those qualities to the surface.

So let yourself be guided by these intuitive feelings and slowly develop your characters into quintessential personifications of their professions and dominant qualities by trial and error, by trying this and that until you create a combination of qualities that gives you goose bumps and chills up your spine.

When you do this with your characters, they will become symbolic. You can put them on a T-shirt, and they will have impact and meaning. If you put Harry Potter, Hannibal Lecter, Archie Bunker or Scrooge on a T-shirt, it will mean something because they personify some important human quality.

When the characters, events and dominant character traits

actually reach these pinnacles and make this psychological connection, they become charismatic, and people will be attracted to them and influenced by them even if they don't know what they mean.

Characters that possess this charisma become like deities: Oedipus, Moses, Hamlet, Romeo and Juliet and King Arthur are unforgettable. And Chaplin's tramp, Rhett Butler, Dorothy, E.T., Dracula, Mickey Mouse, Batman and Superman are definite steps in the right direction. Put Superman on a little boy's pajamas, and he will feel stronger. He'll try to fly around the room. Put Einstein on your T-shirt, and you'll feel smarter. Put Genghis Khan on your leather jacket, and you'll be ready for a Harley. That's charisma.

GLENN GERS

Go Ask Rosenkrantz

GLENN GERS has been a working screenwriter for fifteen years. Glenn's original screenplay for the Showtime movie OFF SEASON was nominated for a Writers Guild Award and won an Emmy. Glenn wrote the caper comedy MAD MONEY and (with Dan Pyne) the legal thriller FRACTURE. He also wrote, directed and coedited the indie feature DISFIGURED, a movie about women and weight.

<pre>
          ROSENKRANTZ
     They had it in for us,
     didn't they? Right from
     the beginning. Who'd have
     thought that we were so
     important?
</pre>

Two men are standing alone on an empty stage. They are lost. They are confused. Their uncertainty about what to do next has forced them to confront a larger uncertainty regarding the meaning of their existence. Yet, strangely, they are not screenwriters.

They are the title characters in Tom Stoppard's dazzling play *Rosenkrantz and Guildenstern Are Dead,* and if you are trying to write a screenplay, they can save your life. Stoppard examines the philosophical and emotional consequences of being a minor character in someone else's tragedy. In doing so, he illuminates a truth so obvious it is easy to neglect: Every character moves through your screenplay unaware that he or she exists for the sake of a plot. They all believe they're the star, the hero, the fulcrum of events. They enter each scene intent upon their own agenda and act according to their own needs.

When Harry met Sally, they were living their own lives. All Twelve Angry Men thought the jury room revolved around them. Central characters and their lowly, doomed messengers are all equally oblivious to the demands of genre and the contraption of your plot. Therefore, in order to write any scene, you need to look at it from each point of view, to understand its meaning within that character's separate story. A scene can be created only out of the conflicts, negotiations or exchanges between those stories in that moment.

The trick, then, is defining each character's needs and managing to weave your story out of such unruly, tangled threads. The best method I've found to help perform this feat of mental macramé is: Examine each character's story within your screenplay as if it were, in fact, *the* story. Take the ride with your characters and make sure the track you've set them on doesn't loop-the-loop or suddenly vanish, only to reappear on the other side of an abysmal chasm.

This is not merely a "character exercise." We are not trying to raise the self-esteem of imaginary people. If your characters do not operate from the rules of cause and effect, objectives and obstacles, then your movie will fall apart. Your story is literally made out of characters.

If you do this right, you will never write exposition again (i.e., characters speaking in order to educate the audience rather than to provoke a reaction from others in the scene). Furthermore, actors and directors will love you for it. Ask them; this is what they need to do their jobs. And screenwriters do not write for the "audience"; they write for actors and directors.

There are, of course, potentially hazardous side effects. You may become too interested in peripheral events. You may feel tempted to write too much stuff. You may realize that something you absolutely *need* a character to do is inconsistent, unbelievable or antidramatic and be forced to rethink your plot. I believe such "troubles" in moderation are useful, but if the symptoms persist, consult the weekend's top-ten list for a healthy dose of "Movies can do just fine making no sense at all."

Even movies that make no sense, though, need us to care about the characters. And we don't care because a character is a type of person or because the character is fashionable or good-looking, or has some freakish quirk. We care because the character wants something we can understand and is doing something to get it. That's what this exercise is about.

EXERCISE

Make a separate outline for each character that lists every scene in which the character appears, in order. Describe, as briefly as possible, what the character does in the scene. Ask yourself and answer—in writing—the following questions about the characters in each scene in each outline:

What is their objective—what do they *want*—in the story as a whole?

What is their objective in this scene?

How does the scene objective help them accomplish the story objective?

What is the obstacle to achieving their objective in this scene?

What action do they take in the scene?

Are the action and objectives specific, concrete and practical in the moment?

Is the action a logical result of what happened in their previous scene?

Does the action of this scene repeat the action of any other earlier scene?

What changes as a result of this action?

When you become lost, indecisive or uninspired, this exercise gets you out of the mire. It whispers to you the most vital sentence in all of screenwriting: *This is what happens now.*

DAVID SKELLY

Character Bones

DAVID SKELLY is a writer and director who was part of the story development team at Pixar Animation Studios that worked on TOY STORY 2, MONSTERS, INC. and CARS. He also wrote the screenplay for JACK & BEN, and recently worked on episodes for a new animated television series with Jennifer Skelly, his wife and writing partner. The Skellys teach story development at CalArts and are working on their upcoming book, *Improv for Writers*.

I don't know about you, but I go to the movies to feel something. I want to laugh out loud and get scared, and I want to let go of my manly façade and shed some tears, dangit! (It's dark in there. No one will see.) I want to go on an emotional journey. And I feel disappointed if I don't. Sure, the plot might be interesting, the settings beautiful, the dialogue snappy . . . but if my heart doesn't race, it all seems academic. And I kind of wish I could get my time and money back. So, writers, how can we write movies that *move* us as well as our audience?

Story structure is important, of course, but focusing only on the form can keep us trapped in the *analytical mind*. How can we get to the heart of our story so that we can get to the hearts of our audience? By playing pretend. Just like we did when we were kids. But wait a second . . . Screenwriting is work, right? It's a profession. A serious craft! What do I mean by *play pretend*? I mean no editing. No self-critique. No filters. Just make-believe. Sound fun? It is. It gets easier with practice—and it's essential to good storytelling.

The key to the following writing exercise is to act without reflection—to react emotionally—like a child. To improvise! This is jazz; let your emotions guide you, and let your characters' emotions guide *them*.

Before you write FADE IN, play this simple game to get to know your main character better. Go deeper than the skin. What is he really made of? Why does he act the way he does? What's his problem? What's his relationship to the other people in his life? That's the bones.

This isn't just backstory; it's autobiography. Written by your character for your character. It's a journal entry. It's a first-person description of how your character feels about what's happened in her life, how she feels about the other people around her. And how she feels will dictate what she does in your story and consequently how your audience will feel.

EXERCISE

1. Get a piece of paper. Yes, paper, the old-fashioned stuff. Set aside your laptop for a moment. You can type up your work later if you want.

2. Write this line: "Hi, my name is _____." It's just a primer. I know we probably wouldn't identify ourselves in the beginning of our own private journal entry, but it's an easy way to take care of that blank piece of paper. Depending on who your character is, he might not say "Hi" but "Hey," instead. Or "Hello." Or "What's up?" So, in a word or two, you've started to make a choice about the tone and voice of your character. Easy, right?

3. Now go for it. Write that journal entry from your character's point of view, in first person. Let your character guide your hand. Whatever comes into your mind. No censoring. You're just the secretary—the stenographer. Get it? What is your character thinking about today? (It needn't have anything at all to do with your script, but it will have everything to do with who your character is—and how he or she will behave in your story.) Need

a little something more to get started? Try using the following questions as springboards:

(a) *Who am I?* This über-question covers all kinds of things like: How old am I? What do I look like? What do I like to wear? And although these attributes may seem like they're superficial, they'll provide a surprising amount of insight into . . .

(b) *Where do I come from?* This is about your character's past. His history. Did I grow up with money? Or did I have to steal to survive? How did that affect me? What was my family like? Was it a loving family? Or was there trouble at home? What was it like where I grew up? Did I go to school? *What were my childhood dreams?* Your character's personal history is what makes him who he is, and it helps us understand . . .

(c) *How do I feel . . . about* everything:—politics, religion, breakfast cereals and, most important, relationships? Who are the people in my life? How do I feel about them?

Don't worry about answering all the questions. (Or any of them, for that matter; these are just examples to point you in the right direction.) Write about things that are relevant to your character today. This is stream-of-consciousness writing. It's not a pass/fail test. Whatever comes up is right, and wherever it leads is correct. Let your characters go. Let them say what they need to say. Let them go on an emotional journey, and your audience will follow.

MARILYN R. ATLAS

The Riddle of the Sphinx

MARILYN ATLAS is an award-winning producer and personal manager who works in the worlds of film, television and live theater. Among her film production credits is REAL WOMEN HAVE CURVES for HBO, which won the Audience Award at the Sundance Film Festival. Marilyn recently produced the musical version of REAL WOMEN HAVE CURVES in Los Angeles. The Goodman Theatre in Chicago will produce the show in 2010, with an eye to a possible run on Broadway.

Once I optioned the script of a young, promising writer. But one of my major concerns was that the character arc seemed too abrupt. I didn't believe in the change that had occurred. So, I wanted to know what this character would be like later in life, to see how traces of that future self would appear in the current incarnation of the character. The writer indulged me by following this exercise and listening to why I felt the character change was not as earned as it should be.

A whole inner life that would later subvert the character's best intentions years later came pouring out from the writer. We had tapped into the writer's secret passion for creating the character in the first place. What initially drew me to the script was the quirky concept and exotic underworld location, but now I felt like I was personally connecting to the protagonist.

It's very important to know the full life of the character, even if you don't plan to show the character at different life stages in your story. This exercise drums up latent issues that may provide texture, while knowing full well that the character will not address these at this particular time. Although a lot of this work will be backstory and not show up on screen, without this knowledge and understanding, you risk your character being flat.

Roles that are finely layered are far more attractive to actors and give them room to play. The more you know, the more flexibility you have to hint at other emotional colors and passions in the subtext, i.e., trauma, fantasy, secret triumphs.

You may also need help narrowing down what will later prove crucial to your character if you have an exciting idea of the internal and external problems the character will wrestle with but no clear priority of what the key goal is. Letting your imagination go in this exercise will help you pinpoint that, and, as a result, what the probable effect on the rest of the character's life will be!

EXERCISE

Write about your character at different ages in his or her life for three minutes. Do not edit. Play close attention to what your character is like physically and psychologically. What is revealed about this character at different ages? How might these characteristics be the same? How are they different? What is revealed about the character at different ages, based on what has transpired?

DOUGLAS J. EBOCH

The Character Diary

DOUGLAS J. EBOCH wrote the original screenplay for the movie SWEET HOME ALABAMA. His script OVERLOAD won the Carl Sautter Award for Best New Voice Features. He teaches screenwriting and pitching at Art Center College of Design, in Pasadena, and lectures internationally on screenwriting and cross-platform storytelling.

One common test of dialogue is to black out the character names in a script and see if you can identify which character is saying each line. The point is that each character should speak in a unique voice. But how do you develop your characters' voices?

Writing a backstory for your characters will give you information that influences how they speak: their socioeconomic background, education level and career, for example. You can also define how characters use language. Are they verbose or reticent? Are they more emotional or more analytical? Are they confident, forthright, deceitful, nervous, shy, mean, sarcastic, polite?

For example, in SWEET HOME ALABAMA it was important to clearly define the differences between the two male corners of the love triangle, Jake and Andrew. I wanted Andrew to represent Melanie's dreams of glamour and sophistication. So I decided he would be from an upper-class New York political family—the kind of guy who would call his parents Mother and Father, not Mom and Dad. He was a sensitive man, in touch with his emotions, but also very controlled. You can see this in the scenes where Melanie rejects him: His pain is obvious but he never loses his cool. Jake, on the other hand, represents Melanie's southern working-class past. He's macho, with southern politeness but volatile emotions, so we sought out southern slang and colloquialisms for him to use.

All of this helps, but I find in practice I write the best dialogue once I start to "hear" the characters in my head. Once that happens I don't have to consciously think about how they would phrase something; the character has become a real person in my mind, and I'm just writing what they say. (If I weren't a writer I suppose I could be hospitalized for this!) And the best tool I have to jump-start those voices in my head is the *character diary*.

The technique is simple: Write diary entries in the voice of the character. Think like an actor. Become the character and just write about an average day. Don't worry about whether your character would actually keep a diary; pretend that he or she would. And if the character is illiterate, write as though it were a verbal, recorded diary.

Of course, like any prewriting task, there is a danger in getting carried away in a subconscious avoidance of facing that blank page. You don't need to write a diary of the character's entire life. You might try doing a couple of entries that person would have written just prior to the start of your story, plus a few spaced out over the course of his or her life and perhaps even an entry set midstory. Sometimes writing a single entry is enough! However, for some projects, doing a bunch of diary entries can be an extremely useful part of your development process.

Here's a practical way I used this technique more extensively on a recent script. I was writing a story about a crew of six on a NASA mission to Mars. Now, most astronauts will have somewhat similar backstories, so I had to really work to differentiate the characters. I figured out their histories, how they got into the space program and what their vocal patterns were. Then I wrote one diary entry for each character for every three months of the two-year training period leading up to the mission. In addition to creating distinctive voices, I was able to explore the interpersonal relationships and conflicts that developed among them prior to the start of the script. As a result, from the very first scene these people felt like characters that had a history together . . . because in a way they did, at least in my mind.

The final technique I can offer for crafting character voices is one I use during the rewriting stage. Once you've got a draft that's working for you from a plot standpoint, go through the script just reading your main character's lines. If you know the character's voice, anything inconsistent should jump out at you. Then repeat the process for all your major characters. But this will only work if you've developed an instinctual understanding of how each character speaks.

EXERCISE

Write a diary entry in the voice of someone you know well who does not speak like you. You might choose someone considerably older or younger or of a different gender or different socioeconomic background. Or you might just choose a friend with a unique way of using language. Push yourself to think about how they would describe the events of their day, not how you would. By practicing writing in someone else's voice you'll develop your abilities to adopt the unique voices of your characters.

LAURA SCHEINER

Getting Inside Your Character's Head
by Becoming Her Pen

LAURA SCHEINER was V. P. Development at Noble House Entertainment. She spent four years as a script consultant at The Script Broker before establishing her own banner, Screenplay Savant. Laura cowrote *Crossed the Line*. Her other screenplay work includes *e-Bride* and *Googled!*

In the beginning there was a protagonist. And she was conflicted and sassy and full of fire and flavor and flair and flaws. In my head she was dazzling and an A-list talent magnet; on paper, not so much. In fact in the early drafts of my earliest scripts, all the characters tended to just lay there, flat as a board that's been run over by all eighteen wheels of an eighteen-wheeler. As I wrote, I'd anxiously wait for the moment my characters would "pop," a time when they'd breathe on their own and feel as real to me as any real-life character I know. That often didn't happen until well into the second act or, in some cases, the second draft.

It's not that I didn't know my characters. I always put in a lot of time doing preliminary work, including intensive "character reconnaissance" before I start beating out a story. To this day, I start every project by doing the exercises in Syd Field's must-have *The Screenwriter's Workbook*. I write detailed biographies so that I know my characters' backstories backward and forward. I become intimately acquainted with their goals, needs, motivations and wounds. I use questionnaires to mold every nuance, from political views to allergies. I've even been known to reach back to my college psych class notes to help me figure out what makes my characters tick and/or provide them with tics.

These are all invaluable tools that help me craft multidimensional characters who have well-defined arcs and whose actions are consonant with their worldviews. But even knowing my characters inside and out does not necessarily place me inside their heads right from the start.

Several years ago I decided to take a stab at writing a novel. I wrote it in the first person, which placed me inside my protagonist's head from the very first word. Even though her worldview was totally different from mine, I found myself writing the story from her worldview, using her voice instead of my own. She popped immediately. I didn't have to write my way into her. She was there on the page in all of her multidimensional, flawed and fierce glory. I knew I had to incorporate a first-person narrative component into my character reconnaissance.

This character exercise has improved the overall quality of my first drafts exponentially. Before I added this exercise, no matter how strong the story and structure of my "first" first drafts were, they were vanilla (no offense to the much maligned, yummy flavor intended). When working on assignment, I'm often required to submit my first drafts under tight deadlines that don't leave me with time to go back and do a second pass to flesh out character. Thanks to this exercise, I can submit my first drafts with confidence. I've shared this exercise with clients and my writer friends, and I'm pleased to share it with you.

EXERCISE

Write three journal/diary entries for your protagonist and all other characters that you do preliminary character work on.

Journal Entry 1: Pick a significant event from your character's biography and write a journal entry that describes her reactions to that event immediately after its occurrence as if you were that character. If in your backstory/biography you have included a moment that has caused the wound your character must heal in your story (i.e., the death of a parent, a moment of rejection or some other trauma that shut the character down), that is the event you should journal. Remember that your journal entry should be written at the time the event occurred, so if your character was eight years old at the time, you should write in the voice and from the perspective of an eight-year-old.

Journal Entry 2: Write a journal entry for the character moments before she appears in your story for the first time. Focus on where her head's at, what she's feeling and thinking, what her priorities and concerns are at that moment.

Journal Entry 3: Pick a significant moment in the story. A from-the-frying-pan-into-the-fire moment, a moment of great conflict when a serious decision must be made or when something happens that throws your character into turmoil. If you choose a beat where a choice must be made, do your journal entry right before your character makes a decision (moments before Sophie makes her choice in SOPHIE'S CHOICE).

If you choose a beat where something happens to your character that throws her into turmoil, write the journal entry moments after she discovers her life is in turmoil (right after Pete Parker discovers his new powers or immediately following his uncle Ben's death in SPIDER-MAN).

Extra Credit: Write Journal Entry 2 for all your characters, even the minor ones. This can help make even the smallest characters pop.

Good luck and have fun!

PAMELA GRAY

Life before FADE IN:

PAMELA GRAY was a poet before she wrote screenplays. Her credits include BETTY ANNE WATERS, MUSIC OF THE HEART and A WALK ON THE MOON. *Variety* named her "One of Ten Screenwriters to Watch."

First, a confession: When I'm writing a screenplay, my characters become as real to me as the people in my life, and as I near a deadline, they become *more* real than the "real" people. My characters and I begin to work together, as cowriters, to move the story forward. This collaboration can't occur, however, unless I have an intimate understanding of what took place before FADE IN.

Characters aren't just beamed into a screenplay; they have lives beforehand, from the moment of birth until the moment they appear in your script. I begin each script by writing character bios, but my characters don't really come to life until they're speaking and taking action in the screenplay. To this end, I now write *backstory scenes* both before and during the screenwriting process. This has become an invaluable tool to deepen my knowledge of both my characters and their story, whether I'm writing a scene that happened five years or five minutes before the movie begins.

The point of this exercise is not to write scenes that will appear in the screenplay (although sometimes that can happen) but to bring you insight. It might just let you know what your character would do next, but it can also lead to dramatic changes, for example, an earlier starting point for the screenplay. You might even realize that there's a different story you want to be telling. (Do this exercise at your own risk!) Whatever the result, the process will help guide you and your characters on the journey toward FADE OUT.

EXERCISE

Take one or more characters and explore, through scene writing, something that happened prior to the beginning of the movie. Tailor the following examples to meet the needs of your screenplay, use them as inspiration or just ask your characters what backstory scenes you should write.

1. Let's say there's an unhappily married young couple in your screenplay.

   Write a scene showing the moment they met.

   Write a scene showing the first time they kissed.

   Write a scene showing their first fight.

   Write a scene showing them at breakfast the day before the screenplay begins.

   Even if this relationship isn't the focus of the movie, you'll have more insight into how these two people interact as a couple.

2. Your main character is a fifty-year-old man who just got laid off from his job of twenty years.

   Write a scene showing him twenty years ago, as he prepared to interview for this job.

   Write a scene that takes place in his eleventh year on the job.

   Write a scene from his childhood when he tells his parents what he wants to be when he grows up.

   Write a scene showing him on a summer job as a teenager.

   Even if you've already planned how this layoff will affect your character, you'll now have a more intimate knowledge of who he is and how his past is affecting his current actions.

3. Let's say your movie opens with a bank robbery.

   Write scenes showing each of the bank robbers getting ready for bed on the night before the robbery.

   Even if you're writing a plot-driven screenplay, backstory scenes can help you flesh out each character and distinguish characters from one another, which can be challenging in an ensemble piece.

Write a scene sequence showing the bank teller's morning before work on the day of the robbery.

Your generic bank teller now becomes a human being who might have overslept and anxiously rushed to work, or perhaps her boyfriend had proposed to her that morning and she sauntered to work, stopping to buy doughnuts for her coworkers. Whatever happened prior to the robbery will inform her reactions to it. And who knows? She may now become a central character, or maybe one of the robbers grabs the box of doughnuts, binges on them during the robbery and then goes into insulin shock as he drives the getaway car . . .

RICHARD WALTER

Loving and Loathing—
How to Get into Your Characters

RICHARD WALTER is the author of *Essentials of Screenwriting* as well as screenplays, fiction and nonfiction. He is a professor at UCLA and longtime chair and co-chair of the Master of Fine Arts in Screenwriting program. He has lectured to screenwriters on four continents. His students have written twelve projects for Steven Spielberg.

A writer's job is to get inside his character's mind and body, acting as the character would act, feeling as the character would feel under the circumstances the writer has created.

This is useful not only in reel life but also in real life. Exactly as a writer needs to enter the psyche of each character in his script, he should do the same with the people in his life: agents, producers, directors and actors. As in chess, the writer must ask: If my opponent made the move I am about to make, what would be my response?

EXERCISE

Choose an issue you feel passionate about. It can be political, social or intellectual. Compose an exchange of dialogue in which two characters argue the issue.

First, however, do not be even-handed, rational and sensible. Dramatic art is supposed to be dramatic. Let this be a passionate exchange.

Second, choose one character as the clear protagonist. Give him the bulk of the dialogue. The second character should simply facilitate; he or she should feed lines to the protagonist in the fashion of a comedic straight man. That character should also help make the interaction an exchange rather than a monologue.

Third, and most important, have the protagonist embrace a view that is totally antithetical to your own. Do you support a woman's right to choose abortion during the first trimester? Have your protagonist argue the opposite.

Do you believe that global warming is a hoax? Argue that it is not. Do you believe that illegal immigration is a serious problem in our nation? Argue that it is in fact trivial. Assert that any patriotic American would welcome to our shores foreigners fleeing political, social or economic oppression. They would see it as wholly in keeping with American history and tradition.

Do you think manned space travel is a costly boondoggle with no useful benefits to humanity? Argue instead that to seek and explore new boundaries is an integral and natural aspect of the human condition.

The key here is not to be sarcastic or sneering in your arguments but sincere. Try to wrap your own mind around your opponents' point of view. Instead of struggling to get your opponent to understand you, endeavor to understand him or her. This will go a long way toward supporting you in your efforts to create characters who are not freeze-dried and paper-thin but palpably fleshy and real and whole and human.

LESLIE LEHR

Getting to Know Your Character

LESLIE LEHR is an MFA prizewinning author and screenwriter whose film HEARTLESS screened in Europe for six years after a three-year run on USA-TV. She is the author of essays, two novels and three nonfiction books. Her essays have appeared in best-selling anthologies and on the *Today* show. She teaches in the Writers' Program at UCLA.

Just as every good story begins with a great character, every good screenplay begins with a great role. In today's film industry, screenplays often go out to actors before they are submitted to producers. With a popular actor attached, you have a much better chance of getting your movie made. So you can't rely on an actor to bring life to your story. You have to write a role that brings your story to life.

So, how do we create a character we can root for? How can we get a good actor to visualize that gold Oscar displayed on his or her mantel? How can we get people to shell out hard cash to watch your hero in action? We make her as complex and fascinating as a flesh-and-blood person.

First, every good hero has some inherent weakness that creates a psychological need. She's unaware of this need, but you better be, because strong characters change or grow during the story.

Second, whatever happens to kick off the action on page one causes your hero to desire something and take steps to get it. Through this action, her weakness is revealed so that ultimately she can fulfill that need and make that all-important change. It's not just the story that has an ending, the character has one too.

Third, while it's vital to know your character's life history, there are a million other details that make a person unique. Since films are a visual medium, we need to show how our hero feels through her actions. To do that, we use action verbs. To choose the right verbs and create believable, unique behavior, we need to know as many details as possible.

As you go about your day tomorrow, think about how your character would handle each situation. It's not just the details alone that are important, but how your character feels about them.

EXERCISE

1. Make three lists: Physical, Psychological and Sociological. Each word can be answered with a fact, but think further. How did this happen? How does your character feel about it?

PHYSICAL	PSYCHOLOGICAL	SOCIOLOGICAL
Age and sex	Optimist/pessimist	Family
Skin color	Nervous/easygoing	Education
Hair (style, color, baldness)	Temperament (angry/sad)	Religion
Clothing style	Depressed/happy	Marital status
Teeth (braces, color, veneers)	Anxiety issues	Politics
		Occupation
Eyes (color, glasses, contacts)	Relaxation techniques	Hometown
Height	Favorite places	Clubs
Posture	Birth order	Social network
Build	Intellect	Favorite TV shows
Exercise habits	Introverted/extroverted	Music preferences
Piercings, tattoos	Addictions	Favorite foods
Jewelry	Judging	Reading habits
Scars, injuries	Controlling	Languages
Sleeping habits	Perfectionism	

continued

PHYSICAL	PSYCHOLOGICAL	SOCIOLOGICAL
Hygiene	Habits	
Hobbies	Dreams/ nightmares	
Manner of speaking		
Sexual habits	Happy memories	
Allergies	Defining moments in past	
Health	Goals	
Eating habits		

2. Using your list above, create contradictions in your character. Is he a mighty warrior who is afraid of bugs? Is she a child therapist who isn't on speaking terms with her children? Is she loyal to a fault? Is she a successful writer who can't type? These contrasting details help make characters human.

The more you know about your character, the easier it will be to show how she behaves in every situation. What does she want? What does she need? How does she react when she gets it or fails to get it? How does she change? The answers will make your character complex and fascinating. That's the kind of role that will bring your story to life!

VERBAL AND NONVERBAL COMMUNICATION

AMY HOLDEN JONES

Find Your Inner Actor

AMY HOLDEN JONES has worked as a writer, editor and director in Holly-
wood. Her writing credits include MYSTIC PIZZA, INDECENT PROPOSAL,
BEETHOVEN, THE GET AWAY and THE RIDE. She wrote and directed
SLUMBER PARTY MASSACRE, LOVE LETTERS, MAID TO ORDER and THE
RICH MAN'S WIFE. She currently works in television creating pilots.

It's notoriously difficult to teach people to write. And writing
a screenplay is a unique skill, nothing like being a playwright,
journalist or novelist. I learned to do it in an unusual way, without ever taking a class or reading a book on screenwriting.

I did not set out to be a writer. I wanted to be a documentary film-
maker. I was passionately in love with real life and with my camera.
Theater, drama, and even feature films, seemed like remote illusions.
I preferred Robert Frank to Irving Penn, and MONTEREY POP to
HAIR. The films I loved most were cinéma verité, shot on the fly
without a screenplay.

In those early days of my career, digital cameras didn't exist.
There wasn't even videotape. We shot film, and it was incredibly
expensive. By the time I was out of school a year, I realized many
working documentarians were independently wealthy. I had to earn
a living. I was about to give up and go back to graduate school when
out of the blue, I got a job as a gofer on a Hollywood feature shooting
in New York City.

From day one, I was in an entirely new world. I had never been
around sets or actors. The first script I ever read was for that film. It
was TAXI DRIVER, by the great Paul Schrader. This was the blueprint for the work done every day by director Martin Scorsese and
his actors. It was all far closer to theater than to documentaries.

In the light of this revelation, I had no clue how I would ever become a movie director, which in my hubris was what I then wanted to become. To direct a film, I'd need a script, and I was not a writer. Miraculously, five years later, the day did come when I was hired to direct a feature for Roger Corman. New World Pictures made two exploitation films. The script for SLUMBER PARTY MASSACRE needed work. Admittedly the bar was not particularly high in this case, but the film still had to work for its intended audience. I had to rewrite, and I had to do it fast. Only one thing made it possible.

Roger insisted that all his directors take acting lessons. He sent me to study with a brilliant character actor named Jeff Corey. Corey had been blacklisted in the fifties and robbed of his career. He became a legendary acting teacher. There wasn't a teacher born who could have made me into a talented actor, but Jeff Corey made me a writer.

So here is my advice: If you wish to write screenplays, learn to act. I learned what acting meant in Corey's class, and it wasn't at all what I expected. It didn't involve putting on a mask and becoming someone else. It involved finding yourself in any character. To act, you have to be on your character's side and see the world through the character's eyes. You have to make up a life history larger than the one on the page. You have to understand the words you speak, and try to convey their meaning. As it turns out, screenwriters have to do all these things.

There are many techniques actors use, too many to go into here. If you are serious, find a good acting teacher and learn all of them. Read *An Actor Prepares* by Stanislavski. Then pick a monologue from a film or play that you love and memorize it.

You'll learn right away why actors like speeches and why most good scripts have at least one (but please, not too many). Perform your monologue in a class. Feel what it feels like to lay yourself bare and risk making a fool of yourself in front of an audience.

Acting requires real bravery. The actor's greatest ally is the writer. Your fates are inextricably intertwined. Great writing is necessary for a great performance, and bad acting will make any dialogue sound appalling.

Acting also teaches you what an actor looks for in a part. Your scripts won't get made unless good actors want to do them. Learning to act will force you to read many scripts and screenplays. Students tend to dodge this step, preferring to look at the films instead. This is cheating and it doesn't work.

Finally, acting makes you learn about subtext, which is so much more important than text. Very often in real life people don't talk about what's actually on their minds. They talk about anything else. Actors know this and learn to perform the lines and convey the emotions that lie beneath the dialogue. I'll give you one exercise to help you understand this.

EXERCISE

Write a scene about nothing at all. I'm not kidding. Make the lines bland and nonspecific, like "How are you?" "Okay." "It's been a while." "Has it?" "Been busy." "You changed your hair." "It's cold in here." "I didn't notice."

The dialogue can be anything as long as it is not in the least compelling. Now get an acting partner and perform this scene in several different contexts. Notice how it plays if you imagine the people talking are a father and daughter who haven't seen each other in years, since the day the daughter stole her father's life savings to finance her drug habit.

Then read the same scene as if it's happening between a former concentration camp guard and a Jewish survivor, or a boy about to ask a girl to the prom, or a husband and wife waiting outside divorce court.

When I did these exercises and others like them long ago in my acting class, there came a day when I realized that, although I was no longer working in documentaries, I hadn't had to give up the thing I loved most. Good writing and good acting are both about finding the breathing, human, flawed souls inside the characters you create in your head. Before I took acting lessons, I thought features were smoke and mirrors, artifice and make-believe. After studying acting, I realized that, to me, good movies are a different form of nonfiction.

They look deep into the human heart to find the contradictions and surprises we see in daily life. Sitting in the dark watching actors on a screen, the greatest pleasure comes from the shock of recognition. This holds true even if your characters are factory workers, vampires, ghosts, superheroes, or Saint Bernards. Only when you find that real breath of life on the page will you have a screenplay.

PETER BRIGGS

On Dialoguing, the Screenwriting Anarchist's Way

A former assistant cinematographer, PETER BRIGGS has been a professional writing monkey for longer than he cares to remember. He
cowrote the screenplay for HELLBOY and his original draft of ALIEN VS.
PREDATOR was featured in *The 50 Greatest Movies Never Made*.

If there's a movie industry rule to be broken, I'll do it. In the par-
lance, I am what used to be termed an *angry young man*.

I was once told not to write a particular project, because
it'd never be read. Within days of submitting it, I'd sold ALIEN VS.
PREDATOR to Twentieth Century–Fox.

I constantly get lambasted not to underline my scene headings
and put them in bold. Nerts to you, bub. It makes them pop. "Don't
use capitalized sound effects; it reads like a comic book." Really? I'm
adapting a comic book for the screen . . . this isn't Russian literature.

I absolutely loathe screenwriting gurus, who by-and-large seem
to be snake-oil salesmen. I constantly advocate tossing their rules
out of the window, because thanks to these bozos, movie scripts are
starting to have the same homogenized taste and texture en masse,
like processed cheese slices.

And another pet peeve of mine: "Don't attend writing groups."
When you realize there are people out there who may be better
than you, it's soul destroying. (Conversely, when you actually realize most of the people out there have no talent for storytelling and
should really give up and go back to their Dairy Queen franchise in
Des Moines, it's sad in a whole different way.) The list goes on.

When I was asked to write this piece, I thought I'd inspire the
Good Readers to become the Screenwriting Anarchists. I was going
to toss out all my sly tricks to the purchasers and let them see what

sticks: using the little cheats favored by Certain Famous and Expensive Screenwriting Programs That Are Badly Coded, which allow you to gain that extra page you so desperately need to get your opus under 120 pages; using business-card-sized index cards instead of the ridiculous larger ones, because that way you can pin an entire intricately structured plot onto a corkboard and gain a faster overview; using a yellow pad and timer on your DVD player to break down several movies of the same genre as something you're working on into descriptions of thirty-second intervals and then taking an overview of each plot and applying it to your own.

However, I soon realized with horror the brevity of this chapter. And I've never been known for writing short. (Indeed, "savage editing" is the best advice I can give to neophytes who've completed their masterwork: "Learn to become a ruthless butcher.")

So what I'm going to put out there this time is this: "Language in film has become familiar," by which I mean that dialogue can have this unfortunate risk, beyond sounding just merely "clichéd." Turns of phrase are subtly ingrained into our shared memory by the stultifying repetition of hack writers making us digest them over and over.

Allow me to pose to you a situation where wiseguys/cowboys/intergalactic mercenaries have just piled into their respective conveyance of choice and yell at the guy at the reins, "Let's get—!" How do you imagine they'll complete that sentence? You'll likely come back with: "—the hell out of here!"; "—the hell out of Dodge!"; or something similar. And there you have it. Writing has rhythms, not just in the repetition of phrases we use, but also in the actual way we say them and in specific anticipation of what is *about* to be said. If your viewing audience falls into the groove of your clichés—if they already *know* what the line of dialogue is going to be before the actor's even spoken it—they'll likely also drift into boredom.

Happily, there are ways around this.

EXERCISE

You can regard this as an exercise if you wish, but as a Screenwriting Anarchist, it should really become the cornerstone of your daily dialogue-writing process. First, load up your writing arsenal with the finest Thesauruses (Thesauri?) you can. Word processing programs (assuming you're not a stubborn Luddite who still pounds his or her Remington) are . . . well . . . slightly crap in the lexicon department. Even a good online thesaurus can usually be bested by a paper one. You need the absolute peachiest Substitution Dinosaur you can get your hands on; if you're doing your job right, it will soon become well-worn (in which case, you should maybe invest in a hardback) and reward you many times over.

You most definitely, and I stress *definitely* (don't be a cheapskate here, reasoning you've already bought a regular one), need at least one slang thesaurus too. There are a number of these, some tailored to specific professions. (I recently purchased a World War II servicemen's slang thesaurus—a fascinating read in itself.)

Okay. Now take a look at your scene and the way it *sounds*, not just *reads*. Screen dialogue is for speaking, not skimming. Practice muttering it to yourself to see if it flows . . . You'll get odd looks, but then you're meant to be a successful writer and therefore halfway bonkers already.

Does your dialogue, first of all, read as though it's from separate characters with different voices? Does your Boston longshoreman sound distinct from the bookish Ivy Leaguer he's been saddled with? If you grudgingly admit he doesn't, try this. Get a list of your characters and "faux cast" your movie, right down to the smallest extra. Even though you've a Popsicle's chance in Hades of getting Leonardo DiCaprio and Sandra Bullock, as you write your characters, *imagine* those particular actors saying the lines. If you've the talent and facility to compartmentalize, I guarantee that your characters will start to individually zing.

Next, when the words are on the page, look at what is being said. You'll probably become aware of the repetition of certain words and phrases. If one character says a word in a sentence like "tonight," for example, and other characters repeat that same word, you should maybe start reaching for that expensive thesaurus again and start substituting.

Another trick is to use inversions and contractions of your sentences, and to alter their punctuation. Look at the individual styles of both Woody Allen and David Mamet. Allen will use circuitous dialogue and go all over the place. Mamet will use punctuation to break his sentences in odd places and then pick up what is being said in a different way. A fantastic (and highly recommended) marriage of both techniques is that of the American writer Damon Runyon, with his highly eccentric vernacular.

So. You should now have dialogue that holds the imagination and stops your audience wandering out or changing the channel to catch that Coke commercial.

Now. Get the hell out of my classroom, and go start breaking some rules.

ANDREW OSBORNE

Nonverbal Communication

ANDREW OSBORNE is a teacher and WGA member whose indie film credits include the Sundance Film Festival premiere ON LINE, the Tribeca Film Festival premiere THE F WORD, and his own directorial debut, APOCALYPSE BOP. Mr. Osborne received an Emmy Award as a staff writer for the Discovery Channel program *Cash Cab*. He has developed scripts for Warner Bros., HBO, MTV and Orion, as well as numerous theatrical, interactive and comic-book projects. He someday hopes to finish the novel he first started writing way back in the previous century.

W hen writing a screenplay, it's important to remember that great dialogue doesn't exist in a vacuum; your characters' words are only truly effective if they're supported by a solid plot, clear character motivations, effective visual descriptions and all the other elements of good screenwriting.

And speaking of visual description, it's also important to remember that dialogue isn't the only way characters (or people) communicate information. In the following scene from the 1975 thriller JAWS by Carl Gottlieb and Peter Benchley (based on his novel), three unlikely companions have been thrown together in a small boat to hunt a deadly great white shark: a crusty old sailor (Quint), a young marine biologist (Hooper) and Brody, a small-town sheriff with a fear of water and virtually no maritime experience whatsoever.

At this point in the script, the group has just fumbled a run-in with the great white, and now Brody is deeply unhappy about the whole situation: the food, his surroundings and the abrasion he suffered during the botched encounter with the shark. Quint, meanwhile, is all business, but there's a sense of grim camaraderie in the air: The old salt shares his home brew with Hooper, a man he's fought with repeatedly in the past, and as the scene continues, Quint tries to lighten Brody's mood by downplaying the abrasion while sharing a humorous story from his past:

Quint bends forward and pulls his hair aside to show something near the crown.

> QUINT
> That's not so bad. Look
> at this: . . . St. Paddy's
> Day in Knocko Nolan's,
> in Boston, where some
> sunovabitch winged me
> upside the head with a
> spittoon.

Brody looks politely. Hooper stirs himself.

> HOOPER
> Look here.
> (extends a forearm)
> Steve Kaplan bit me during
> recess.

Quint is amused. He presents his own formidable forearm.

> QUINT
> Wire burn. Tried to stop
> a backstay from taking my
> head off.

```
                    HOOPER
          (rolling up a sleeve)
       Moray eel. Bit right
       through a wet suit.
```

Brody is fascinated. Quint and Hooper take a long
pull from the bottle.

Note how nonverbal communication is used to counterpoint the spoken words. Brody doesn't say anything, but he's still an active part of the scene as the conversation perks him up: The one-upmanship between Hooper and Quint over their battle scars has the intended effect of making Brody weirdly proud of his "manly" abrasion.

Meanwhile, the brief action descriptions (Hooper stirring himself, Quint presenting his forearm) ground the dialogue in physicality, which not only communicates nonverbal information (like Quint and Hooper getting looser, drunker and more relaxed with each other, as indicated by the shared long pulls from the bottle) but also helps to avoid what I call radio-play syndrome, where too much dialogue and too little description causes a reader to merely "hear" a scene rather than fully visualize it.

Which brings us to . . .

EXERCISE

Write a conversation using neutral dialogue ("Hello," "Nice to meet you," etc.) in which the true meaning of the scene is communicated nonverbally.

AND/OR

Write a scene establishing two or more characters in a dramatic situation using only visual description and body language: action, appearance, expression and other nonverbal cues.

MARK EVAN SCHWARTZ

The Big Eavesdrop

MARK EVAN SCHWARTZ is associate dean and associate professor of screenwriting at Loyola Marymount University School of Film and Television in Los Angeles. He has writing credits on over a dozen produced feature films and television movies and is the author of *How to Write: A Screenplay*. He has an MFA from Boston University College of Fine Arts.

A story had been gnawing at me for years, a true one I'd grown up hearing about and one that I thought had cinematic value. It was set in the late twenties in a textile mill village in my hometown, Piedmont, North Carolina, a place I'd moved away from decades before.

Returning to visit my family one summer, in anticipation of finally beginning to turn this story into a screenplay, I spent countless hours in the local library, pouring through books, scouring microfilmed clippings, talking to people about memories passed down to them by their parents and grandparents, learning everything I could about the violent events upon which I wanted to base the story.

Soon, I felt I had the facts—boxes full of them. But my objective was not to write a documentary; it was to create a dramatic narrative, a historic fiction. And I knew that what I lacked were traits for the principal characters, their voices and nuances. I had not yet found the humanity of the relationship that drives the story. Sure, I could sit back and use my imagination, but I was looking for something more, something that would spark creativity in ways that didn't readily come to mind. So I ventured out to find it.

For the next week or so I made it a point to snack at a small mom-and-pop diner in the mill village where the story took place. Alone, I'd sit quietly at the counter, sipping a cheery smash, nibbling a pressed sandwich of vinegary barbecue and slaw. I discreetly observed and listened to the locals, absorbing their syntax and slang, their postures and gaits. One day a couple dining with a young girl grabbed my attention.

The man, dressed in pressed overalls, appeared to be in his late thirties. The woman, who was maybe ten years younger, was wearing a bargain-basement flowered dress. The girl, preteen, was similarly clad. There was awkwardness in their interaction. He was fidgeting with his fork, spoon and knife, straightening them while talking shyly about a game. The woman would nod, saying nothing, feigning interest. The girl was clearly bored. A waitress arrived with their meals, and the man offhandedly suggested to the girl that she put her napkin in her lap. She cringed and shot him a look, but before she uttered a word, the woman tapped her hand and simply said "Hon?" Heeding what sounded like a warning, the girl managed an annoyed smile and put the napkin in her lap.

Eureka. I found it.

Modeled off the central relationship of this triangle, the screen story took shape in my mind's eye from the point of view of a brooding preteen girl, loyal to her mother, resentful of the fastidious man she's seeing and selfishly using.

EXERCISE

One of the great traits of most screenwriters is the ability to observe or to eavesdrop, if you will. It's in our nature to drift to the outside of circles and quietly peer in. And it's part of our mindset to imagine scenarios involving the people and situations inhabiting it. This is an exercise about doing exactly that.

You've got an idea for a story, and it's percolating. It's time to do some research, to authenticate your characters and make them credible.

Go to a place where people who are similar to the character (or characters) you're writing about might hang out. It could be a library, playground, sporting event, courthouse, college campus, bar . . . whatever. The key is to not draw attention to yourself, to make yourself as invisible and unobtrusive as possible, and then eavesdrop.

Listen to the conversations and watch the interactions. Observe. Take in manners of speech, topics discussed, body language, choices of clothing, surrounding noises and sounds, environmental and/or musical. Consider everything these people are doing. Make mental notes, but don't write down anything; that would make people self-conscious.

Later, as soon as possible, write down everything that you've seen and heard. Create bios detailing who you imagine the people you've observed to be. And then rewrite those bios, bringing them into the world of your screen story.

The Twitch: Objects as Emotions

WILLIAM C. MARTELL is a professional screenwriter with nineteen scripts carelessly slapped onto celluloid, including a handful of HBO World Premiere Movies in the action and thriller genres. His out-of-print book, *The Secrets of Action Screenwriting*, has sold for over $320, used, on eBay. He can often be found on some far-off film festival jury or battling bad script notes in Hollywood.

Screenwriting is writing for the screen, telling the story visually through the actions of the characters. Just like in real life, actions speak louder than words. What a character says is usually what he wishes were true, or what he wants the others in the scene to believe is true.

But good stories need characters to wrestle with inner demons, to overcome fears and to solve emotional conflicts. How do we display a character's emotional conflict on screen without thought balloons or voice-overs? How do you show feelings and thoughts on screen?

Though there are at least a dozen techniques to show what a character is thinking or feeling on screen, I use a method I call "The Twitch." Probably after seeing some strange double bill of ONCE UPON A TIME IN THE WEST and THE PINK PANTHER, I realized an object could be used as a symbol of the turmoil bubbling within the character's mind.

In the original Pink Panther movies, whenever Clouseau's name was mentioned around Inspector Dreyfus he began twitching uncontrollably, and we knew how he felt and could easily imagine what he was thinking. In ONCE UPON A TIME IN THE WEST, Charles Bronson's character has a harmonica on a lanyard around his neck, but he plays it only in the presence of Henry Fonda's gunslinger.

That harmonica has some hidden meaning that won't be revealed to us until near the end of the film.

A Twitch is an object that symbolizes an emotional conflict or unresolved problem; a Touchstone is an object that is usually used to show memories of a more peaceful time. The cliché Touchstone is that family photo every soldier in a foxhole looks at in the scene before he is killed. That same photo could become a Twitch if the soldier's family had been killed in an attack, and his motivations were revenge. Instead of looking at the photo and feeling peace, he would be feeling anger.

The problem with using a photo is that it's all surface, two dimensional and obvious. Better to find an object with some personality or significance. In Robert Rodat's THE PATRIOT, before Mel Gibson's character leaves his family to go off to war, his son gives him his collection of lead toy soldiers. As the war goes on, Gibson melts the toy soldiers one by one to make ammunition for his musket. The full bag of toys begins to empty. Every time he melts one, we know that he's not only missing his family but also thinking about how he is losing his humanity . . . melting away those things that make him a good father and husband, to be a soldier. Toy soldiers being turned into something that will kill soldiers—not only better than a picture of his family, but also thematic.

I have used wedding bands and money clips and compasses and retirement watches and children's toys . . . and a Hershey's chocolate bar, which was split between father and son before the boy was kidnapped, and for the rest of the script, whenever either of them eats one of his six sections of the candy bar, we know what he is thinking and feeling. Also, with every section that's consumed, we know that time is running out.

The key is to find the object that fits the characters, the story, and the theme. Then either introduce that object into a scene that gives it meaning, like a father sharing a snack with his son, or turn it into a mystery and reveal the meaning at the end, as in the Leone spaghetti westerns. Whenever the character pulls the object from his or her pocket and looks at it, we'll know exactly what he or she is thinking and feeling. No need for pesky dialogue!

EXERCISE

What is the emotional issue your character is struggling with? Usually in a screenplay the protagonist is forced to resolve an emotional problem in order to deal with a physical conflict. Hamlet has to deal with his responsibility issues to avenge his father's murder. In THE DARK KNIGHT, good guy Harvey Dent struggles with his rage after being burned in a fire. In UP, Karl Fredrickson must deal with the loss of his wife as he goes on the big adventure they never got a chance to take while she was alive.

Now make a list of all of the potential objects you can use to symbolize this emotional conflict. Brainstorm as many as you can, so that you can select the best. Find the object that also connects to your story's theme, the object that will best resonate with the audience.

Now do it in reverse. Look at some random object and try to figure out what emotional conflict it might be a symbol for.

Funny Faces: Tips on Writing Animation

AYDREA WALDEN TEN BOSCH is a Los Angeles–based writer who has written for Nickelodeon's *ChalkZone*, Disney's *Yin Yang Yo* and Hawaii Film Partners' *Guardians of the Power Masks*. She recently completed her first live-action feature film.

Animation is a wonderful field to write in because you get to escape the bounds of human reality. Whether you are writing a traditional cartoon with personified animals or a "realistic" cartoon with humans as lead characters, these beings can do things that we cannot. They can abuse their bodies, stretch their faces and go to physical extremes to express their feelings. They are not bound by laws of gravity or physics. They can tolerate levels of pain and discomfort that would be tragic to experience but hilarious to watch.

Cartoon writing is all about heightening. Making more of whatever it is that your character is doing. Your cartoon characters generally can do more than walk out of the room: They can *zip* or *dash* or *bolt* or *slink* or *mope* out of the room. Your characters don't have to just pick something off a counter; they can "*Yoink!* Grab it fast!" or "*Swipe* it away" or "*Pounce* on the shelf" to get what they want.

Your character's face can do more than "look sad." Instead, the character's jaw can: "*Clank!* Hit the floor as her eyes *bug* out." Your character doesn't have to simply "smile"; instead her grin can "slowly spread from ear to ear, past the edges of her cheeks."

When writing a script for an animated production, it is necessary to insert some *cartoonishness* into your language. You are writing a script or outline that an artist is going to draw out. You are helping that artist's imagination, so you have to liven up your script with sounds and descriptions that capture attitude, emotion and movement in a more extreme way than you would for a live-action script that must be acted out by humans who can only do so much with their bodies before a trip to the hospital.

Following is an exercise I use to help me get in the right frame of mind to write as animatedly as my characters are to become.

EXERCISE

Think about what you would love to do with your body if you could. Would you fly high above the clouds? Leap a tall building? Do a perfect swan dive? Do the splits as you catch something falling off a high shelf? Tiptoe on the very top of your toes? Slither away from an uncomfortable situation on your belly? Well, you cannot do these things, but your characters can!

As you write, put your mind in the body of the character. As your character reacts to what is happening to him or her, let yourself feel what you could do if you were able to. If you get embarrassed, do you ever feel like sinking into the floor or flattening yourself against the wall? If you get excited, do you feel like hugging someone so hard that he or she cinches in the middle like a balloon animal? If you get cold, do you feel like shaking so hard that you vibrate the fibers out of your clothes?

As you write, get up, walk around, allow yourself to react to what your character is thinking and feeling. Then heighten what it is you're doing, and you're on your way to a great animated script!

DAVID FREEMAN

False Emotion

DAVID FREEMAN has sold or optioned scripts and ideas to Sony Pictures, Columbia Pictures, MGM, Paramount Pictures and many other film and TV companies. His screenwriting class, Beyond Structure, is taught in Los Angeles, New York and London. David is also interested in interactive narrative and has included several hundred writing techniques, most of which apply to screenwriting, in his book *Creating Emotion in Games*.

Did you ever see AMERICAN BEAUTY by writer Alan Ball? If you haven't, you should. One reason is because it's great. The second reason is because this chapter will make more sense if you've viewed it. But I'll try my best to make it useful, even if you haven't seen the film.

Ricky Fitts (Wes Bentley) is a teen with an almost Zen-like view of the beauty behind all things—or so it seems. But real Zen masters don't, as Ricky does, sell drugs; they don't, as is the case with Ricky, allow themselves to be beaten to a pulp by their fathers. They also don't insist on staying detached from the world (viewing everything through a video camera), and they don't become fascinated by death and speak about it frequently. In fact, Ricky's supposed serenity is a cover for his real state of mind: an apathy deeper even than grief (thus his fascination with death). Ricky's apathy, we eventually learn, stems back to when he was wrongly put in a mental institution and drugged.

When a character has a false emotion (in this case, serenity), which covers a real emotion (in this case, apathy), it's one of many ways to give a character depth. Thus I call it a character-deepening technique.

I call this particular technique *false emotion*.

Though Ricky's serenity is false, this doesn't negate his eloquent insights into the beauty behind all things. When a character is either artistic or has an aesthetic awareness, as Ricky does, that's another *character-deepening technique*. (There are many, many *character-deepening techniques*.)

We also see a *false emotion* in the classic film CASABLANCA. Rick Blaine (Humphrey Bogart) seems to have a bemused, bored demeanor. Unexpectedly, his ex-lover, Ilsa Lund (Ingrid Bergman), whom he thought he'd never see again, happens into his Casablanca nightclub. We then see Rick's real emotion—deep depression—as he drinks himself into an alcoholic stupor.

There are two other components of this technique: (1) It's usually best to "fake out" the audience by introducing the *false emotion* first. Then it's something of a revelation when the audience realizes that the character is not as upbeat as he or she seems. (Remember that even a state of boredom is "upbeat" if the character's real emotion is depression.) (2) The character is usually not "pretending." The character almost always believes his or her false emotion is the real emotion. If you told Ricky Fitts he was apathetic, he'd deny it. And Rick Blaine would deny being deeply depressed.

This is just like real life, for in real life many people also have false emotions, but are in denial about their true, darker emotional state.

Although the character might deny what's really going on, you, the writer, should leave telltale evidence of the character's real emotion. The audience is smart; they'll figure it out, and feel quite smart in doing so.

EXERCISE

In this exercise, you'll write a short scene. Have one of the characters appear to be feeling one of five *false* emotions: lightly sarcastic, bored, mildly interested in life, cheerful, or spiritually serene.

Before writing, choose what the character's *real* emotion is.

Choose one of these five: angry, sad, anxious, very depressed, or apathetic. The character's pretense should be good enough that, at least at the beginning of the scene, we believe that the character's false (more upbeat) emotion is real. But sprinkle into the scene at least one or two little things that slip out of the character's mouth—or one or two things that the character does—that give us the feeling (or allow us to figure out) that this character's emotion is false.

If someone can read your scene and figure out both the character's false emotion (the lighter one) and the character's real emotion (the darker one), you've done a good job. You've done a good job even if someone reading the scene can figure out that the character's apparent emotion is false, even if the reader can't exactly pinpoint what the character's real emotion is.

JUDY KELLEM

Building Between the Lines

Since 2001, JUDY KELLEM has been a partner in Hollywoodscript.com. She has previously worked as a researcher for Universal and has done screenplay/manuscript coverage for Fox Studios. Judy has an MA in English/creative writing.

One of the key, most challenging aspects of screenwriting is the use of "attitudes" and "visual aids" between the lines of dialogue. The narrative descriptions and stage directions threaded throughout character voices are the screenwriter's word-built director/camera within the script. These elements help to guide the reader's emotions and inner eye, dictating what details are worthy of noting as the characters speak: the gun in the corner of a room, the taboo clasp of hands under a table, the compliment delivered with profound sarcasm. They are tools that build story, mood, tone and subtext.

But many writers struggle with the management of these techniques. Some think they should leave all dramatic detail to the director or the actor, and their material can become overly amorphous. Others show so much unnecessary detail that the script is novel-like and the pace is brought to a slug's run. Hitting the right balance is vital to great screenwriting, for when properly laced, these director-like/cameralike descriptions can be part of the genius of a script. While re-viewing THE GODFATHER, I meditated on this very notion. At the film's core, it's a character study of the Al Pacino character, Michael, who, despite all early intentions to be an upstanding citizen, winds up becoming the ultimate mobster. His character arc is often dramatized via silent beats where we simply watch him and observe how he shifts inside from being an innocent to a killer to a powerful criminal. I wondered how much of this was written, versus directed or performed, and skimmed the screenplay. The script is exploding with both stage directions [things such as: MICHAEL (coldly); SUNNY (almost in tears)] and narrative ["Michael is petrified; quickly, he takes each edition, drops a dollar in the tray and hungrily reads through them. Kay knows to keep silent."] The writer's concise use of these key elements helped provide the narrative connective tissue that brought the entire story together.

As you write your script, bear in mind that you are entitled and expected to show the reader what is crucial to know in order for the story to be aptly dramatized. It's your prerogative to cultivate and fully exploit the aid of that word-built director/camera. Careful use of this valuable tool can make all the difference between what we simply "read" and what we actually experience.

EXERCISE

Take a look at a scene you have already written or think about a scene you want to write. Focus on what unspoken details are essential to the moment. For example, when your hero's wife says, "I love you," perhaps it's totally insincere. Provide this detail, for the dialogue isn't telling us, and your former characterization of her may not do the job of making us "assume" it. Dramatization can be done via a stage direction:

```
                    WIFE
          (totally insincere)
      I love you.
```

Or via narrative:

```
                    WIFE
      I love you.
```

He studies her face. He can see in her eyes that she doesn't mean it.

As another example, say you have a scene where your hero drives his little boy to school and, despite tender smiles and chitchat with his son, is contemplating suicide. Here is how you might show this important story component using a stage direction. . . .

> SON
> Today in science class
> we're gonna dissect a frog.

> DAD
> (pointedly)
> Lucky frog.

Or via narrative:

> SON
> Today in science class
> we're gonna dissect a frog.
> Dad smiles fondly, then
> painfully peers out the
> car window as if he'd like
> to be that frog.

Bottom line: Remember that juicy story details given in rich, brief prose along the way are part of the very pulse of the tale you, the writer, are unfolding. If those little gems are not on the page, you risk losing the full impact of your creative intention and, in turn, the heart of your reader.

STEVE KAPLAN

Using Metaphors in Comedy

STEVE KAPLAN has taught screenwriting workshops at NYU, Yale School of Drama and UCLA as well as for companies such as DreamWorks Animation, Disney Animation and Aardman Animation. His lectures have been presented in Los Angeles, New York, Vancouver, London, Sydney, Melbourne and Singapore. Some of Steve's students have gone on to write for shows such as *Sex and the City*, *Ugly Betty*, and *Big Love*.

One of my favorite plays (and films and TV shows, for that matter) was Neil Simon's THE ODD COUPLE, in which a pair of mismatched friends, one divorced and one soon-to-be, decide to room together. On the surface, Oscar Madison and Felix Unger are friends and roommates. As the story progresses, however, their relationship undergoes a subtle but startling transformation: Their growing antagonism begins to resemble that of an old married couple.

Take, for example, the scene in which Oscar has set up a date with two stewardesses for himself and Felix. As Oscar comes home, he finds Felix, wearing an apron, meeting him at the door with arms folded. What follows is a scene that almost any wayward husband might recognize, as Felix peppers Oscar with: "Do you know what time it is? Where were you? Why didn't you call me? Do you know that the meatloaf is all dried out now?" Finally, Oscar blurts out what we all might be thinking: "Wait a minute. I want to get this down on a tape recorder because nobody's going to believe me. You mean now I got to call you if I'm coming home late for dinner?"

This is a technique I call *metaphorical relationships*. A metaphor, like a simile, is a comparison or analogy that shows how two otherwise unlike objects are similar in some way. I define a *metaphorical relationship* as the essential, somewhat hidden relationship that lies or is perceived beneath the surface relationship. By grafting the squabbling behavior of an old married couple onto the bachelor roommates, Felix and Oscar, Neil Simon creates an instant comic situation. *Metaphorical relationships* work because, while they show the characters behaving in ludicrous ways, the behavior itself is both recognizable and believable.

Imagine an adult couple having an argument over money. Now imagine the same couple fighting as though they were kids in the backseat of a car. The content they cover may be similar, but now the couple might be pushing each other, sticking their tongue out and punctuating their points with: "Did not!" "Did too!" "Did not!" "Too!" "Not!" "Too!" "Not to a thousand!" "Too to infinity!" (Pause) "Not to infinity . . . plus one!" The metaphor takes a serious, perhaps dry, exchange and makes it comic while keeping it connected to a recognizable reality.

EXERCISE

Take a conversation between two or more characters. Now place one or all of those characters in a *metaphorical relationship*. They can both treat each other metaphorically, like the kids in the back of the car, or one can be in the *metaphorical relationship*, like Felix treating Oscar as though he were the wife, while the other reacts to the odd behavior, like Oscar does.

Or you can have them treat the entire scene in a metaphorical way. For instance, in an episode of *Seinfeld*, Jerry remembers that he has an old library book he's forgotten to return. When he attempts to return it, though, there's a librarian who claims to be a "library detective." All of a sudden, the entire episode becomes a film noir, with all the dialogue and characters reacting as though they were in that style of cinema.

The trick is to keep the characters reacting honestly within the metaphorical situation without destroying or denying the given reality of the scene. For example, in THE ODD COUPLE, while Felix and Oscar behave like an old married couple, it would be incorrect for Felix to actually *think* that Oscar was his husband and do something like call him "darling" or try to kiss him. Oscar's his friend and roommate; Felix just *behaves* as though Oscar were his husband. In a *metaphorical relationship*, it's important to maintain the reality of the surface relationship.

JENNIFER SKELLY

Pick Up a Party Line

JENNIFER SKELLY, a professional actor, writer and scientist, was the story and science advisor for the animated series *The Zula Patrol*, which aired on PBS and NBC. She and her husband and writing partner, David Skelly, recently wrote MISS TWIGGLEY'S TREE, a live-action feature adaptation for BixPix Entertainment, and several episodes of a new animated television series for Nicktoons. The Skellys teach story development at CalArts and are working on a book, *Improv for Writers*.

Dialogue should be the easiest part of writing, shouldn't it? I mean, we all talk. Every day. All the time. We're experts in talking, experts in dialogue. And yet, in my opinion, writing truthful dialogue is one of the biggest challenges we screenwriters face.

As a writer, I strive to make an audience believe that what they're seeing—and hearing—is real. An audience knows when something doesn't ring true, because every person sitting in the audience is just as much of an expert in dialogue as I am. So is every actor. And if an actor doesn't buy the words he's saying, an audience certainly won't.

As an actor, some of my favorite writers are Tina Fey, Woody Allen, Aaron Sorkin and David Mamet (there's always a lot of fun swearing in Mamet). I like to say their words. They understand the gritty, fluid, loose, chaotic way in which people actually converse. They don't try to write pretty dialogue. It's not about vocabulary (well, with Sorkin there are always lots of big government-y words). It's not about diction. It's not about impressing the audience with their witticisms (although Fey and Allen are about as witty as you can get). It's about writing *truthful* dialogue for *real* people.

So, how do people *really* talk? We all know, but getting what we know down on paper isn't as easy as it sounds. Here is an exercise to help us tune our ear (and guide our pen) to truthful dialogue:

EXERCISE

1. Head out to your local coffee shop (or other public place) and set up camp near a cell phone conversation. It shouldn't be hard to find one; people on cell phones are usually the loudest ones around. Open your laptop, or even a notebook (as in paper), so you seem busy and won't look suspicious. And you don't want to look suspicious because you will be engaging in suspicious activity.

2. Listen in on the phone conversation. Write down what's being said. Do your best to note as much as you can. It's okay if you don't get every word, but try to get some full phrases. (You'll probably notice that most of the sentences aren't complete. People don't really pay much attention to grammar when they talk.)

3. Next, fill in the gaps with dialogue from the other side of the conversation. Who is the cell phone talker talking to? (If you got a name, use it! If not, make one up.) What's their relationship? What do they want from each other?

4. Transcribe the conversation into screenplay format. Then flesh out your screenplay with action lines: Instead of a phone call, create a new scenario altogether.

5. Now write the next scene. When do these two characters meet again? What happens next? Write the preceding scene, too. What led them to this meeting?

Hint: While you're out and about, log as many cell phone conversations as you can. People often forget they're in public when talking on their phones, so you'll likely overhear some rather intimate—and truthful—dialogue. It's a great opportunity to note how real people really talk.

Have fun with this exercise! And don't worry about getting it "right"—we aren't trying to accurately depict the life stories of random coffee drinkers. We're trying to get to the truth of a real conversation.

Actively eavesdropping on dialogue is like taking an immersion course in a foreign language; it's the best way to learn it. Once we've listened to how people talk, we can write dialogue in their unique voices, and we can apply their unique voices to our own writing, so that our characters speak truthfully.

REVISION

PILAR ALESSANDRA

Backward Brainstorming

PILAR ALESSANDRA is the director of the writing program On the Page. She's worked as a senior story analyst for DreamWorks and Radar pictures and trains the Fellowship Writers for ABC/Disney. Her students and clients have sold to Disney, DreamWorks, Warner Brothers and Sony, and have won prestigious competitions such as the Austin Film Festival Screenplay Competition and the Nicholls Fellowship. She is the author of *The Coffee Break Screenwriter*.

Many writers feel they need to do a page-one rewrite, when, in truth, what they really need is a page seventy-five rewrite. They've honored their concept, created some great set pieces in act two, set a terrific premise for act three . . . and then they got stuck. If you've faked your way through a third act, hoping that the reader will forgive, think again. Think about the times that you've left a movie and been disappointed by the ending. Everything that came before it suddenly didn't matter.

But rethinking your ending is easier said than done. It's difficult to find cool ways to solve problems. In your screenplay, you know that your sweethearts marry, your cop gets the robber, and your good guy defeats the bad guy. But just how does all of that happen? How does the character get there?

Often, the answer can be found in the small, clever details—what I call the trigger moments that lead to the big revelation.

In ETERNAL SUNSHINE OF THE SPOTLESS MIND, Jim Carrey's character is given the cassette tape that talks about Kate Winslet being his former girlfriend, triggering him to reclaim his memories.

In PRIMAL FEAR, Ed Norton's character slips up by accidentally breaking his own character's rule in which he supposedly doesn't remember anything that happens when he's in the persona of his alter ego. Again, one small moment, in this case a slip of the tongue, triggers a "lightbulb" moment, which leads to the answer.

How do you find those trigger moments? Sometimes it helps to work backward. Start with what you do know, and ask questions that help you find clever ways of getting there.

EXERCISE

1. Start with the final reveal: what does the character discover that is most painful, shocking, surprising or delightful?

2. Where did that person discover it?

3. What physical clue led him to that place?

4. What was said that triggered the character to search for that clue?

5. What event occurred that caused that character to say what he or she said?

6. What problem occurred that created that event?

7. How did the main character's own actions create that problem?

8. What goal did the main character have that caused him to behave badly enough to create this problem?

9. What circumstances in the main character's world inspired that goal?

By asking these questions, you should have at least one new way of moving toward your big third-act revelation. A sequence of clever details that push a character toward a truth is a much more interesting journey than one in which she simply trips on the answer, or worse, is just told!

PAUL GUAY

Hurt Me, Hurt Me!
(Oh, and Help Me Make My Script Better)

PAUL GUAY conceived and cowrote LIAR, LIAR, which, at the time of its
release, was the sixth-highest-grossing comedy in history. The screenplay received an Honorable Mention in *Script Magazine*'s list of the
Best Scripts of the Past 10 Years. He also wrote THE LITTLE RASCALS
and HEARTBREAKERS, the latter of which he co-licensed to MGM for
production as a stage musical. He leads screenwriting workshops and
is a script consultant.

The second semester of my junior year in high school, Robert
W. F. Jones—Menlo School director of studies, Spanish teacher,
faculty advisor, advisor to the student newspaper (the editing
of which I got in hot water for), track coach (I ran the 440 and 880, and
when I didn't, I walked fast) and six-foot, five-inch American original—began teaching creative writing.

As I was the only student in the class for that semester and for all
of my senior year, I think it's fair to say he started the class just for
me. Guess I was the teacher's pet.

Over the course of those three semesters I turned in something
like a thousand poems, lyrics and short stories for that class. Mr. Jones
read them all. And to this day I still treasure some of his comments:
"Destroy this evidence" was scrawled across one of my poems; the
simple but eloquent, "Yuckadoo" adorned another; and the cryptic
note "I have dealt with your story as I saw fit" accompanied an envelope filled with ashes.

Ah, to be the teacher's pet again . . .

Did I take this disrespect lying down? Of course not, I mailed him a fish head.

Back came the note: "The fish head was tasty, although a bit chewy."

He even criticized my fish head.

To this day, Mr. Jones is one of my best friends, not only because we love horror, science fiction and fantasy films; not only because we both worship 2001: A SPACE ODYSSEY and THE WIZARD OF OZ and he introduced me to HAROLD AND MAUDE; not only because he directed me in two productions of *The Zoo Story* and I cut my hand when we used a real knife in one of them; but also because of that class.

Why?

Because he took me seriously enough to read every poem, every lyric, every short story I wrote for a year and a half.

So I had a reader, someone who wasn't my mother or my dad.

So I kept writing.

And because, while it may not have been his intention, and while I didn't realize it at the time, he taught me to grow a thick skin and to be able to listen to criticism.

I took a number of creative-writing classes at Pomona College, where my work—now not only poems, lyrics and short stories but also comedy sketches and plays—was incisively (sometimes derisively) critiqued by my teachers and my peers. What they said didn't upset me; they couldn't top Mr. Jones's ashes. I took what I could use of their comments—whatever I thought would improve the work in question—and let the rest slide off me like water off tooth enamel.

When I worked for five years at Producers Sales Organization writing marketing, advertising and publicity material for the films we produced or distributed overseas, including taglines, trailers and new titles for some of them, I read hundreds of screenplays and analyzed and critiqued a few. I started learning what works, what doesn't and why. And getting the assignment to polish THE NEVERENDING STORY in thirty-six hours, to take a (wonderful) script that read like it had been translated that morning from the German and turn it into something idiomatic and colloquial enough to attract financing from a U.S. distributor didn't hurt.

It was during that time that I began cowriting my own screenplays. When they were "finished," I gave them to five or ten friends (mostly screenwriters) for comments.

My wife, Susan, still remembers the first such critique. The friend was brutal. He eviscerated the script. Everything we'd poured our talent and craft into, everything we'd spent months of our lives writing was called into question, up for grabs.

After the ordeal was over, Susan came into the room to comfort me. To her surprise, I wasn't whimpering under the desk. I wasn't bent over a trash can, puking my guts out. I wasn't shaking with rage. I was, instead, scribbling on binder paper, finishing my notes.

I looked up and saw her expression. "What?" I asked, being a master of dialogue. "No, it was great."

I welcomed the comments, and I welcomed the next five or ten sets that came in.

Would I have enjoyed it if my readers had loved my work and told me it was perfect as is?

A part of me would have. Even now, many scripts later, though I'm a produced writer who should know better (and a script consultant who should *really* know better), a part of me still would love to be stroked and told how good my work is. (I'm *wait*-ing . . .)

But you know what? A much larger part—the part that thinks, the professional part, the part that wants to write the best scripts I'm capable of, scripts that get bought and made into movies that are artistically satisfying enough to justify my existence on this Earth and commercial enough to pay the bills—is delighted at the comments.

You know that the world of screenwriting is incredibly competitive. Your script has to stand out from its 180,000 competitors, so it had better be as close to perfect as you can possibly make it.

Far better that your friends tell you where you've come up short, when you still have time to fix it, than that a potential buyer see the infelicity and you blow a sale.

EXERCISE

Step 1: Make your screenplay perfect.

Step 2: Find five to ten friends and acquaintances—if possible, professional screenwriters or people who read tons of screenplays in their line of work; if not, screenwriters who are working to become pros—and ask them to read your screenplay.

After they read it, start out by asking, "What are your thoughts?" Then listen to their comments *without making any of your own*. Do not give them any feedback or "direct" them in any way. Don't fight. Don't defend. Don't wince. Don't sob.

If they're puffing you up or being too polite, tell them to be as straightforward and honest as possible. Tell them writing may be a holy chore, but it's also a contact sport—and you want to get your game up to the highest level.

Tell them that however tough they are, the marketplace is going to be much tougher.

Tell them a variation of what I tell my clients: You don't want them to blow smoke and tell you your screenplay is perfect as is. If you are a professional or want to be one, such coddling is a waste of your time and theirs. Instead, you want to find out how to make your screenplay better.

Now that you've emboldened them to be direct (and therefore helpful), write down everything they say. This will enable you to look at their comments at leisure rather than in the heat of the moment, when if they make one more caustic criticism you want to grab your laptop and jam it up their snarky, smug, patronizing, condescending, superior tailpipe.

And it will enable you to compare their comments with those of your other readers. Not that you should ignore a point because only one reader makes it. But I'd certainly be taking an especially close look at any point brought up by half or more of my readers.

After your readers have finished responding to your general opening query, ask specific questions, without directing them toward any specific answer.

Here are the questions I ask my readers, in roughly this order:

What gave you problems?

What worked for you?

What are your thoughts about the title?

What are your thoughts about the length (both the page count and how the script reads)?

Are there any scenes that go on too long?

What are your thoughts about the pace? (You'll notice that several times I ask essentially the same question in slightly different ways. That's because sometimes one phrasing will produce more or different information than another, plus I want to see if they're awake.)

What is the script about? What is its theme? How would you describe the movie?

What's the log line? (As with a number of my questions, the answers to this one will not only help me market the project but also let me know whether I'm conveying what I think I'm conveying.)

What's the tagline?

Do you have any ideas for the poster art?

What genre is it? What subgenre? (If I think I've written a comedy-action film and my readers think I've written a romantic comedy, I want to know. If they think I've written a horror musical, I really want to know.)

What are your thoughts about the stakes?

What are your thoughts about the budget?

What are your thoughts about the tone?

What are your thoughts about the believability?

What's the rating? (If I think I've written a PG-13 film, and my readers think I've written an R, I may need to make adjustments. If they think I've written an NC-17, I may need to see their copy of the script.)

What was unclear?

Now I'll ask questions *specific to the project*, like "What are your thoughts about Christopher?" and "What are your thoughts about Christopher's backstory?" and "What are your thoughts about Christopher and Semolina's relationship?" and "What are your thoughts about Mr. Stanton's plan?"

Then I'll return to more general questions:

What are your thoughts about the read? For example, was it smooth?

What are your thoughts about the verbal humor? (This is best asked if you're writing a comedy.)

What are your thoughts about the visual humor?

Does it read comedically?

Did you laugh out loud?

Is there tension?

What is the hook?

What would you put in the trailer?

Who is the audience?

Would you go to see a movie based on this script?

Would you enjoy it?

Would you buy this screenplay?

What's the best thing about the screenplay?

What's the worst thing?

Are there any typos, misspellings, grammar problems, punctuation problems or format problems?

How would you sell it?

What films would you compare it to?

What directors or producers or studios come to mind as being right for this kind of film?

Whom would you cast?

What are my chances of starring in this film? (Just kidding. Sort of.)

Okay, now your session is over.

Whew! That was fun. What next?

You thank them for taking the time to read your script and for giving you their comments.

You compare their comments with those of your other readers.

You implement those changes that will improve your screenplay artistically and/or commercially.

And if you feel undernurtured and your fury still rages, then and only then do you mail them a fish head.

JIM STRAIN

The Jewel Case Outline

JIM STRAIN'S feature film credits include JUMANJI, BINGO and SUM-
MER OF THE MONKEYS. His most recent original screenplay, ZAPPER,
is in preproduction. He is adapting *Alien X-mas*, a children's book he
coauthored, for a stop-motion animated feature, and he is cowriting
SPACE CAMP with Stan Chervin, for United Studios Entertainment
Productions. A visiting assistant professor, he teaches graduate-level
screenwriting at UCLA's Department of Film, Television and Digital
Media.

All screenwriters like to fuss with dialogue, write crisp evocative prose, and create stunning visual images. But in the
end, story structure is the most important component of a
screenplay. Without it, the rest is flummery.

There are a variety of structural story models that screenwriters
rely on, and each has its own merits. I am most comfortable with the
template that identifies the inciting incident, act one escalation, midpoint event, second act crisis, and resolution. But regardless of which
model you prefer, it's important to understand that you are building
the dramatic armature for your story.

Creating the story beats that complete the armature is the next
challenge. Some writers jump into writing the screenplay itself and
work out the details as they go along. Others go to outlines or treatments, which can become very lengthy and complicated as well.

It's easy to get lost in the details of a scene and lose sight of its
function within the overall story. And the most beautifully written
scene on earth is useless if it doesn't serve the whole. The trick is to
keep the bigger picture in mind.

Oddly enough, I have found that DVDs provide a useful tool: the scene index, sometimes called chapter headings. Written to fit a jewel case, scene indexes are, in fact, one-page structural outlines. Once you convert the often-cryptic headings to a brief plot beat, you have the film in a nutshell. Here are a few examples from BONNIE AND CLYDE, one of my all-time favorites:

Chapter Title: *The things that turn up in the street*

Story beat summary: Bonnie meets Clyde when he tries to steal her car.

Chapter Title: *Home bodies*

Story beat summary: Barrows on vacation. Bonnie's conflict with Blanche escalates.

Chapter Title: *Velma Davis and Eugene Grizzard*

Story beat summary: Gang kidnaps undertaker and girlfriend. Foreshadows death. Triggers visit home.

In the end you wind up with a concise thirty-six-point outline of the story beats: the big picture on a single typewritten page. Within that format, it's relatively easy to identify the major structural tent poles.

Of course, chapter headings or scene indexes are written after the fact. But it occurred to me that thinking in those terms at the outset of a project might be a useful tool. A few years back, I began requiring my UCLA graduate screenwriting students to submit a jewel case outline prior to beginning their first drafts. What I have discovered is that it is one of the most difficult assignments and yet one of the most fruitful, because it requires a big-picture overview and reduces stories to their essential beats.

This is not easy, but the exercise quickly identifies problem areas and muddy thinking. It clears the shrubbery and forces a writer to determine the fundamental purpose of a scene or sequence within the context of the entire screenplay. That is not to say that the resulting beat sheet becomes a straightjacket that confines the subsequent writing process. Any screenwriter will tell you that a work evolves as the characters come to life and the details emerge. As philosopher Alfred Korzybski once said, "The map is not the territory." But I've found that the jewel case outline can be a useful structural touchstone.

EXERCISE

1. To get the hang of the process, choose a favorite DVD and convert the chapter headings or scene indexes into brief story beat summaries. Confine your summaries to a single descriptive line. There are likely to be multiple story elements you can identify in each chapter, but prune your way to the most important.

2. Now do the same with an existing screenplay you are about to rewrite. Oftentimes the jewel case outline will help you diagnose fundamental story problems that have been masked by your sparkling prose or lively dialogue. The result might also suggest that your foundation is strong and that you can now focus on aspects of character or scene details.

3. Finally, take a crack at writing a jewel case outline for a project you are about to begin. Confine your outline to thirty-six story beats. If you don't know them all, leave blanks. Identify the inciting incident, the act one break, the midpoint, and the second act crisis point. If you haven't nailed down every beat, don't let that deter you. Many problems won't be solved until you throw yourself into the draft. Don't allow a "perfect" outline to become an excuse for not writing. You are creating a reference tool, not an immutable blueprint.

JAYCE BARTOK

"'Aloud,' He Cried!"

JAYCE BARTOK wrote the screenplay THE CAKE EATERS and has three more screenplays currently in development. Shortly he will step into the realm of feature directing with his screenplay RED RIVER, a true-crime thriller about a seemingly normal family in Wisconsin who are connected to a bizarre series of deaths in the Mississippi River.

Movies are, at their core, a hypnotic stream of images flickering at twenty-four frames per second, a sensual marriage of sight and sound that transports a group of strangers in a dark, cool theater to a place of communal fiction. In the purest sense, movies must be seen in a *theater* with an *audience* that hangs on every word in your screen*play*. Maybe you see where I'm going here. Movies are the big bad bastard child of the theater. They are the spoiled overgrown tantrum-throwing edge-of-your-seat explosion-filled spectacle-fest relation of that ancient art form of the Greeks known as the *play*.

Hamlet tells us, "The play's the thing!" As fledgling screenwriters, we write and write and rewrite . . . and cry. But one thing we don't usually do is think of our screenplay as a living, breathing, moving thing with parts that will engage and move a live audience with just the words on your page sans big crane shots and famous movie star mugs.

Hearing your words aloud, brought to life by a group of talented actors—whether they be famous thespians, friends, or relatives—is the most invaluable litmus test for your developing screenplay. There is nothing more humbling and simultaneously exhilarating, whether in a theater rented for the night with an audience filled with producers and potential investors or before a group of folding chairs set in a circle in your living room with an audience of friends and pets. You will immediately get a sense of what works and what doesn't in your screenplay. It is the first road test of many that your script will endure at the hands of readers and covering agents throughout the land, so I recommend putting yourself through this right out of the gate so you can fix the problems and also stand by your work; because if you can't stand by it, no one else will.

In those early drafts, so many fanciful things take hold of your imagination—they are powerful and important fancies in forming a truly original story—yet under the discriminating eye of a warm and supportive audience (not a bunch of killjoys, mind you), these early fancies can seem a step too far. That certain monologue that makes you cry every time you read it might not be necessary. That knife fight at the end of a small town indie drama may seem to clash tonally with the rest of your story. That extended hospital scene where every character says his piece may better serve the story if seen in silence, without any dialogue at all.

The feedback and notes you will get from hearing your words read aloud in front of an audience is more valuable than any screenwriting course you could ever take, so try to leave your ego at home. Instead, just nod and write down all the notes from all the generous people who decide to give you their opinions. As much as you may want to strangle them at the time, as you desperately try to down your seltzer, mopping sweat off your forehead, crowded up against a wall in the swirling post-reading atmosphere of a hot theater or living room, just smile and say, "Thanks for coming." It's these notes that, once the dust has settled and you've licked your wounds, will be the iron rebar of your new drafts to come.

EXERCISE

1. I recommend getting your screenplay to at least the third or preferably the fifth draft before you trot it out for the masses. That way it will at least begin to resemble the Oscar-winning work of art that it will soon become.

2. Find a space to hold the reading, but don't spend more than $500 for the rental fee and food/wine for the night, because you don't have it.

3. Gather a great group of actors. Actors will do anything for a good part. They will walk over broken glass to shine under the footlights and hopefully impress you, so that when your masterwork gets financed, you will offer up their name in a casting session. If you don't have access to a roster of actors, for a small fee you can always hire a casting director if you are in New York, Los Angeles, or Chicago. Or you can post listings online or go to your local community theater. You'd be surprised what talent lurks beneath your very eyes.

4. Pick a date, and make it a party: wine, cheese, art.

5. Gather your notes, either in the form of harried after-reading encounters, e-mails, or coffee meet-ups. I recommend saying: "E-mail me your thoughts." And really try to be open to the feedback. You'll be surprised where it will lead you.

6. Finally, a few weeks after the reading, begin again but, this time, knowing you have looked the dragon in the face and triumphed. Heck, they even applauded.

CHARLES DEEMER

Screenwriters: Stop Shooting Yourself in the Foot!

CHARLES DEEMER is the author of *Practical Screenwriting* and *Screenwright*, an electronic screenwriting tutorial. Three of his short scripts have been produced, and many feature scripts optioned. Deemer now makes his own digital films as artistic director of Small Screen Video. His DVDs include THE HEIRS: A SILENT COMEDY and KARAOKE TONITE!, a mockumentary. He teaches screenwriting at Portland State University.

I'm at the age where I'm asked to judge screenwriting contests from time to time, and the experience has been enlightening. As a screenwriting professor, I've long been aware of the common problems beginning screenwriters share, but I did not realize that so many wannabes were so consistently their own worst enemies. This is unfortunate because their errors are so easily correctable. But why do they happen in the first place? Clearly, considerable misunderstanding is at work.

Beginning screenwriters write what are called *spec scripts*—scripts written on speculation that they will sell after being written—and herein lies the problem. Screenplays that get published are *shooting scripts*, which are a different animal. Therefore, a beginning screenwriter who checks a screenplay out of the library and uses it as a model of what to write already has two strikes against him or her! It's the wrong model.

To understand the nature of spec scripts, consider how they are read in the real world. They are not read for pleasure; they are read for business. They are read by readers hired by producers to evaluate them, and these readers get paid by the script. What does this tell you? The longer a reader takes to read a script, the more complicated the script's language and the less he or she gets paid. In other words, the way to get on a reader's good side—and my good side when I'm judging a contest—is to write in a style that is quickly read and easily understood.

Such a style is not what is commonly thought of as literary prose. Screenplays require a rhetoric that is totally different from that of prose. The first mistake made by most beginning screenwriters is that they set out to write a literary document. A screenplay is *not* a literary document but a *blueprint* for a film. It must read like a blueprint, not like a short story.

The cardinal sin in spec-script screenwriting is this: Your writing gets in the way of your story. What a thing to say about any kind of writing! *Your writing gets in the way of your story.* In other words, screenplays are story driven, not rhetoric driven. No one cares about your "writing." They want to know your story. If you write "literary prose," you shoot yourself in the foot by making your story too hard to find. *A screenplay is a blueprint for a movie.* Write accordingly, which is to write simply.

Here are some tips for writing an effective spec screenplay:

- Use short, simple sentences, not long, complex sentences.

- Don't be afraid to use sentence fragments.

- Write generically: You are not the costume designer, or the set designer, or the actor, or the director. In prose, detail makes for good writing—but *not* in screenwriting! Only use detail that is dramatically important to the story. If detail has no dramatic function, be generic, such as: "It's a typical teen girl's bedroom, full of stuffed animals and rock band posters." Someone else will decide which animals and which posters. A screenwriter is a collaborator.

- Write vertically. The more your script invites a vertical reading rather than a horizontal reading, the less it looks like prose, and the more it looks like a screenplay. This point is worth elaborating.

Consider this paragraph from a student screenplay:

> *One showgirl heads toward the back of the store, not even looking at the clerk as he watches her backside. She is an excellent distraction. The other girl walks directly to the counter and smiles at the young man. He can't tell what she looks like since her face is made up and she is wearing oversized false eyelashes.*

To someone unfamiliar with screenwriting, this might read "simply" enough, but this passage is overwritten and has too much text density. Readers often reject text density unread! Let me rewrite this as follows:

> *One showgirl heads toward the back of the store.*
> *The clerk watches her.*
> *The other showgirl comes to the counter.*
> *She wears oversized false eyelashes. She smiles at the clerk.*

Take a moment to compare these two passages without reading them. The first looks like prose. The second looks like an outline or list. This is what screenwriting should look like, a blueprint for a movie. As a reader, when I have a pile of a hundred scripts on the desk and pick them up one by one, first impressions matter. When I see the proselike text density of the first example, I assume the writer doesn't know much about screenwriting. Right or wrong, this is the first impression. The first writer is shooting himself in the foot.

Opening up your script to a more listlike, outlinelike appearance is called adding verticality. In fact, this technique has an important visual function. Here is a handy rule to follow: When your writing implies a new image, begin a new paragraph. Notice how this explains the paragraphs of my rewrite above. First image: The woman walks to the back of the store. Second image: The clerk watches. Third: The other approaches the counter. Fourth: A closer angle, to see the false eyelashes and smile. Cameras are never mentioned in a spec screenplay, but by beginning a new paragraph with each new image, you can, in fact, write your script as if you are directing it. It's subtle, but it works and it adds verticality to your script. It makes the script much more inviting to read (and readers often skim as much as read, so your writing style must be easily skimmed).

EXERCISE

Go through your screenplay, paragraph by paragraph, one sentence at a time. If the sentence implies a new image on the screen, start a new paragraph. Notice how much verticality is added to your script this way, how much more it begins to resemble an outline or blueprint and less the prose of "normal" writing.

Look at your writing style. Change all complex sentences to two or more simple sentences. Don't be afraid to use sentence fragments.

Look at your descriptions. Make sure detail has a dramatic function; otherwise be more generic, leaving clues for the costume designer, clues for the set designer, etc. Be a good collaborator.

Above all, don't let your writing get in the way of your story. Never forget that a screenplay is a blueprint for a movie, not a literary document. This is not the form for showing off your writing ability. This is the form for showing off your storytelling ability.

KEN ROTCOP

The First Ten Pages

KEN ROTCOP is the winner of the Writers Guild Award, the Image Award and the Neil Simon Award for the writing and producing of FOR US THE LIVING: THE STORY OF MEDGAR EVERS. He has been the creative head at four major studios and is the author of *The Perfect Pitch* series.

Once you've finished your screenplay, then comes the hard part: getting someone to read it! Someone of influence who can turn your script into a movie.

Convincing someone requires persuasiveness, enthusiasm and the ability to verbally communicate your passion for your story. This procedure is called "The Pitch." Here are some rules to follow:

1. Keep your pitch under two minutes.

2. Do *not* tell the whole story, only a piece of business that will captivate the listener, something that is unique or different about your story.

3. Remember, movies are about people, people caught in a web of conflict or intrigue. Always start your pitch with: "This is the story of a man (or woman) who . . ."

4. Sometimes the pitch should be about the villain, the antagonist, rather than the hero, the protagonist. Villains always put the story into action and most times they are infinitely more interesting than the protagonist.

5. And, finally, if your listener asks you to send a synopsis, send the first ten pages of your screenplay instead.

There is no way you can bring your story to life in a synopsis or write a condensation that communicates the innuendos, the shadings, the twists and turns or the flavor of the screenplay. It just can't be done. Instead, send those first ten pages with the following cover letter:

> *Dear [Name of Producer]:*
>
> *Per our phone conversation of [date], I know you asked me to send a synopsis of my screenplay [title]. Instead, I am taking the liberty of sending you the first ten pages of my script. Please take eight minutes to read these ten pages.*
>
> *They will not only tell you what my story is about but also show you my ability to write.*
>
> *I hope you will then ask for the rest of the screenplay, which I will send you immediately.*
>
> *I may be reached at [your phone number] or my e-mail address, which is [e-mail address].*
>
> *[Then, if you already have representation, you may also include your agent's name and contact info here.]*
>
> *Awaiting your response,*
> *[Your signature]*

Numerous studios and producers are now using this method. Rather than ask for a synopsis, they're asking for the first ten pages.

EXERCISE

In order to entice an executive to read your entire screenplay, the first ten pages must answer the following questions:

1. Who is the protagonist?

2. What does she want?

3. Who or what is stopping the protagonist from reaching her goal?

4. Why do I care about the protagonist and whether she reaches her goal or not?

5. Have I established the genre in these ten pages? (Comedy, action-adventure, drama, etc.)

6. Have I taken the protagonist out of her comfort zone and placed her in a situation from which she can never go back to the way things were?

Answer these half dozen questions to your satisfaction and you're ready to submit those very important first ten pages.

BILLY FROLICK

Prose (and Cons)

BILLY FROLICK's screenwriting credits include DreamWorks Animation's MADAGASCAR, and IT IS WHAT IT IS, his award-winning directorial debut, which stars Jonathan Silverman. Billy's journalism has appeared in *The New Yorker*, *Entertainment Weekly* and the *Los Angeles Times*. He is the author of five books, including *What I Really Want to Do Is Direct: Seven Film School Graduates Go to Hollywood*, and teaches feature screenwriting at NYU's Tisch School of the Arts.

In the 1980s. There was a trend. To write. Screenplay description. This way.

Who led this staccato stampede, William Shatner? Actually, Shane Black often gets the credit (or blame). But at least with "modern noir" projects like LETHAL WEAPON, Black was plying a genre that justified this hard-boiled style.

With rare exceptions, though, sentence fragments in scene description need to go the way of the mullet, Chia Pets and leg warmers. We may be living in a golden era of attention deficit disorder, but if the day arrives when complete sentences become just too inconvenient, literacy must officially be pronounced dead.

Too often devalued and considered wasted effort that won't end up in the movie, the descriptive passage is an important tool in the screenwriter's box. That's not to say that these paragraphs should resemble your old college essays. But effective prose—tight, yet colorful and vivid—is crucial to evoking detail and atmosphere and maintaining a story's tone. The first audience for any script is not a moviegoer but a reader, be it friend, story analyst, agent or producer. And the screenwriter's job is to earn that individual's attention and to maintain it through clarity and economy.

The average script reader's tolerance threshold for shoddy craftsmanship is low. A perceived lack of discipline and focus usually leads one to conclude, often as early as the second or third page, that the writer is not in control. (Trust me. I started as a reader.) Just think about how quickly you get bored watching a movie . . . then double that speed.

A common by-product of thoughtless prose writing is redundancy—and if I've said this once, I've said it a thousand times. Does "rundown gas station" require any further description? Is one character telling another about an event we've already seen? Does a guy introduced as being "fat" really need to be subsequently identified as "portly," "rotund" and "overweight"? Yawn. Get me a pillow!

Unlike novels, playwriting and poetry, there is little margin for error in scriptwriting. You may be a natural storyteller with a great ear for dialogue, but these gifts may go unnoticed if you don't respect the importance of grammar, punctuation and syntax.

"I didn't have time to write a short letter," Mark Twain once said, "so I wrote a long one instead." With a screenplay, take however much time it requires to write it best.

And then. Script long. And. Prosper.

EXERCISE

Pick up the published screenplay—one you haven't read—of a film you admire, let's say the Coen Brothers' FARGO. (What screenwriter doesn't admire that one?) Before you read it, watch a five- to ten-minute scene from the movie. Watch it as many times as you need to in order to write it in screenplay form. You don't need to transcribe the dialogue.

Read your scene over and rework it until you feel it reaches a professional standard and articulates what's on screen, even if that involves looking at the scene yet again.

Then read the published scene. What details did you leave out? What unnecessary information did you put in? How clear and compelling is the scene in the actual screenplay compared with your version? Which specific *words* evoked the tone that ended up on screen?

Even if the published screenplay is a shooting script or transcript of the finished film, this exercise will help you to achieve fluency and confidence in your prose writing.

If you haven't—or even if you have—read Strunk and White's *The Elements of Style.* Consider taking a basic mechanical-writing class, frequently offered in continuing education programs. All of these rudiments will help make your scripts more "readable," with the right combination of flow, rhythm, word economy and efficiency of expression.

PETER MYERS

What to Do When You're Stuck on a Creative Problem

PETER MYERS is a Hollywood-based screenwriter, producer and script consultant who works with fellow screenwriters as well as producers and directors. Two films based on screenplays rewritten according to his analyses were shot in 2009.

Frankly, I'm not much into "exercises" when I write scripts. I just write them.

But I will give you one thing that has worked for me for many years, even before I was a screenwriter—when I was still a sculptor.

It is the solution to the problem of how do I get through this scene or bit of dialogue, or how do I write a great log line for this premise. It's the answer to the "How do I . . ." question, when the writer is just plain stuck and can't think of a way to solve a problem or create what he or she wants to create.

Here's the answer:

EXERCISE

When you're stuck, return to what originally inspired you to write the script, to write that scene, to write that particular line of dialogue or to create anything, for that matter.

This may involve physically returning to a place, or a person, or again listening to a piece of music or just mentally returning to that moment when you were inspired by something. But, when you get back to what originally inspired you and you relive that moment of inspiration, the answer will come to you. It's really inevitable, and this has worked for me countless times.

Getting stuck mid-process can happen sometimes; artists of any kind can go down various side roads and get distracted from communicating what they want to communicate. The danger is they can lose sight of why they began that particular artistic journey in the first place! And, as they wander, inevitably they will stumble, because they're off course from their true inner creative purpose, which started them on that journey.

So if you have a problem on your journey, return to what started you on that road at the beginning. The source of inspiration is like an ever-flowing spring, from which ideas will just appear, as if by magic—as long as whatever inspired you manages to retain your interest.

Which leads to something else, I might as well mention: You create the interest in whatever it is that you're interested in. That thing, or person or idea does not create the interest. You do. So, if your interest in a particular thing or your inspiration is lagging, no sweat. Just find something else about it to be interested in. You do this by communicating more deeply with whatever that is. If it's a person, talk to him or her some more. If it's a place, revisit it. If it was a piece of music, play it on the iPod again.

If you're a screenwriter, the chances are ninety-nine out of a hundred that you write about people. And one thing I've observed about people: There's no one I meet who, after I speak with him for five or ten minutes, doesn't reveal something interesting about himself, or what has happened to him or what he's observed in life that wouldn't fit into a film or even be worthy of the central subject for a film. But it's *me* creating my interest in them.

So, in essence, you are the source of your own inspiration, because you are the one finding interest in something in life. As long as you have that, as long as you return to that, you'll never stay stuck on a script, a scene, a novel chapter, a line of dialogue, for very long. So, have at it, and have fun writing!

DEVORAH CUTLER-RUBENSTEIN

Button It—The Cure for Overwriting

DEVORAH CUTLER-RUBENSTEIN has participated in every creative and business aspect of motion pictures and television. A former studio exec and now at The Script Broker®, a division of Noble House Entertainment, Inc., she helps writers connect with the marketplace. She is an adjunct professor at USC's School of Cinema/TV and author of *What's "the Big Idea?" Writing Shorts.*

Just like a dress shirt that's buttoned incorrectly and is one button off, even a great scene that goes beyond its natural conclusion feels unkempt, uncared for and unprofessional. For a professional writer, *buttoning* is a term commonly used in writing or performing comedy. A director collaborating with a show runner (writer/producer who "runs" a TV show) will say, "Great button for that scene," when something that's been set up pays off comedically or emotionally.

Buttoning a scene is a tool rarely talked about, an oft-overlooked wrench in a writer's tool kit. The "button moment" of a scene is critical to the lifeblood of a script. Not knowing where to end a song, scene or story can be deadly. At the very least, it can be annoying to the point where a studio reader will just put the script down and pick up another one in its place.

In my own writing, a button can lend a kind of rhythm-inducing (or rhythm-enhancing) musical note that completes an action for my characters. It's an "aha" moment that creates a sense of completion of a mission, great or small, and it's a way of feeling closer to my characters.

When I first started writing screenplays, under the tutelage of

Alexander Mackendrick at CalArts Film School, I drastically over-wrote. It was not Professor Mackendrick's fault—he was a master of brevity—but I just felt the need to overwrite to explore my char-acters. Inevitably, I included "too much fat," which did not advance the story. In the beginning, my scripts ended up in the recycle pile because I was too lazy, too in love with my words or plain ignorant about where to end a scene. Improvisation was the key for me under-standing buttons.

Improv usually consists of short scenes with a beginning, middle and end. When the houselights come up, the audience applauds or not. You get instant feedback. But as a writer, in the privacy of your own mind, how do you get feedback? My sister, a professional improviser who teaches improv to writers, said she feels the teeth of a scene during a performance, and she bites down hard when she needs a button to wrap things up. Perhaps learning to button is a way of thinking, and improvisation is where a writer can flex and tone mental muscles?

As an adjunct professor at USC working on story with student directors and student writers, I invariably have them get up and improvise a scene with their actors. This helps them keep it alive, see it from the characters' POV and feel the spot where a scene wants (and needs) to end. An improv class helps improve the spontaneity and urgency of your writing, and it'll definitely help you become more aware of the endings and beginnings of scenes—those seem-ingly elusive buttons.

EXERCISE

Start by getting a group of writers together and maybe one actor who'll help the group conquer any performance anxiety. After all, this is not about performance; it's about working out in your mental gym. One writer selects volunteers from the group to do an improv of an existing scene from his screenplay that's overwritten and in need of a button. The writer describes only: (1) location (2) relationship (3) goals . . . Opposing goals are best. The writer of the scene calls, "Action," and the improv begins.

While watching the scene unfold, when the writer senses the button for his scene, he then says, "That's the button . . . End scene!" If the scene goes on too long, start the scene over with another writer in the group assigned to call out the button.

GLEN MAZZARA

Finishing a Script—The Actor Pass

GLEN MAZZARA is currently executive producer and show runner of *Hawthorne*. He was the creator and show runner of the first season of *Crash* and has also written for *The Shield*, *Life* and *Nash Bridges*. He is currently writing the features HATER and HANCOCK 2.

Many aspiring film and TV writers ask me, "When do I know a script is finished?" There's always another friend to read it, always another round of notes. Always some little tweak to be made, and, if you're like me, it can be difficult to let go. How do we know when it's done?

When I first moved to L.A., scripts were still hand-delivered—none of this e-mailing pdf file stuff. I once finished a spec script, printed it out, inserted the right brads, drove it to my agent's office, parked, got out, then jumped back in and drove all the way home to cut a line. It threw the formatting off, and, of course, I had to reprint the entire script. Neurotic? I like to think "meticulous." But that's baloney—I just had no idea if the script was any good. It was all so terrifying.

Since then, I've published many scripts and have found that what's always surprising is how they are read, particularly by actors. The story, the nuances, the clever turn of a phrase—these are all glossed over by the actor reading a script. They scan the scenes to see how many they are in. The young ones may count lines. The smart ones don't; they look at their *moments*, those little snippets of their character that they can invest in, those glimpses into the inner workings of their character's humanity that only they can bring to life. The moments when they get to shine, when they get to do good work, when they get to act. It's these moments that resonate with the audience, not the clever turn of a phrase. The look of heartbreak and betrayal a young wife has on her face when she learns her husband is cheating stays with us. The pithy action line reminding the director to get that shot remains invisible. The wife may or may not have a line of dialogue. The best writers will realize the actor will carry the day and not write one. The smart actor will probably ask to cut the line and say, "Can't I just play that with a look?" And she will be right. Her look will say it all.

So after the script is done, after you've typed THE END, and polished it countless times, and cut for length, and cut each scene to the bone, and moved scenes around, and you're deep in the story's tunnel, no longer sure if it makes sense, if you've even remembered to use verbs, the last thing you do is an *actor pass*.

EXERCISE

Read your script as if you are the lead actor, #1 on the call sheet. Read only your scenes and only your dialogue. Polish as necessary. Cut. Tighten. Punch up the dialogue. Broom out all extraneous, confusing loose ends. Delete all precious writing that calls attention to itself. You'll find that perhaps this character drops out of the story for twenty-five pages, or that he is angry in one scene but enters the next joking instead of seething. That doesn't track, and by doing a pass for that character, you'll pick it up, smooth it out and tie the entire script together.

Most important, you'll determine if your character is passive instead of driving the action. If there is a scene running several pages, and your lead only says, "Got it," "What?" and "Call you back," any actor of merit is going to ask what they're doing in the scene. They're not driving the action; they have no moment. You've wasted an opportunity.

The actor pass moves you from writer to actor. You start to see how others will read your script. It's about to go out into the world; your baby is about to be born. You begin the process of letting go.

After you finish this lead-character pass, go back and read the script as your second most important character. Read the script all the way through again, but with that character's eyes. Punch it up as necessary. Do not look at any scene #2 is not in. Then go through as character #3, then #4, etc. These multiple passes deepen the work and add layers. By the time you are polishing things from Clerk #2's perspective, trust me, you're done. Time to send off that file and enter the next rung of screenwriter hell: waiting for feedback. Congratulations.

NOW WHAT?

BILL LUNDY

Creating the Killer Log Line

BILL LUNDY has written two movies for the Sci-Fi Channel, has sold stories to *Star Trek: Voyager,* and currently has several feature projects in development. A top script consultant and teacher, he's been nick-named "The Log Line Doctor" and has taught classes at Screenwriting Expo, the Scriptwriters Network, Learning Tree University and other venues.

So you've written a really great script. Honed it to perfection. Made the characters come alive, the dialogue sing, the action punch the reader in the gut. You're ready to set it loose on the world, convinced it's going to sell or at least get you noticed by Very Important People in Hollywood.

But you're still missing one very important item. It's the answer to the big question: *How* are you going to get people to read your script? No one's going to read it just on blind faith or simply because you ask them to. They're going to want to read it based on one thing: *What's It About*? What's the story, what's the hook, what's going to make them want to take two hours out of their busy lives to read your precious pages?

That's where your *log line* comes in. For the uninitiated, a *log line* is a one- or two-sentence description of your story. It's arguably the single biggest selling tool a writer uses. And yet too many writers have no idea how to create a good one. They either tell too much or don't tell enough. Or they just don't make it interesting: "Boy meets girl, boy loses girl, boy wins girl back." *Bleh.*

EXERCISE

So how do you create a killer log line, one guaranteed to grab some-one's interest? It's really a very simple formula, which I'll break down into the following five steps:

1. Lead with Your Title.

   A good title is a selling point unto itself, but you'd be sur-prised how many pitches I've heard or query letters I've seen over the years in which the writer forgets to mention the title. Train yourself to always start with your title when giving your log line or pitching your story in a longer format.

2. Indicate the Genre.

   The next step is also one that many writers forget about and which is almost as important as the title: the *genre*. Indicating the genre of the script right off the bat helps orient the reader/lis-tener to what he or she is about to read or hear. If you say, "It's a comedy about . . ." then the person you're telling it to is more likely to think your idea is funny or at least has the potential to be. Or, saying "It's an action-thriller about . . ." better prepares the listener/reader to be thrilled or excited. If your script is based on a true story or another source (book, comic book, play), this is where you mention that as well.

3. Introduce Your Protagonist and Your Protagonist's Situation.

   Okay, you've got your *title* and your *genre*. Now you're ready to delve into the log line proper. Besides the question "What's it about?" a good log line also answers a few secondary questions while giving an accurate, succinct overview of your story.

   The first of those secondary questions is: *Who* is it about? Here's where you introduce your Main Character (or Protago-nist) in a general but cool way. Don't give the person's name, just describe who this person is. Some examples from famous movies:

   A naïve but ambitious farm boy (STAR WARS)

CREATING THE KILLER LOG LINE

A tortured billionaire (THE DARK KNIGHT)

A greedy, compulsively lying lawyer (LIAR, LIAR)

If you want to embellish it a little bit, you can add something about your protagonist's situation at the beginning of your story. This helps to give an overview of both the story arc and the protagonist's *character arc*, i.e., the physical and emotional journey through which the events of the story will take the character.

A naïve but ambitious farm boy from a backwater desert planet . . .

A tortured billionaire using his resources and fighting skills to secretly battle crime in his beloved city . . .

A greedy, compulsively lying lawyer on the fast track to a partnership . . .

4. Describe the Central Conflict.

The next step is to describe your *central conflict* and, usually, mention your *primary antagonist* or *antagonistic force*. This really is your answer to "What's it about?" or, more precisely, "What happens to your protagonist?"

It's the centerpiece of your log line and needs to relay the basic plot of your story as entertainingly and concisely as possible. This is also where you can introduce key supporting characters if they're central to the main plot. Let's continue with some of the examples we've used earlier, starting from the beginning with each:

STAR WARS—A science-fiction fantasy about a naïve but ambitious farm boy from a backwater desert planet who teams up with a feisty princess, a mercenary space pilot and an old wizard warrior to lead a ragtag rebellion against the sinister forces of the evil Galactic Empire.

THE DARK KNIGHT—A noir fantasy based on the classic *Batman* comic books about a tortured billionaire who uses his resources and fighting skills to secretly battle crime in his beloved city and who tries to save the woman he loves and a crusading district attorney from a deformed, amoral, chaos-loving maniac.

LIAR LIAR—A comedy about a greedy, compulsively lying lawyer on the fast track to a partnership, whose life gets turned

327

upside down when a magical birthday wish by his neglected son forces him to tell only the truth for an entire day.

As you can see, we're almost there. All of these give a pretty good overview of the basic story. Now it's time to add the final ingredient, the one that really makes your log line soar and stand out from the crowd.

5. Sketch In the Protagonist's Arc.

This answers the final secondary question, which is something along the lines of "What does your protagonist learn?" or "How does your protagonist change?" Adding a bit of detail about the protagonist's character arc gives your log line a crucial emotional element, allowing your reader/listener to really connect with the story you're trying to tell. Expanding on the examples used above, notice the different ways the arc is integrated into the log line (in italics):

STAR WARS—A science-fiction fantasy about a naïve but ambitious farm boy from a backwater desert planet *who discovers powers he never knew he had* when he teams up with a feisty princess, a mercenary space pilot and an old wizard warrior to lead a ragtag rebellion against the sinister forces of the evil Galactic Empire.

THE DARK KNIGHT—A noir fantasy based on the classic *Batman* comic book series about a tortured billionaire who uses his resources and fighting skills to secretly battle crime in his beloved city and *who struggles with his sense of justice and purpose* while trying to save the woman he loves and a crusading district attorney from a deformed, amoral, chaos-loving maniac.

LIAR LIAR—A comedy about a greedy, compulsively lying lawyer on the fast track to a partnership *who learns what's really important in life* when a magical birthday wish by his neglected son forces him to tell only the truth for an entire day.

That's pretty much all there is to it. Using this five-step formula will help you craft solid, enticing log lines that will be the key marketing tools for your scripts.

A word of caution: If you have trouble using this technique to create a log line for one of your stories, chances are it's the story itself that's the problem. In my experience, a script that can't be boiled down to a good log line is usually one that needs work and isn't ready to go out yet. Either the protagonist or central conflict isn't really well defined, or the overall story hasn't come into focus yet and is clouded by too many unnecessary subplots or characters. Many writers actually use this technique before they even begin writing their script, as a way of homing in on the actual story they're trying to tell. You can use it as a reference while you're writing, to make sure you're staying on track.

HEATHER HALE

What If It Were Your Money?

HEATHER HALE wrote, directed and executive-produced the pilot *Ghost Writer*. Her other credits include about fifty hours of award-winning productions, including a 2000 Lifetime Original Movie. Her work has garnered two Emmys, two Tellys and "Best New Series Pilot" for *The Evidence*. Heather is a member of the Television Academy and Showbiz Mensa.

I thought I'd offer a completely different perspective (one that I think gets ignored all too often in the speculative market): *What if it were your money? I mean . . . really your money.*

If you've ever produced your own independent film, you know what I'm talking about: Entire scenes get slashed because *there just isn't time* or, more accurately, never enough money.

But even in development of big-budget studio features, writers must reduce their scripts to only the essential. Each and every scene must simultaneously forward plot, develop character and reveal theme—all while delivering on the audience's expectations for the genre.

Think of it as a reduction sauce: You start with all these great colorful, flavorful ingredients (moments, characters, images). Maybe you sauté them individually to bring out their rich, unique flavors—but ultimately, everything gets dumped into the same pot to be patiently and diligently boiled down—for hours, days—evaporating all the unnecessary watery dilution until it is condensed to its wonderful essence.

Let's figure out how to reduce your script to everything—and nothing—but what must be shot to powerfully and cinematically tell your story.

EXERCISE

1. Pretend it's your money making your film.

    (a) Let's say you just won the lottery. After taxes (and relatives you never knew you had come out of the woodwork), you net a cool $10 million. Yay. *Just walk with me for a moment in this possibility* . . .

    (b) Now you can finally self-finance that brilliant hundred-page script that's been collecting dust on your Ikea shelf for over a decade! You can actually—dare I say—put your money where your pitch is!

    (c) You can add or subtract a zero if you like (to plan your $1 million indie or your $100-million studio summer tent pole flick), but just to keep the math easy:

    $10,000,000 Fantasy Lottery Winnings Budget, 100-Page Script = $100,000 Cost per Page
    (REMEMBER: It's out of your pocket!)
    Now let's see how this new perspective changes things. . . .

2. First: Set your script aside. Take your favorite pen and paper to your most effective writing environment: a quiet beach, noisy coffee house, hole-in-the-wall dive bar, library, cramped airplane seat, living room filled with the chaos of children—whatever and wherever it is. Don't even bring your script or laptop. Make a list of the twenty-five most memorable moments from your script.
    What are the:

    • most conflict-rich scenes?

    • images that most resonate with you?

    • beats that get the most laughs or lean-ins during pitches?

    • lines of dialogue that distill the whole story?

    • the trailer moments (script your trailer even!)?

    • the "decisions resulting in visible action" that if you had to take money out of your own pocket for, this story could not be told without?

Don't worry about chronological sequence or even order of priority; just jot them down as they come to you. What might alarm you (or crack you up) are the scenes you can't even remember. This is perhaps one of the best lessons of this exercise. If you (who have written, what, seventeen drafts of this script?) can't even remember a particular scene (or a character or a subplot), do you really think anyone in your audience will remember it? Probably not. If it's not worth shooting, what's it doing taking up precious real estate and slackening the pace in your spec script? Dead page space. Why risk the sale over something you wouldn't even shoot?

3. Now set the twenty-five ingredients for your reduction sauce script recipe aside (yes, it can be sixteen or thirty-one—don't be anal . . . creativity, like cooking, is not a precise science) and try to remember what inspired you to write this script in the first place. Really think about it: *Do you remember?* Was it a heartbreak? A betrayal? A stranger's intriguing comment? An image you passed while traveling? The combination of something you were reading colliding with a memory? What got so far under your skin that compelled you to spend this much time of your life trying to express it?

   Does the same theme or pattern pop up over and over in your writing even if it shows up in different eras and genres? Is it all the same story? The issues you're working through at this time in your life? I encourage you to keep a journal or track your inspirations as much as the changes you made in each draft (why and for whom); this can be an invaluable paper trail as you navigate the development process.

4. Now you *finally* get to open that last draft of your poor, neglected script. By now, I promise you, it's going to look very different to you. The pages that can be ruthlessly slashed will go slinking off, embarrassed, of their own accord. Suddenly, when it's your money, you're not so eager to save that on-the-nose, boring expositional scene of "How are you?" "Fine. And you?" "Good. Say, how long have we been friends?"

And suddenly that three-page throwaway transition that gets your heroine from the haunted mansion back to her magazine office isn't worth trading for your dream beach house or convertible Jaguar or trip to Greece.

5. Now that you've taken a fine paring knife to the extra fat in your script, look at what's left. Is it as crisp and clean as it can be? *Mise-en-place? Mise-en-scène?* (Everything in its place and a place for everything?) Feng shui the clutter out of your screenplay. Clean it up. I write a sentence per shot, a paragraph per point of view. Emulate the viewing experience in your reader's mind's eye. Unfold your story cinematically, using the tools in your arsenal: Your grammar and punctuation can *imply* the camera position and moves while still leaving white space for your actors—seat of the pants to the seat of the chair. Great writing is rewriting. Enjoy the process!

MICHELE WALLERSTEIN

How to Find and Get an Agent

MICHELE WALLERSTEIN is a screenplay, novel and career consultant, who has spent many years as a literary agent in Hollywood. Michele has been a guest speaker at numerous film festivals, pitch fests and writers' conferences and groups all across the United States. She teaches the ins and outs of the writing business as well as how to get the most out of one's material.

After many years of being a literary agent in Hollywood, I know how difficult it is for new writers to connect to the bona fide agents they need so that they can pursue their writing careers. Most writers are stymied by the process and think that the whole business of entertainment is closed to them. It feels particularly difficult for people who do not live in the Los Angeles or New York area. While it is true that finding agents is difficult, it is certainly much more possible than you think.

The key to locating and securing the services of those agents is in knowing that they are looking for you just as much as you are looking for them. This is a secret well kept from most new writers. The Hollywood community is in constant need of new ideas, new screenplays and the new writers that are coming up with those projects. Often professional writers are booked up with work, or have run out of new ideas or stop working, for any number of personal or business reasons. We need to fill those spots with new and exciting clients. To prove my point, simply attend any film festival or pitch fest or writers' conference in your local town and you'll see that the lineup of visiting pros, including producers' representatives as well as agents, is astounding.

The people who attend these events are, indeed, looking for you.

They are not there simply to sit on a dais with other pros and talk about Tinseltown. They are not there just to give a speech about the movie and television business and then disappear. They are there to find the next new hot writer they might sign and sell. They are looking for outstanding talent to add to their client list. They are looking for bright and shining new screenplays to bring to their world. It's their job to find you.

Today, there is such a huge proliferation of communication tools that finding these elusive professionals is a lot easier than it used to be. There are loads of resource books with all of the information you need that you can access online. In most colleges there are film classes with information for you. There is a plethora of books in local bookstores and libraries where you will be able to discover the names, addresses, e-mail addresses, phone numbers and even the client lists of hundreds of good agents. There is no reason not to write a simple query letter to these agents to see if you can entice them to read your newest script by writing a great paragraph or two about the story. The key to this endeavor is to follow up with a phone call.

Another great way to connect is to attend as many writers' conferences and pitch fests as possible. This is where you will really be able to score a one-on-one meeting with the folks who are on the inside of Hollywood. Sign up for as many pitches as you can and be prepared to answer questions about your project. Ask for the business cards or e-mail information of all you meet, then follow-up with a note to thank them for their time, information, help, advice or anything that you felt they gave to you. This will establish a potential ongoing relationship. This one small e-mail is essential to your future.

EXERCISE

Sign up for a writers' conference in your area and be sure to practice your "pitch" many times prior to attending the event. Make sure you pitch a completed screenplay that you feel is ready to present to a professional. If someone likes your idea and wants to see the project, you must send it to him immediately, with a brief cover letter reminding him that you met at that event and that he expressed interest in this project. Wait two to three weeks, and then follow up with a phone call to see:

1. If your screenplay was received.

2. If it has been read.

3. If he likes your work.

If he likes your work but the script isn't right for him, be prepared to suggest another script that you would like to send to him. Always have the next script or idea ready.

AUTHOR WEBSITES

Michael Ajakwe, Jr.	www.ajakwetv.com
Will Akers	www.yourscreenplaysucks.com
Pilar Alessandra	www.onthepage.tv
Howard Allen	www.scriptdoctor.com
Scott Anderson	www.hssw.info
Jayce Bartok	www.vinylfoote.com
Glenn M. Benest	www.glennbenest.com
James Bonnet	www.storymaking.com
Aydrea Walden ten Bosch	www.theoreoexperience.com
Paula C. Brancato	www.paulabrancatowriter.com
Michael Ray Brown	www.storysense.com
Allison Burnett	www.allisonburnett.com
Daniel Calvisi	www.actfourscreenplays.com
Paul Chitlik	www.rewritementor.com
Christine Conradt	www.christineconradt.com
Linda Cowgill	www.plotsinc.com
Devorah Cutler-Rubenstein	www.thescriptbroker.com
Charles Deemer	www.screenwright.com
Madeline DiMaggio	www.cre8ascript.com
Michael Feit Dougan	www.21stcenturyscreenplay.com
Steve Duncan	www.steveduncanproductions.com
Doug Eboch	www.letsschmooze.blogspot.com
Barri Evins	www.bigbigideas.com
Syd Field	www.sydfield.com
David Freeman	www.beyondstructure.com
Billy Frolick	www.billyfrolick.com
Glenn Gers	www.disfiguredmovie.com
Jen Grisanti	www.jengrisanticonsultancy.com
Paul Guay	www.letsschmooze.com/PaulGuay.html
Heather Hale	www.heatherhale.com
Larry Hama	en.wikipedia.org/wiki/Larry_Hama
Michael Hauge	www.screenplaymastery.com

Marilyn Horowitz	www.marilynhorowitz.com
Karl Iglesias	www.karliglesias.com
Bill Johnson	www.storyispromise.com
Steve Kaplan	www.kaplancomedy.com
Craig Kellem	www.hollywoodscript.com
Judy Kellem	www.hollywoodscript.com
Susan Kougell	www.su-city-pictures.com
Neil Landau	www.neillandau.com
Leslie Lehr	www.leslielehr.com
Billy Lundy	www.scifiscreenwriter.com
T. J. Lynch	www.writingisrewriting.com
Bonnie MacBird	www.writesideofbrain.com
William Martell	www.scriptsecrets.net
Billy Mernit	www.billymernit.com
Peter Myers	www.myspace.com/petermyers
Andrew Osborne	www.newenglandscreenwriters.com
Brad Riddell	www.twitter.com/bradriddell
Stephen Rivele	www.stephenrivele.com
Ken Rotcop	www.pitchmart.com
Danny Rubin	www.dannyrubin.com
Laura Scheiner	www.screenplaysavant.com
Hester Schell	www.bayareacasting.com
Barbara Schiffman	www.hypnopitch.com
Brad Schreiber	www.thewritersjourney.com
Linda Seger	www.lindaseger.com
Mark Sevi	www.ocscreenwriters.com
David Skelly	www.improvforwriters.com
Jennifer Skelly	www.improvforwriters.com
Chris Soth	www.yourscreenplaymentor.com
Richard Stefanik	www.themegahitmovies.com
David Trottier	www.keepwriting.com
Michele Wallerstein	www.novelconsultant.com
Richard Walter	www.richardwalter.com
Alan Watt	www.lawriterslab.com
Sam Zalutsky	www.sazamproductions.com

ACKNOWLEDGMENTS

With heartfelt gratitude to our agent, Susan Schulman, and to our editor, Gabrielle Moss.

CREDITS

"Start with a Conflict" by Mardik Martin (edited by Hunter Hughes) © 2010 by Mardik Martin

"The Cringe Exercise" by Hal Ackerman © 2010 by Hal Ackerman

"Trusting Yourself" by Alan Watt © 2010 by Alan Watt

"Note Card R&D" by Brad Riddell © 2010 by Brad Riddell

"Concept Is King" by Chandus Jackson © 2010 by Chandus Jackson

"When Sally Met Harry" by Barri Evins © 2010 by Barri Evins

"The Comfort Zone" by Christina M. Kim © 2010 by Christina M. Kim

"Finding Your Story" by Paula C. Brancato © 2010 by Paula C. Brancato

"Binding and Gagging the Internal Critic" by Kim Krizan © 2010 by Kim Krizan

"The Talking Cure" by Wesley Strick © 2010 by Wesley Strick

"The Almighty Verb" by Beth Serlin © 2010 by Beth Serlin

"Throw the Book Away" by Alexander Woo © 2010 by Alexander Woo

"Feeling the Music" by Daniel Calvisi © 2010 by Daniel Calvisi

"It's the Read—Writing Great Film Narrative" by Glenn M. Benest © 2010 by Glenn M. Benest

"Dream On" by Nicholas Kazan © 2010 by Nicholas Kazan

"Random Thoughts" by William M. Akers © 2010 by William M. Akers

"Analyzing Your Characters" by Susan Kouguell © 2010 by Susan Kouguell

"The Power of Negative Thinking" by Kevin Cecil © 2010 by Kevin Cecil

"When Great Writing Meets a Great Actor: Writing for a Star" by Hester Schell © 2010 by Hester Schell

"Police Investigation" by Brad Schreiber © 2010 by Brad Schreiber

"Write Truthfully in Imaginary Circumstances: The Mythology Inside You" by Mark Sevi © 2010 by Mark Sevi

"Postcards from the Edge of Creativity" by Sam Zalutsky © 2010 by Sam Zalutsky

"Found in Translation" by Coleman Hough © 2010 by Coleman Hough

"The Most Important Thing I Know and Teach" by Chris Soth © 2010 by Chris Soth

"The Character/Action Grid" by David Trottier © 2010 by David Trottier, excerpted from *The Screenwriter's Bible* by David Trottier, reprinted courtesy of Silman-James Press

"Writing in the Dark" by Jim Herzfeld © 2010 by Jim Herzfeld

"The Newspaper Exercise" by Linda Seger © 2010 by Linda Seger

"21 Questions to Keep You On Track" by Neil Landau © 2010 by Neil Landau

"Key Things to Know About Your Script Before You Write" by Barbara Schiffman © 2010 by Barbara Schiffman

"Four Magic Questions of Screenwriting" by Marilyn Horowitz © 2010 by Marilyn Horowitz

"Creating Unpredictability Using Subgoals and Plot Twists" by Richard Stefanik © 2010 by Richard Stefanik

"Your Outline Is Your Lifeline" by Michael Ajakwe, Jr. © 2010 by Michael Ajakwe, Jr.

"The Tool Kit—James V. Hart's Resuscitative Remedy for Writer's Block and Blank-Page Elimination" by James V. Hart © 2010 by James V. Hart

"The Genre Game" by Bonnie MacBird © 2010 by Bonnie MacBird

"How to Move a Pile of Dirt" by Danny Rubin © 2010 by Danny Rubin
"The Emotionally Charged Icon" by Karey Kirkpatrick © 2010 by Karey Kirkpatrick
"True Love" by Michael Hauge © 2010 by Michael Hauge
"Finding Universal Themes" by Jen Grisanti © 2010 by Jen Grisanti
"Refining the Idea" by Stephen Rivele © 2010 by Stephen Rivele
"The Thematic Line of Dialogue" by Barry Brodsky © 2010 by Barry Brodsky
"The Emotional Outline" by Karl Iglesias © 2010 by Karl Iglesias
"Writing from Experience, or Grandma's Teeth Fell into the Soup Again" by Paul Chitlik © 2010 by Paul Chitlik
"Change Your Perspective" by Michael Ray Brown © 2010 by Michael Ray Brown
"The Union of Opposites" by Scott Anderson © 2010 by Scott Anderson
"From End to End: The Creative Compass" by Michael Feit Dougan © 2010 by Michael Feit Dougan
"Rhythms, Levels and the Proper Respect" by Michael Genet © 2010 by Michael Genet
"Some Things Are Better Left Unsaid" by Colleen McGuinness © 2010 by Colleen McGuinness
"Self-Knowledge Availed Us Plenty" by Tommy Swerdlow © 2010 by Tommy Swerdlow
"What Happens Next?" by Sara Caldwell © 2010 by Sara Caldwell
"Scenes as Concepts" by Craig Kellum © 2010 by Craig Kellum
"Crafting the Kick-Ass Scene" by David Atkins © 2010 by David Atkins
"Visual Storytelling" by Larry Hama © 2010 by Larry Hama
"What Lies Beneath" by Allison Burnett © 2010 by Allison Burnett
"Write Cinematic Scenes" by Stephen Duncan © 2010 by Stephen Duncan
"I Know What You're Thinking: Dialogue, Context, Subtext" by T. J. Lynch © 2010 by T. J. Lynch
"One-Page Character Introduction" by Valerie Alexander © 2010 by Valerie Alexander
"Better Than Irony" by Howard Allen © 2010 by Howard Allen
"On Creating Character" by Syd Field © 2010 by Syd Field
"Give Mea Dramatic Truth or Give Me Death" by Bill Johnson © 2010 by Bill Johnson
"Creating Characters Who Work for You, Not Against You" by Linda Cowgill © 2010 by Linda Cowgill
"Approach Character Like an Actor . . . from the Inside Out!" by Madeline DiMaggio © 2010 by Madeline DiMaggio
"The Character's Trailer Shot" by Billy Mernit © 2010 by Billy Mernit
"The Scene That Doesn't Exist" by Christine Conradt © 2010 by Christine Conradt
"The Key to Charismatic Characters" by James Bonnet © 2010 by James Bonnet
"Go Ask Rosenkrantz" by Glenn Gers © 2010 by Glenn Gers
"Character Bones" by David Skelly © 2010 by David Skelly
"The Riddle of the Sphinx" by Marilyn R. Atlas © 2010 by Marilyn R. Atlas
"The Character Diary" by Douglas J. Eboch © 2010 by Douglas J. Eboch
"Getting Inside Your Character's Head by Becoming Her Pen" by Laura Scheiner © 2010 by Laura Scheiner
"Life Before FADE IN:" by Pamela Gray © 2010 by Pamela Gray
"Loving and Loathing—How to Get into Your Characters" by Richard Walter © 2010 by Richard Walter
"Getting to Know Your Character" by Leslie Lehr © 2010 by Leslie Lehr
"Find Your Inner Actor" by Amy Holden Jones © 2010 by Amy Holden Jones
"On Dialoguing, the Screenwriting Anarchist's Way" by Peter Briggs © 2010 by Peter Briggs
"Nonverbal Communication" by Andrew Osborne © 2010 by Andrew Osborne
"The Big Eavesdrop" by Mark Evan Schwartz © 2010 by Mark Evan Schwartz
"The Twitch: Objects as Emotions" by William C. Martell © 2010 by William C. Martell

"Funny Faces: Tips on Writing Animation" by Aydrea Walden ten Bosch © 2010 by Aydrea Walden ten Bosch

"False Emotion" by David Freeman © 2010 by David Freeman

"Building Between the Lines" by Judy Kellem © 2010 by Judy Kellem

"Using Metaphors in Comedy" by Steve Kaplan © 2010 by Steve Kaplan

"Pick Up a Party Line" by Jennifer Skelly © 2010 by Jennifer Skelly

"Backward Brainstorming" by Pilar Alessandra © 2010 by Pilar Alessandra, excerpted from *The Coffee Break Screenwriter* by Pilar Alessandra, reprinted courtesy Michael Wiese Productions

"Hurt Me, Hurt Me! (Oh, and Help Me Make My Script Better)" by Paul Guay © 2009 by Paul Guay

"The Jewel Case Outline" by Jim Strain © 2010 by Jim Strain

"'Aloud,' He Cried!" by Jayce Bartok © 2010 by Jayce Bartok

"Screenwriters: Stop Shooting Yourself in the Foot!" by Charles Deemer © 2010 by Charles Deemer

"The First Ten Pages" by Ken Rotcop © 2010 by Ken Rotcop

"Prose (and Cons)" by Billy Frolick © 2010 by Billy Frolick

"What to Do When You're Stuck on a Creative Problem" by Peter Myers © 2010 by Peter Myers

"Button It—The Cure for Overwriting" by Devorah Cutler-Rubenstein © 2010 by Devorah Cutler-Rubenstein

"Finishing a Script—The Actor Pass" by Glen Mazzara © 2010 by Glen Mazzara

"Creating the Killer Log Line" by Bill Lundy © 2010 by Bill Lundy

"What If It Were Your Money?" by Heather Hale © 2010 by Heather Hale

"How to Find and Get an Agent" by Michele Wallerstein © 2010 by Michele Wallerstein

ABOUT THE AUTHORS

SHERRY ELLIS is the editor of *Now Write!* (Fiction) and *Now Write! Nonfiction. Now Write!* (Fiction) was recognized by the *Writer* magazine as one of the best writing books of 2006. Her author interviews have been published in literary magazines and are anthologized in *Illuminating Fiction*. She is a screenwriter, author of fiction, a writing coach and a writing teacher.

LAURIE LAMSON is a writer, filmmaker and book editor. She recently adapted a book for the screen (*Don't Shoot! I'm the Guitar Man*) and edited a nonfiction book. She is Sherry Ellis's niece.